Caste Discrimination

Caste Discrimination

Edited by

Jagan Karade

RAWAT PUBLICATIONS

Jaipur • New Delhi • Bangalore • Hyderabad • Guwahati • Kolkata

ISBN 978-81-316-0703-9

Published by
Prem Rawat for **Rawat Publications**
Satyam Apts, Sector 3, Jawahar Nagar, Jaipur 302 004 (India)
Phone: 0141 265 1748 / 7006 Fax: 0141 265 1748
E-mail: info@rawatbooks.com
Website: www.rawatbooks.com

New Delhi Office
4858/24, Ansari Road, Daryaganj, New Delhi 110 002
Phone: 011 2326 3290

Also at *Bangalore, Hyderabad, Guwahati* and *Kolkata*

Typeset by Rawat Computers, Jaipur
Printed at Chaman Enterprises, New Delhi

Dedicated to

Jyotiba Phule

the pioneer of education and equality in modern India.

Contents

List of Tables

Chapter 4

Chapter 5

Chapter 9

Foreword

The book *Caste Discrimination* edited by Jagan Karade is one more useful volume in the series of books on the topic of caste in the recent years. This volume will be a very useful research material for students of sociology and social work. Though caste discrimination is an old and historical issue, it needs to be researched from time to time. This book looks at the contemporary process of discrimination.

The book has several chapters: some are very well written and lengthy. The book makes very useful contribution in the field of sociological studies on discrimination in Indian civil society. Discrimination is a process that results in dehumanization of social forces that have contributed to national growth and development.

Caste is a cultural category that has fragmented the Indian society for centuries. That fragmentation has resulted into enormous backwardness of the nation over the years. Right from the days of Buddha moving on to Mahatma Jyotirao Phule and Dr B.R. Ambedkar, the struggle against castes and caste discrimination has been a major problem in Indian civil society and state. But for long time, the social researchers of India and of other countries, who worked on Indian social system remained completely indifferent to the caste and the question of untouchability.

Theoretically, the issue of discrimination has acquired the global importance. But the international academic space has been completely used for examining the discriminative practices of Western societies. However, the eastern societies – particularly a society like the Indian society – where most brutal practices, such as caste and untouchability existed for centuries, the global researchers never tried to examine them seriously. But in the recent past, quite a few studies are being done to examine the impact of these institutions on the life of all sections of people.

For centuries, caste has crippled the Indian social life. It has institutionalized many forms of discrimination. These institutions of discrimination have created conditions of social exclusion of multiple layers. Each community, excluded from the other, suffers enormous amount of social and cultural exploitation and oppression. Unlike ethnic discrimination, racial or sexual discrimination, caste discrimination invokes the divine sanction of Hindu scriptures and also philosophers. The Hindu scriptures such as *Vedas*, *Vedangas* and *Upanishads* say that the Hindu Gods were born in superior castes. The Hindu philosophers, both ancient and modern, believed that caste discrimination is a divine entity and no system of ideology can change it.

Caste discrimination introduced brutal oppressive forms in day-to-day life of human beings. It constructed concepts such as bodily pollution and purity, food pollution and purity. Therefore, intermarriage and inter-dining between castes were abolished with strict ritualistic laws. It constructed theories of occupational discrimination. Certain occupations were defined as pure and certain occupations were defined as impure. Though major threats to such wrong social concepts and human practices came from Buddhism in ancient period and Islam in late medieval and early modern period, such religions were attacked and marginalized. In the contemporary times, Christianity and Ambedkarite Buddhism are once again challenging the Hindu discriminative structures but they too are facing massive onslaughts.

A new and very powerful modernist discourse has started to abolish caste and untouchability. The modern state, though constitutional in nature, is more Hinduistic in nature than being democratic. This Hindu character of the state makes the struggle for abolition of caste difficult. However, in several modes, anticaste struggle and scholarly efforts to abolish castes are on.

This volume is one more addition to the existing literature on this very important issue. This volume has very important material that can be used by researchers working on caste. It contains multidimensional aspects of caste and Indian culture.

Kancha Ilaiah
Director,
Centre for the Study of Social Exclusion and Inclusive Policy,
Maulana Azad National Urdu University, Hyderabad.

Acknowledgement

The issue of caste discrimination has haunted the Indian psyche for ages. A large section of Indian society who was earlier called untouchables (or *Shudras*) suffered this caste discrimination at all levels. The present volume deals with this issue of caste discrimination in various sectors such as political, educational, economical, cultural and social life of the Dalits in modern India. The articles in this book have been contributed by eminent personalities, academicians, experts and research scholars all over India. I would like to thank the writers and eminent personalities who helped me to shape the book. I also thank all those who directly or indirectly rendered their help and cooperation in making this venture a success. I would like to express my deep sense of gratitude to the authors who contributed their articles and without whose support this book would not have become complete.

I am very grateful to the renowned writer and thinker Dr Kancha Ilaiah (Hyderabad), who kindly accepted my request to write the Foreword for this book.

I must thank the eminent personalities Dr Bhalchandra Mungekar (Member, Rajya Sabha, Government of India), Dr Uttamrao Bhoite (Ex. Vice Chancellor, Yashwantrao Chavan Maharashtra Open University, Nashik, and Bharati Vidyapeeth University, Pune) and my research guide Dr P.G. Jogdand

(Mumbai University, Mumbai) for motivating me to write this book. I would also like to thank Dr Sharmila Rege (Pune), Dr Pradip Aglave (Nagpur), Dr S.L. Gaikwad (Aurangabad), Dr B.K. Nagla (Haryana), Dr M.H. Makwana (Gujarat), Dr S.N. Pawar and D. Shrikant (Kolhapur).

Special thanks to Dr N.J. Pawar (Vice Chancellor, Shivaji University, Kolhapur), Dr D.V. Muley (Registrar, Shivaji University, Kolhapur) and the faculty members especially Dr R.B. Patil, Dr R.N. Salve, Dr Pratibha Desai and Dr P.M. Mane who encouraged me. I also thank Dr Praveen Jadhav, Shankar Bhoir, Sanjay Khilare and Sunil Ogale for their motivation. Also I thank Dr Manish Wankhede (Nagpur) and Dr Richard Pais (Mangalore) for taking pains in clearing the pre-publication works.

Words cannot express my feeling for my family members: My mother Indumati, my wife Dr Sujata, children Utkarsha and Ujjwal. I also express my feelings to my parents-in-law Advocate S.G. Sudarshani and Mrs Sudarshani.

At last but not the least, I express my gratitude to the publisher Rawat Publications and their associates, photographer Mr Raju Tipare and artist-friend Mr Raju Dabade without whose help this book would not have been completed.

Jagan Karade

Contributors

BIBHUTI BHUSHAN MALIK is the Director of Dr Ambedkar Studies Centre and an Associate Professor of Sociology at Babasaheb Bhimrao Ambedkar University (a Central University), Lucknow. He completed his M.A., M.Phil and Ph.D. from the Centre for the Study of Social Systems at the Jawaharlal Nehru University, New Delhi. He was awarded Junior Research Fellowship as well as Senior Research Fellowship by the University Grants Commission, New Delhi, for his research work. He started his academic career as a Lecturer at Dayalbagh Educational Institute (Deemed University), Dayalbagh, Agra. He has also worked briefly as a Research Officer cum Faculty Member at National Institute of Social Work and Social Sciences, Bhubaneswar. Further, he also worked as Reader in Sociology at M.G. Kashi Vidyapeeth, Varanasi. He has contributed a number of articles and research papers in English and Hindi in various national and international journals. His areas of specialization are Sociology of Ecology, Sociology of Development, Sociology of Weaker Sections, Dalits and Ambedkar Studies. He has published a book entitled *Poverty in India: Fundamental Issues – A Social Science Perspective.* At present Dr Malik is engaged in Major Research Project funded by University Grants Commission, New Delhi. (E-mail: bbmalik57@gmail.com)

DHANRAJ A. PATIL is an Assistant Professor and Head of Department of Sociology, Walchand College of Arts and Science, Solapur. He holds dual masters degree in Sociology and Journalism and Ph.D. in

Development Communication. His research explores the impact of ICTs and globalization on marginalized (indigenous) communities with a focus on community informatics and digital divide, political economy of development and new social movements. He is a fellow of Indian Council of Social Science Research (ICSSR). Presently Dr Patil is engaged in Major Research Project funded by University Grants Commission, New Delhi. (E-mail: dr.dhanraj9@gmail.com)

JAGAN KARADE is working as Associate Professor in the Department of Sociology, Shivaji University, Kolhapur. He is an ICSSR Fellow. He obtained his M.A. and M.Phil from Shivaji University, Kolhapur and Ph.D. from University of Mumbai, Mumbai. He is the author of three books entitled *Reservation Policy and Reality, Nationalistic Dr. Ambedkar* and *Occupational Mobility among Scheduled Castes* and three edited books entitled, *The Effects of Religious Conversion, Globalization and Indian Challenges* and *Development of Scheduled Castes and Scheduled Tribes in India.* His several articles are published in reputed journals and edited books. He has completed a Major Research Project which has funded by UGC, New Delhi. Dr. Karade is Member, Management Council, Indian Sociological Society. At present he is engaged in a Major Research Project on 'Interaction Patterns of SCs in Maharashtra' which is funded by ICSSR, New Delhi. (e-mail: jagankarade@yahoo.co.in)

M.H. MAKWANA is the Head and Professor of Sociology Department, School of Social Science and Chair Professor, Dr Babasaheb Ambedkar Chair, Gujarat University, Ahmedabad. He has published eight books entitled *Mahatma Jyotirao Phule: Bharatiya Samajik Kranti, Anusuchit Jati Ma Udhyog Sahasikta, Gujarat Vidhyapeeth Mandal, Atyachar Nivaran Dharo: Amal, Vastavikta ane Dalit Vikas, Gujarat Ma Anusuchit Jatiyo, Dr Ambedkar's Vision and Social Justice, Gujarat Na Vankaro: Ek Adhyayan, Anthony Giddens: Adhunikta Ane Anu Adhunikta* and *Samaj Vyavstha Ma Dalit Nari.* He has 90 research papers presented in international, national and state level seminars and conferences and 38 research articles are published in edited books and reputed journals. (E-mail: dr_mhm001@yahoo.co.in)

M.S. WANKHEDE is an Assistant Professor of English, Dhanwate National College, Nagpur. He obtained his M.A. (English, Linguistics, Dr Ambedkar Thought), and Ph.D. and B.Ed. degrees from RTM. University, Nagpur. He is gold-medallist in M.A. and has two books to his credit – *English and Business Communication* and *Arnold's Culture and Modernity.* He has attended more than 80 state, national and international seminars and conferences and presented more than 50 papers there. Some of his papers have been published in the national journals. Under his guidance 19 scholars have completed their MPhil successfully and 4 scholars have submitted their thesis for Ph.D. In addition, he is an executive member of the Association of English Studies of India, which is a body of All India English Teachers. He is a bilingual creative writer and writes poems and stories in English and Marathi. Some of his poems are also published. He is the executive editor of the recently launched weekly *Yuvabhiman*. (E-mail: mswankhede@rediffmail.com)

PRADIP PRAJAPATI is an Associate Professor of Economics at Gujarat University, Ahmedabad, with 24 years teaching experience at various levels. He is a socio-economist having specialization in econometrics – a dynamic subject. He has published more than 35 articles and research papers in various state level and national journals on various eco-politico-socio-religo-philo-psycho aspects. He has guided more than 30 MPhil and 8 Ph.D students. And he was also a Dean of Arts Faculty, Member of Senate of Gujarat University, Ahmedabad.

PRAKASH KAMBLE is working as an Associate Professor, Department of Economics, Shivaji University, Kolhapur. Five MPhil and three Ph.D. students completed their research under his guidance, and currently six students for Ph.D. and seven students are working for M.Phil. More than 75 of his research papers are published in the reputed research journals, edited books and magazines. He has received two awards for Best Research Papers. He has published two books and presently he is engaged in Major Research Project funded by University Grants Commission, New Delhi. (E-mail: pskamble2007@rediffmail.com)

PRAVEEN K. JADHAV is the Head and Professor of Economics Department in Tilak Maharashtra University, Pune. He is the author of four books titled, *Socio-Economic Status of Scheduled Castes: Comparative Study*, *Ambedkar's People in India*, *Environmental Economics* and *Deprived Communities in Contemporary India*. Twenty-five of his articles have been published in the reputed journals and newsletters. (E-mail: praveenjadhav7@yahoo.co.in)

RAVSAHEB JANU KATTI is working as an Associate Professor in the Department of Sociology in Government College, Khanapur (Karnataka). He obtained his M.A., M.Phil and Ph.D. from Shivaji University, Kolhapur. His fifteen articles have been published in national and state level journals. He has completed Minor Research Project on *Surplus Land Distribution Programme in Karnataka* funded by the University Grants Commission, New Delhi. (E-mail: ravasaheb.katti@gmail.com)

SMRITI BHOSALE is working as an Associate Professor and Head, Department of Sociology, LJNJ College, Mumbai. She has obtained M.A., MPhil and Ph.D. degrees. She has been guiding MPhil and Ph.D. students and writing research papers and articles for reputed journals, chapters in edited books and has also authored books. She has worked on research projects sponsored by ICSSR, UNICEF and UGC. From the year 2000, she has been actively involved in the academic activities of SNDT Women's University. She was the Chairperson of the Board of Studies in Sociology and also as a member of the Academic Council, Faculty of Social Sciences, Research and Recognition Committee, BUTR Committee and other academic bodies during 2000–2005. At present, she is the Chairperson of Adhoc Board of Foundation courses and member of Management Council, Senate, Grievance Committee and Board of Studies in Sociology of SNDT Women's University. She has received University Special NSS award for dedicated and sincere service spanning 16 years. (E-mail: smriti69@rediffmail.com)

SUJATA KARADE is working as the Head and an Associate Professor, Department of Sociology, Smt Champaben Balchand Shah Women's College, Sangli. She has obtained her M.A. and MPhil from Shivaji University, Kolhapur, and Ph.D. from Tilak Maharashtra University, Pune. She has presented 20 research papers in international, national and state level seminars and conferences and 20 articles are published in edited books, journals and newsletters. (E-mail: sujatakarade76@gmail.com).

VIKAS SUDAM KAMBLE is working as the Head, Department of Criminal Psychology in Smt Kasturbai Walchand College of Arts and Science, Sangli, Maharashtra. He has published eight articles at national and international level. He has completed a minor research project funded by University Grants Commission, New Delhi. (E-mail: vsk_kwc@yahoo.com, vikasminchekar@yahoo.com)

VISHAL JADHAV is an Assistant Professor, Tilak Maharashtra Vidyapeeth, Pune and Visiting Fellow of the Institute of Development Studies (IDS), University of Sussex, 2003 and 2004. He was awarded the *Dudley Seers Memorial Award* for best article in *Journal of Development Studies* (2006). He was also selected for the International Sociological Association's doctoral workshop held at Moscow, 2008. Presently, he is pursuing doctoral studies from University of Pune. (E-mail: gharja@rediffmail.com)

1

Caste Discrimination

An Introduction

Jagan Karade

Indian population is growing rapidly but there is significant stratification among them. Supreme Court points out, 'The one billion population of India consists of six main ethnic groups and fifty two major tribes; six major religions and 6,400 castes and sub-castes; eighteen major languages and 1,600 minor languages and dialects'.[1] The Green Revolution of the 1960s and 1970s has increased agricultural output. (The Green Revolution was a movement that improved farming methods to increase agricultural output.) Industry has grown rapidly, especially in the area of high-tech industries. As a result of globalization, irrigation system has been improved by using canals and reservoirs to store rain water. But when we think of social stratification, we understand that the social institutions have been changing day by day, but caste system has not changed in modern India.

The caste system is one of the most significant features of the Indian society. As Mumtaz Ali Khan said, 'Though the caste system as such has undergone significant changes for the last several decades, the role of the caste system is still prominent. In spite of modernization, urbanization and Westernization, caste

This chapter is based on the 'Major Research Project' sanctioned by Indian Council of Social Science (ICSSR), New Delhi. The author is grateful to ICSSR, New Delhi, for extending the financial support for the project.

system is still a governing principle of the Hindu social order'.[2] The caste system is a form of social and economic governance which is based on principles and customary rules in Indian society. Caste system involves the division of people into the social groups (castes), where assignments of rights are determined by birth, are fixed and are hereditary. The assignment of basic rights among various castes are unequal and hierarchical, with the group at the top enjoying more rights coupled with least duties and those at the bottom, performing more duties coupled with no rights. Therefore, we consider/see that the caste discrimination involves massive violations of educational, civil, political, economic, social and cultural rights.

History

The caste system is a powerful tool of social discrimination. It runs deep in the mind of Indians and its application in the day-to-day life. In India, caste discrimination is traditionally rooted in the Hindu Caste System. Supported by the philosophical trends, caste system constructs the moral, social and legal foundations of Hindu society. Dalits are outcastes or the people who fall outside the fourfold caste system consisting as the *Brahmin, Kshatriya, Vaishya* and *Shudra*. Dalits are also referred as the *Panchamas* or people of the fifth order. *'Shudras'* known as *Chandalas, Nishadas, Panchamas* or Untouchables are out of *varnas*.[3]

The early Pali texts often mention the five despised castes as *Chandala, Nishada, Vena, Rathakara* and *Pukkasa*. They are described as belonging to the low status families *(nicha kula)* or inferior birth (*Hina jati*). But *Dharmasutras* did not treat them all untouchables, only the *Chandalas* and the *Nishadas* were considered as untouchables in later Vedic society, collectively. The untouchables were known as the *Antyas* or *Bahyas*. 'The Harijans have, thus, been relegated to a position outside the pale remain a part of the of Hinduism and yet remain a part of the structure of village society'.[4] And those, who fall outside the caste system, are considered lesser human beings, impure and thus polluting the other caste groups. They are known as untouchables and subjected to the so-called 'untouchability practices' in both public and private spheres. Untouchables are often forcibly assigned the most dirty, menial and hazardous jobs, such as cleaning human waste. The work they do adds to the stigmatization they face from the surrounding society.[5] The exclusion of caste-affected communities by other groups in society and the inherent structural inequality in these social relationships lead to high levels of poverty among affected population groups and exclusion from, or reduced benefits from development processes and generally precludes their involvement in decision making and meaningful participation in public and civil life.

The original Vedic system called *varnashrama* was legitimate and virtuous. It had divided society into four natural groups depending on individual characteristics and dispositions, which was prescribed in *Shastras* as the four *varnas*. Over a period, the fourfold *varna* system became a deviation into many hundreds and thousands of other *varnas*, castes or *jatis*. Most of such *jatis* are the people of a particular geographical or linguistic region. Thus, each member within a *varna* would often act accordingly and marry within the similar *varna*. However, Kshatriyas were often excluded from such nuances. 'The original caste or *varna* system existed all over India and has been considered by many sociologists and social anthropologists as pan Indian phenomenon. Since the castes and caste system existing today originated from the earlier *varna* system or caste system in the broader sense, it also developed and spread throughout India though there does not exist uniformity, neither in their local names nor in their ranks in the local caste-hierarchy'.[6] Ghurye views, 'the caste system gave rise to hierarchical gradation and social discrimination regarding privileges, marriage, social inter-course, choice of occupation, etc.'[7]

Dr Ambedkar mentioned, in the report of 1910, 'the Hindu people were divided in three classes, viz. 1. Hindus 2. Tribes 3. Dalits'.[8] During the British period, new phrases were coined to denote the Dalits. For example, for the first time the existence of the Depressed Classes was recognized in the text of the Act of 1919.[9] In 1931, the Census superintendent of Assam made a suggestion to change the title from the Depressed Classes to the Exterior Castes. The argument for this suggestion was that, 'it is a broader title, because its connotation does not limit itself to "outcaste" people (which mean people who are outside the caste system) on the other hand, "Exterior Castes" would include those who had been cast out because of some breach of caste rules'.[10]

Constitutional Safeguards

In the nineteenth and twentieth centuries, many social reformers, such as Jyotiba Phule, Periyar Ramaswamy, Dr Ambedkar, and some institutions, such as Brahmo Samaj and Arya Samaj, fought discrimination on the basis of caste. The result was that the Constitution of India prohibited discrimination on the grounds of religion, race, caste, sex, place of birth or any of them (Article 15, 15(4), 16, 16 (4), 17, 23, 25 (b), 29 (2) 325, 330, 333, 338, 341). These laws were passed against the practice of untouchability and discrimination of those, who are considered to be of lower castes and some of these have already been enacted. A great number of constitutional bodies, special legislative measures and executive orders have been passed to enable the 'scheduled castes' and the 'scheduled tribes' to seek redress for human rights violations in India. Moreover, several national commissions and state institutions have been established for the same purpose. Indian Constitution has a specific article forbidding untouchability (Article 17), along with Article 25 (2b) to throw open Hindu religious institutions to all sections of the Hindus and Article 15 (4) to permit the state to make special provisions for scheduled castes, scheduled tribes and other backward classes.

Since the last 66 years of independence, the Constitution of India has provided protection to scheduled castes and scheduled tribes. These constitutional and legislative measures to protect the rights of scheduled castes, scheduled tribes and other backward classes have been enacted in most affected states and the implementation of such laws remains alarmingly weak and insufficient.

One critical example is the lack of implementation of the Scheduled Castes and Scheduled Tribes (Prevention of Atrocities) Act, passed in India in 1989. While this law was specifically enacted to prevent and to protect Dalits from atrocities committed against them by non-Dalits, the low conviction rates show that this act does not live up to its objectives. For example, the Scheduled Castes and Scheduled Tribes (Prevention of Atrocities) Act 1989 criminalizes atrocities committed against members of the Dalit community and other lower castes. The rules formulated in accordance with the legislation also provide for the protection to the lower castes and are more preventive in nature. However, the laws and rules are limited. They do not address the root cause

– the caste system itself. In cases where compensation is awarded, the amount of the damages is far below as compared to international standards. The twentieth anniversary of the act presents a historic opportunity to work for enhanced implementation of the SC/ST Act and to critically review its performance in realization of its objectives and provisions.

Koli has strongly argued, 'Law is a powerful weapon to bring about social change in a given society, but unless it is flawless and its implementation is free from bias, its purpose cannot be accomplished. The atrocities against scheduled castes and scheduled tribes are more related to the hearts, minds, desires, attitudes and thinking of individuals than the situation and circumstances'.[11] 'The caste Hindus had the monopoly of their share in administration for a long time. In a democratic country like India, where number plays a significant role, it would be unfair to continue to neglect the weaker sections of the society, who constitute the bulk of the population. To remove this imbalance, the government has laid down the policy of reservation for the scheduled castes and scheduled tribes in particular'.[12] Therefore, the government has adopted protective discrimination policy.

Even after having the reservation policy in India, the higher-class posts in the governmental administrative set-up have not been filled. Therefore, the backlog is carried forward. This type of caste discrimination is observed by Gaikwad and he points out that, 'Social legislations are enacted with a view to motivating people to move in the desired direction and secure social justice. There are many cases where SC candidates are neglected. University committee argue, "For the concerned post, the candidate is available but is not eligible".'[13] And the result is that the reservation backlog is still continuously unfilled in the government and non-governmental jobs.

Despite the fact that caste discrimination is prohibited in Indian Constitution, the implementation is problematic. Numerous reports, statistics and cases document persistent patterns of discrimination against Dalits. Perpetrators often enjoy impunity for acts of exclusion and heinous crimes against Dalits. Many cases are not registered due to threats by dominant castes and negligence of the police. Moreover, lower caste people who are victims of caste discrimination many times are not aware of the Prevention and Atrocity Act. There is a systemic discrimination in access to employment, education and health, budgetary allocations for Dalit development and in the criminal justice administration system.

In this way, the Constitution of India provides certain safeguards against caste discrimination. However, the constitutional remedy is often inaccessible to Dalits and lower castes. Therefore, the Dalits are denied their legitimate share in equality quotient of human rights. Considering India's vastness and its limited resources and poverty, the possibility of a victim, who is otherwise deprived of basic standards of living, approaching a constitutional court is most unlikely. Compounded by the burden of expenses in litigation and the immense time taken for reaching a final verdict such legal steps are rarely taken by the victims.

Caste Discrimination in Modern India

Many sociologists and anthropologists have found caste as a major form of social and economical stratification all over India. Caste discrimination is not related to only uneducated people but also with educated people. This discrimination in the society is based on caste, therefore the sociologists G.S. Ghurye says that without a proper understanding of caste, our study in sociology will not be complete. A.R. Desai has very strongly argued that the village economy should also be studied from the point of view of caste. It is the caste which mainly determines the economic life of people, despite diversification in village economy and even today traditional occupations determine the wealth status of the people. Today, mostly in the rural area, Dalits have no right of education. For instance, Rajput farmers proudly proclaim that no Dalit may sit in their presence. In some villages, Dalits are forced to dismount their cycles and remove their shoes when passing by the upper caste people. This phenomenon is present in the remote rural areas. André Béteille argues, 'Caste not only remains a salient feature of the social morphology, it is still manifestly correlated with every form of social stratification, whether based on wealth, occupation, income, education, or some other criterion. In all public institutions, those in superior positions are likely to be of higher and those in inferior positions to be of lower caste'.[14] A number of human rights violations occur in relation to the caste discrimination: the right to adequate food, water, sanitation, clothing and housing, education, physical security and life; the right to be free from violence, right to health, the right to fair access to justice, to equal access to public and social services, to equal opportunity and free choice of employment, to marriage on free will. (When we see the matrimonial advertisements in popular daily newspaper, it is clearly mentioned that we are agreeing to inter-caste and inter-religious marriage but the excuse for scheduled caste and scheduled tribes is indicated.)

K.L. Sharma has observed in his study of Rajasthan, 'The Rajputs, Jats and Brahmins now do not hesitate to touch the untouchables. Occasionally, the Jats would not mind to share smoking with the lower castes'.[15] According to Sharma, this kind of change is characterized as *desanskritization*. Another example of *desanskritization*, which happened before the independence, is that the upper castes have controlled every water tank and a particular place was not allowed to be used by the lower caste persons but, in modern India, the Constitution has made the rule of atrocity, but still the upper castes people do not use the places used by the lower caste people. Shankar Gaikwad points out in his study, 'In the nature of discrimination faced and reported by the respondents nearly 30.15 per cent out of 136 respondents who faced discrimination reported that they have had to face caste based treatment, for instance, offering tea or water in separate utensils, pouring water from a distance, maintaining a certain distance while having meals, separate line for scheduled castes, no entry in the temple and their houses, etc.'[16]

In the state of Andhra Pradesh, the Dalits are not allowed inside the temples. Barbers don't shave the lower caste persons. Upper caste school children stay away from Dalits. If a cow dies, they ask the lower caste people to carry carcass. The shopkeepers from upper caste don't permit Dalits for tea inside the shop. They keep their cups and plates of food separate in the hotel. The backward caste's children are kept separate in the school because of untouchability. Meanwhile, untouchability is not an issue when it comes to sexual abuse (prostitution). In Maharashtra, the horrific incident of caste discrimination unfolded on the evening of 29 September 2006, when a group of villagers (upper caste) descended on the Bhotmange family in Khairlanji village in Bhandara district. They dragged out Surekha Bhaiyyalal

Bhotmange (age 44), her sons Roshan (age 23), Sudhir (age 21) and daughter Priyanka (age 18), assaulted them brutally, paraded them naked in the village, sexually abused them with sticks and then hacked them to death.

In India, the sufferings of Dalit communities affected by the disasters have been exacerbated due to caste-based discrimination in the provision of relief supplies and other assistance. The world is unaware and the Government of India has not acknowledged that the relief operations are being carried out with caste as a determining factor. The Tsunami relief operations in South India are indicative of persistent caste discrimination throughout the country. In the state of Maharashtra, massive evictions from tribal lands in Nasik District have been witnessed in the recent past. The claim for land by the Maharashtra State Farming Corporation deprived the basic rights of the tribal community in Maharashtra. In West Bengal, the eviction from Belilious Park was because of the apprehension that the presence of Dalits would pollute the shrine atmosphere of the upper caste in the locality. In West Bengal, even the High Court affixed its seal of approval for the eviction ignoring the basic legal virtue of fair hearing of *audi alteram partem*. However, evictions do not remain as the one and only form of discrimination. The forced labour of manual scavenging and carrying of night soil, slave practices in granite quarries in Karnataka and Tamil Nadu, denial of education in Orissa and starvation deaths in Maharashtra, Bihar and Kerala are all shocking realities of the Dalits in India and their position in the caste-based social structure. Mumtaz Ali Khan has mentioned, 'Generally, neither do the scheduled castes invite caste Hindus nor do the caste Hindus invite the scheduled castes for private social functions'.[17]

Dalit doctor Suman Bhaskar, an assistant professor in All India Institute of Medical Science, Delhi, complained to National Commission of Scheduled Castes and mentioned that 'the upper caste students do not give any response when he goes for round in hospital. In the same college hostel, a separate wing is allotted for Dalit students'.[18] Pais also noted that 'Many of the talented students were not allowed to represent the school or college in sports and games because of their caste background. It was also the case in National Cadet Corps (NCC) or National Service Scheme (NSS) and in such other extracurricular activities'.[19]

A total of 160 million Indians are born outside the four castes of the *varna* system. They are called the 'untouchables'. Every political party is thinking of how to capture power. This society has discriminated the backward caste people in each and every sector.

When we think of social change, the question is who is willing and who is not willing for a social change? Many people have implemented the stages of development for the upper caste community but they do not think anything about the development of lower castes and the result is that the caste violence is lashed and armed conflicts are experienced between Dalits and upper caste landlords. M.G. Kulkarni conclude, 'Within the village, such upward mobility has been still a difficult task for the scheduled castes to achieve'.[20]

In the era of globalization, the young generation is not aware of the caste system in their childhood but when they come at the stage of marriage and think about the life partner they do not think about another caste, likewise the family also forces them to find a partner from their own caste. Additionally, when a person wants to search for service or wants to get engaged in any business, s/he must be aware of the caste. 'Over the past few centuries, many Dalits have also converted to Christianity and have often, by this means, raised their socio-economic status. However, Christians of Dalit origin often suffer from discrimination by Christians and others – of higher caste backgrounds'.[21] Caste system and the ensuing caste discrimination have spread into Christian and Muslim communities too.

Because of the caste, the violation of international human rights standards occurs whereas domestic law prohibits caste-based discrimination. But it still continues to exercise a debilitating influence on the lives of millions daily in India. The national- and state-level human rights commissions do not have any authority to take an affirmative action after receiving a complaint whether it is of the caste-based discrimination or otherwise. The powers of these institutions are not legally enforceable. Sections 12 and 13 of the Scheduled Castes and Scheduled Tribes (Prevention of Atrocities) Act are limiting the authority of the rights of commissions to receive complaints, inquiries and inspection. Later, they decide to either refer the matter to the appropriate authority for further action or provide an advice to the government. This limitation makes the institutions incapable of protecting human rights. Their orders are limited for recommending the government to collect a fine from a perpetrator and disburse an amount to the victim. If the perpetrator is not an employee of the government, possibly, the order will be implemented slow. Even when the perpetrator is a government employee the order is often not executed. This makes a mockery of the system and discourages victims from approaching these institutions.

Summary

The message, 'India Untouched' underlines that, even though we are stepping into the twenty-first century, our social and political relationships with others are continuously being governed by unsound and illogical notions and traditions of purity, pollution, inferiority and superiority. Every religion has its own prejudices about casteism. When we travel to the remote corners to shoot specific instances of how it is practiced, then we see that the Dalits have been discriminated against by upper caste people in different fields.

The Constitution has given more rights to protect the scheduled castes and scheduled tribes, but question is whether these communities are aware of their rights. We can't say they are aware of their rights because majority of them are illiterate. Therefore, we can say that we have been given tinted optical glasses treating us to be a blind person. In this way, neither they are aware of discrimination taking place nor have they any idea about the leader for the community such as Dr Babasaheb Ambedkar, who would stand firm against the social discrimination based on caste.

Notes

1. Supreme Court Judgment, Case No. (Civil) 5041 of 12.8. 2005, *P.A. Inamdar V/s Government of Maharashtra and Others*, Para 158.
2. Mumtaz Ali Khan, 1994, *Identity Formation and Self Identity Among Harijan Elite*, Uppal Publishing House, New Delhi, pp. 210–211.
3. P.V. Kane, *History of Dharma Sutra*, Vol. II, pp. 120–121 and 154.
4. Patwardhan Sunanda, 1973, Change among India's Harijans: Maharashtra: A Case Study, Orient Longman Limited, New Delhi, pp. 6.
5. www.castediscrimination

6. Nandu Ram, 1995, *Beyond Ambedkar: Essays on Dalits in India*, Haranand Publications, New Delhi, p. 58.
7. G.S. Ghurye, 1959, *Caste and Class in India*, The Popular Prakashan Bombay, pp. 15–17.
8. *Dr Babasaheb Ambedkar, Writings and Speeches*, Vol. 7, Book–2, Education Department, Government of Maharashtra, 1990, p. 311.
9. G.S. Lokhande, 1982, *Bhimrao Ramji Ambedkar*, New Delhi, p. 181.
10. J.H. Hutton, 1946, *Caste in India*, Oxford University Press, Delhi, p. 167.
11. Manohar Koli, 2008, 'A Study of Social and Legal Dimensions of Atrocities against Scheduled Castes and Scheduled Tribes', Article published in *Development of Scheduled Castes and Scheduled Tribes in India*, Edited by Jagan Karade, Cambridge Scholars Publishing, United Kingdom, p. 32.
12. Mumtaz Ali Khan, 1994, *Identity Formation and Self Identity among Harijan Elite*, Uppal Publishing House, New Delhi, p. 163.
13. Shankar Gaikwad, 1999, *Protective Discrimination Policy and Social Change: An Analytical Study of State Action on Scheduled Castes in Aurangabad City*, Rawat Publications, Jaipur, p. 66.
14. André Béteille, 1999, 'The Reproduction of Inequality: Occupation, Caste and Family', Article published in *Social Inequality in India*, Edited by K.L. Sharma, Rawat Publications, Jaipur, p. 148.
15. K.L. Sharma, 1997, *Rural Society in India*, Rawat Publications, Jaipur, p. 183.
16. Shankar Gaikwad, 1999, *Protective Discrimination Policy and Social Change*, Rawat Publications, Jaipur, p. 146.
17. Mumtaz Ali Khan, 1980, *Scheduled Castes and Their Status in India*, Uppal Publishing House, New Delhi, p. 229.
18. Editorial, *Aajcha Sudharak (Marathi)*, 2008, Vol. XIX-I, April, p. 4.
19. Richard Pais, 2004, *Scheduled Castes: A Study in Employment and Social Mobility*, Mangala Publications, Mangalore, p. 80.
20. M.G. Kulkarni, 1969, 'The Scheduled Castes in Maharashtra: A Study of Social Change with Particular Reference to Mahars (Buddhists)', Marathwada University, Journal Vol. IX, July, Re-quoted by Dahiwale, S.M. 1989, *Emerging Entrepreneurship among Scheduled Castes of Contemporary India: A Study of Kolhapur City*, Concept Publishing Company, New Delhi, p. 5.
21. Harpreet Kaur and R.K. Suri, 2009, *Reservation in India: Recent Perspectives in Higher Education*, Pentagon Press, New Delhi, p. 12.

2

Caste-based Discrimination in Indian Society

Smriti Bhosale

Caste denotes a system of rigid social stratification into ranked groups defined by descent and occupation. More than 250 million people worldwide continue to suffer under what is often a hidden apartheid of segregation, modern-day slavery and other extreme forms of discrimination, exploitation and violence. Caste imposes enormous obstacles to their complete attainment of civil, political, economic, social and cultural rights. Under various caste systems throughout the world, caste divisions also dominate in households, marriages and general social interactions-divisions that are reinforced through the practice and threat of social exclusion, economic boycotts and even physical violence.

Indian caste system describes social stratification and social restrictions in the Indian subcontinent, in which social classes are defined by thousands of endogamous hereditary groups, often termed as *jatis* or castes. A person is considered a member of the caste into which he or she is born and remains within that caste until death, although the particular ranking of that caste may vary among regions and over time. Differences in status are traditionally justified by the religious doctrine of *karma*, a belief that one's place in life is determined by one's deeds in previous life.

Each caste has its own customs that restrict the occupations and dietary habits of its members and social contact with other castes. Social status is determined by the caste of one's birth and may only rarely be transcended. The caste has the function of maintaining the status quo in a society. The Indian term for caste is *jati,* which generally designates a group varying in size from a handful to many thousands. There are thousands of such *jatis,* and each has its distinctive rules, customs and modes of government. The term *varna* (literally meaning 'colour') refers to the ancient and somewhat ideal fourfold division of Hindu society: (i) the Brahmans, the priestly and learned class; (ii) the Kshatriyas, the warriors and rulers; (iii) the Vaishyas, farmers and merchants; and (iv) the *Shudras*, peasants and labourers. These divisions may have corresponded to what were formerly large, broad, undifferentiated social classes. Below the category of *Shudras* were the untouchables, or Panchamas (literally 'fifth division'), who performed the most menial tasks.

Although there has been much confusion between the two, *jati* and *varna* are different in origin as well as functions. The various castes in any given region in India are hierarchically organized, with each caste corresponding roughly to one or the other of the *varna* categories. Traditionally, caste mobility had taken the form of movement up or down the *varna* scale. Indian castes are rigidly differentiated by rituals and beliefs that pervade all thought and conduct. In Hinduism, *Dharma* is the doctrine of the religious and moral rights and duties of each individual; it generally refers to religious duty, but it may also mean social order, right conduct or simply virtuous life.

There are about 3,000 castes, or *jatis* and more than 25,000 subcastes in India. Extreme upper and lower castes differ so widely in habits of everyday life and worship that only the close integrating of intervening castes and the intercaste language communities serve to hold them together within the single framework of Indian society. The explanation that Indian castes were originally based on colour lines to preserve the racial and cultural purity of conquering groups is inadequate historically to account for the physical and cultural variety of such groups. Castes may reflect distinctiveness of religious practice, occupation, locale, culture, status or tribal affiliation, either exclusively or in part. Divergence within a caste on any of these lines will tend to produce fission that may, in time, result in the formation of new castes. Every type of social group, as it appears, may be fitted into this system of organizing society.

Within the boundaries of settlement of each Indian nationality, the castes form a hierarchical structure. Already in early medieval society, the upper stratum of the caste hierarchy was composed of the *Brahman* and warrior-landowner castes. These were the castes from which the class of feudal lords was created, along with the class of village community members with complete rights (e.g. *Rajputs, Kunbi, Nayars, Reddy, Vellala* and *Jats*). A high place in the hierarchy was also occupied by the urban trading and money-lending castes (such as the *Baniya*). Standing somewhat lower were the lessees and craftsmen in certain specialties (weavers, jewellers, potters, carpenters, blacksmiths and so forth). The lowest level of the class-caste hierarchy was occupied by castes whose members did not enjoy the communal rights and use of lands. Most of them belonged to a stratum of semi-slaves and semi-serfs who were exploited by the feudal upper classes of the community. This group included castes that performed jobs that, according to Hindu tradition, were considered 'unclean', such as sweepers, leatherworkers and laundrywomen. Widespread and numerous social restrictions were imposed on these castes; contact with them was considered defiling for persons belonging to higher castes. Hence, they acquired the term 'untouchables'.

The development of capitalism led to a disruption of the traditional connections of caste members with particular occupations and particular permanent regions of settlement. The restrictions on social intercourse between the members of different castes weakened, mainly in cities, which were outside the traditional way of life. The most persistent features of the caste system have been endogamy and the hereditary transfer of caste membership.

Changes in the Caste System

Untouchability conveys 'a sense of impurity and defilement. It implies certain socio-religious disabilities. It includes customs, practices sanctioned by the rigid Indian caste system whereby persons belonging to the scheduled castes were prohibited from entering Hindu temples, public places, streets, public conveyances eating places, educational institutions, etc.' There are other disadvantages: segregation in colonies in the village, denial of land rights, low wages for manual work, denial of access to services, e.g.

by barbers and washer men, to health care and education. Untouchables belong to castes that have the lowest ritual standing and often are in the most depressed economic condition.

In course of time, occupations have changed and many Dalits are now engaged in agriculture as landless labourers, as this activity has been opened to all. But this is not so in the case of other occupations to which access is not permitted by caste traditions. It is not merely the indignities heaped on Dalits that make them oppressed people. Because of the social ostracism and economic deprivation they suffer, they often fall prey to the most serious forms of persecution in their society, including killings, mutilation, rape, arson, destruction of property and other forms of violence when they attempt to assert their rights.

The occupational barriers among Indian castes have been breaking down slowly under economic pressures since the nineteenth century, but social distinctions have been more persistent. During the British Raj, this sentiment gathered steam, and many Hindu reform movements such as Brahmo Samaj and Arya Samaj renounced caste-based discrimination. The inclusion of the so-called untouchables into the mainstream was argued for by many social reformers. Attitudes towards the untouchables began to change in the 1930s by the influence of Mahatma Gandhi. Mahatma Gandhi called them *Harijans* (children of God), although that term is now considered patronizing and the term Dalit (downtrodden) is the more commonly used term.

The practice of untouchability was formally outlawed by the Constitution of India in 1950 and has declined significantly since then. In accordance with the 1950 Indian Constitution, all castes have equal rights. Caste discrimination has been prohibited by law (1955) and special measures have been undertaken to improve the economic and social status of the scheduled castes and scheduled tribes. The Government of India has taken several steps to prohibit the practice of untouchability. First and foremost, the government has recognized the existence of the problem. Second, the government has made determined efforts to deal with it.

The Government of India has officially documented castes and subcastes, primarily to determine those deserving reservation (positive discrimination in education and jobs) through the Census. The Indian reservation policy, though limited in scope, relies entirely on quotas. The government lists consist of scheduled castes, scheduled tribes and other backward classes.

Scheduled Castes

Scheduled castes generally consist of former untouchables (the term Dalit is now preferred). Their present population is 16 per cent of the total population of India. For example, Delhi has 49 castes listed as scheduled castes.

Scheduled Tribes

Scheduled tribes generally consist of tribal groups. Their present population is 7 per cent of the total population of India, that is around 70 million.

Other Backward Classes

The Mandal Commission covered more than 3,000 castes under OBC category and stated that OBCs form around 52 per cent of the Indian population. However, the National Sample Survey puts the figure at 32 per cent. Constitution of India, in its Bill of Rights (Part III), besides guaranteeing to all citizens the basic civil and political rights and fundamental freedom has special provisions that deal with the practice of caste discrimination:

- Article 15 prohibits subjection of persons to a disadvantage based on caste with respect to access to shops and public restaurants or to the use of wells, roads and public places maintained by the state funds.
- Article 16 prohibits discrimination on the ground of caste or descent with respect to employment under the state.
- Article 17 abolishes untouchability and prohibits its practice in any form.
- Article 23 prohibits forced labour and discrimination on the ground of caste when imposing compulsory service for public purposes.
- Article 29 (2) prohibits denial of admission to any educational institution on the ground of caste.
- There are also positive duties imposed on the state to redress imbalances due to past injustices against untouchables.
- Article 15 (4) permits the state to make special provisions for the advancement of any socially and educationally Backward Class of citizens, including scheduled castes and scheduled tribes.

- Article 16 (4) permits the state to reserve appointments for members of backward classes not adequately represented in the state services.
- Articles 15 (4) and 16 (4) recognize beneficial discrimination or protective/compensatory/preferential discrimination or simply affirmative action. Indeed, in the governance of the country, the state is enjoined by a directive principle of state policy (Article 46) to 'promote with special care the educational and economic interests of the weaker sections of the people, and in particular, of the scheduled castes and the scheduled tribes and to protect them from social injustice and all forms of exploitation'. But it is important to note that in the implementation of these provisions, the efficiency of the administration is not to be sacrificed (Article 355).

Other provisions in the Constitution addressing caste discrimination are as follows:

- Article 325 prohibits disfranchisement on the ground of caste.
- Articles 330 and 333 provide for reserving of seats for members of scheduled castes and scheduled tribes in union and state legislatures according to the scheduled caste population in each constituency.
- Article 338 mandates the appointment of a National Commission for Scheduled Castes and Scheduled Tribes. The commission has been appointed and investigates and monitors all matters relating to the safeguards provided for scheduled castes.
- Article 341 makes possible the legal identification of scheduled castes or untouchables by means of lists prepared for each state and union territory. The list, when published by the President, is final as to the castes or groups within castes deemed to be scheduled castes. The current state and union lists, when totalled, contain more than 1,000 castes but, given the fact that the same castes appear in the different state lists, the estimate given of 76 scheduled castes is probably correct.

To bolster the Constitutional Provisions, India has passed several laws:

- The Protection of Civil Rights (Anti-Untouchability) Act, 1955, strengthened by an amendment in 1973, punishes offences that amount to the observance of untouchability, such as prohibiting entry to temples or insulting someone on the basis of his caste.

- The Bonded Labour (Abolition) Act, 1976, aims at the release of labourers (usually Dalits) who work in slave-like conditions in order to pay off a debt due to a high caste employer, by cancelling any outstanding debt and prohibiting the creation of new bondage agreements.
- The Scheduled Castes and Scheduled Tribes (Prevention of Atrocities) Act, 1989. This important law was needed because of the high incidence of recurrent acts of violence against helpless Dalits throughout the country. Eighteen atrocities are listed, including violence against women, dispossession of a Dalit of his land, mischief by fire and destruction of property. Penal Code offences carrying a punishment of 10 years' imprisonment if committed against a member of a scheduled caste are punishable by imprisonment for life. There are special courts to provide speedy trials and special prosecutors to conduct cases. In 1999, rules were enacted under the act to strengthen the investigation process and make provision for payment of compensation to victims.
- The Employment of Manual Scavengers and Construction of Dry Latrines (Prohibition) Act, 1993. This special law was considered necessary to deal with the most distressing discrimination based on work indecent. There are an estimated 800,000 people, mainly women, who are engaged in cleaning dry latrines using the most primitive methods. The law itself describes this as a 'dehumanizing practice' and is intended to make it obligatory to convert dry latrines into water-seal latrines. For the implementation of the act, the National Commission for Safai Karamcharis was appointed. In its 1997 report the commission found that manual scavengers are 'totally cut off from the mainstream of progress and are still subjected to the worst kind of oppression and indignities'. What is more pathetic is the fact that manual scavenging is still largely a hereditary occupation. Safai Karamcharis are no doubt the most oppressed and disadvantaged section of the population. Unfortunately there is evidence that manual scavengers are considered untouchable by other untouchables.

Land Reform Laws to Redistribute Land to the Landless

It is an impressive list of the actions that have been taken by the Government of India. There improvements have taken place and cannot be doubted and credit should probably go to the National Human Rights Commission, the National Commission for Women, the Scheduled Castes and Scheduled Tribes Commission and the National Commission for Safai Karamcharis. The practice of untouchability and resultant discrimination has reduced in the public sphere, such as in panchayat offices, schools, use of public roads, public transport, health and medical services, services of shops (for buying goods) and services rendered by the tailor, barber, eating places and tea shops in large villages and urban areas.

The Mandal Commission was established in 1979 to 'identify the socially or educationally backward' and to consider the question of seat reservations and quotas for people to redress caste discrimination. In 1980, the commission's report affirmed the affirmative action practice under Indian law whereby members of lower castes were given exclusive access to a certain portion of government jobs and slots in public universities.

But even discrimination in various subtle forms prevails even today. In urban areas, it is more the hidden or invisible discrimination that a Dalit would encounter, in rural areas where three-fourths of the Dalits live open discrimination is practiced in all forms and is fairly widespread. The overall picture is depressing. In school education, there is a marked literacy gap between the scheduled castes and the rest of the population. It is reported that reserved quotas in the universities are not filled, especially in the technical and professional courses. There is reportedly poor representation of scheduled castes in teaching posts and caste clustering. There has been inadequate distribution of lands among the scheduled castes promised under the Ceiling of Land Acts. The shame of bonded labour still remains for millions, including a large number of children. The occupation of manual scavenging continues except in a few states. If reports are to be believed, no real effort has been made to improve the conditions of work for these wretched people who out of sheer necessity find that it is their lot to clean dry latrines.

The reservation of quotas in government employment and education has run into a vexed problem of having to determine whether caste alone should be the test or whether caste should be combined with economic need. The quota reservations in state employment are being filled in lower category jobs such as sweepers, peons and clerks. In the absence of quotas, there is hardly any representation in the defence forces, scientific establishments and the judiciary. The scheduled castes have not benefited from the economic progress made in the country even after 60 years of independence as there has been no policy on the allocation of resources. In the rapidly growing private sector, there are no opportunities for advancement for members of scheduled castes and scheduled tribes.

At the same time, atrocities are being committed almost daily against Dalits and they go unpunished. These have been researched and documented, mainly by Dalit organizations, in several publications in horrifying detail. The laws are there, but there is a lack of will on the part of law enforcement officers (the police and courts) to take action owing to caste prejudice.

Nevertheless, caste differences are still used, primarily in villages, to intensify the exploitation of labourers, especially those who belong to the lowest castes. Caste is also a factor in the politics of India. Many political parties in India have openly indulged in caste-based vote bank politics. In elections to local and the central legislative organs, all political parties take into consideration the caste composition of the voters. In the Indian republic, changes in the socio-economic position of castes led to sharp caste conflicts during the 1950s and 1960s and the efforts of a number of castes to raise their status in the caste hierarchy. At the same time, there was a massive attempt to eliminate the category of untouchability. The Communist Party of India and other progressive forces are fighting for de facto caste equality and against caste discrimination.

The present situation in India could not have been better expressed than in the words of the National Scheduled Caste and Scheduled Tribes Commission: 'The task ahead is clearly, therefore, to focus on the basic needs and requirements of scheduled castes/scheduled tribes and give them the social dignity and the economic capability to come on par with other sections of the society and become part of the mainstream which had been the charter visualized by the Constitution framers. Such a strategy would not only control the feeling of alienation, frustration and rising military and civil strife but would also make the scheduled castes/scheduled tribes active partners in nation building'.

Casteism in India

In very simple words, we can say that, casteism is a blind group loyalty towards one's own caste or subcaste, which does not care for interests of other castes and seeks to realize the social, economic, political and other interests of its own group.

There are various factors that act as causes of casteism in India, some of them are as follows:

- Sense of Caste Prestige: There is a hidden desire in people belonging to a particular caste to uplift or enhance the prestige of their own caste. So, the members of this particular caste are provided with special privileges and benefits to raise their social status and living conditions. As a result, casteism is popularized and accelerated.
- Marriage Restrictions: It is also well known that under normal conditions, any family still prefers to get their children married to individuals belonging to their own caste. This is one of the biggest accelerators of casteism.
- Political Issues: There are many politicians who, in order to fulfil their political benefits, raise the issues of casteism and repeat same stunts to attract votes. Indian voters fall an easy prey to them.
- Improvement in Transport and Technology: As a matter of fact, even the technological advancement in India intensifies casteism. People can now meet each other and hold gatherings and conferences of their own caste members and discuss issues with much more ease than earlier when there were certain difficulties due to distances.

India's caste system is perhaps the world's longest surviving social hierarchy. In India, the government has committed itself to developing policies aimed at the social and economic advancement of the Dalit population. In 1998, the Independent Downtrodden and Oppressed Community Council was formed with the objective of coordinating policies and supervising programmes to benefit Dalits. However, the caste discrimination, especially in rural areas, is still in practice. The so-called untouchables cannot even enter the houses of the people of the so-called higher and middle-class castes. On one hand, they are socially suppressed by the upper classes and, on the other hand, they suffer from poverty; the intensity of poverty seems to be higher in socially backward people.

Caste Discrimination in Society

Social Barriers in Marriages

Often rigid social norms of purity are socially enforced through strict prohibitions on marriage or other social interaction between castes. While economic and social indicators other than caste have gained in significance, allowing intermarriage among the upper castes, on many countries strong social barriers remain in place against marriage between lower and higher castes.

In India, the condemnation can be quite severe, ranging from social exclusion to punitive violence. The public lynching was punishment for refusing to end an intercaste relationship. Intercaste marriages can also lead to large-scale attacks on lower-caste communities. Dalits are often forbidden from performing marriage or funeral rites in public areas or, in some areas, from speaking to members of upper castes.

Restricted Occupations

Most Dalits in India continue to live in extreme poverty, without land or opportunities for better employment or education. With the exception of a minority who have benefited from India's policy of quotas in education and government jobs, Dalits are relegated to the most menial of tasks as removers of human waste and dead animals, leather work, street sweeping and cobbling. Allocation of labour on the basis of caste is one of the fundamental tenets of many caste systems, with lower castes typically restricted to tasks and occupations that are deemed too filthy or polluting for higher-caste communities.

Nearly one million Dalits in India are manual scavengers who clear faeces from public and private latrines and dispose dead animals; unofficial estimates are much higher. Handling of human waste is a caste-based occupation, deemed too polluting and filthy for anyone but Dalits. Manual scavengers exist under different caste names throughout the country. Members of these communities are invariably placed at the very bottom of the caste hierarchy and even the hierarchy of Dalit subcastes. They are made to clear faeces from public and private latrines and carry waste to dumping grounds and disposal sites. Though long outlawed, the practice of manual scavenging continues in most states.

Debt Bondage and Slavery

The poor remuneration of manual scavenging, agricultural labour and other forms of low-caste employment often force families of lower castes or caste-like groups into bondage. A lack of enforcement of relevant legislation prohibiting debt bondage in most of the concerned countries allows for this practice to continue unabatedly. There is an estimated 40 million people in India, among them approximately 15 million children are working under slave-like conditions as bonded labourers in order to pay off debts. Due to the high interest rates charged, the employers' control over records and the abysmally low wages paid, the debts are seldom settled. Bonded labourers are frequently low-caste, illiterate and extremely poor, while the employers are usually higher-caste, literate comparatively wealthy and relatively more powerful members of the community. The Bonded Labour System (Abolition) Act, 1976, abolishes all agreements and obligations arising out of the bonded labour system. It aims to release all labourers from bondage, cancel any outstanding debt, prohibit the creation of new bondage agreements and order the economic rehabilitation of freed bonded labourers by the state. However, relatively few bonded labourers have been identified, released and rehabilitated in the country. In India, children often inherit their families' debts and remain trapped in a cycle of debt bondage.

Socio-economic Disparities

Significant economic and educational disparities persist between lower- and higher-caste communities. The lower-caste communities are often plagued by low literacy levels and a lack of access to health care and education. A lack of formal education or training, as well as discrimination that effectively bars them from many forms of employment, and the non-enforcement of protective legislation, perpetuates caste-based employment and keeps its hereditary nature alive.

In India, awareness creation, income generation, education and health facilities programmes were implemented to address the problems of the backward communities. However, the gap between the so-called higher and lower castes has not been narrowed. There have hardly been any changes in the society or in the living standard of the poor. Consequently, the people of backward communities have felt discriminated against and could not believe that the government was actually doing nothing for their welfare and development. The main reasons for this are: lack of integrated programmes, weak implementation and sustainability, failure to mainstream backward communities and repressed people into the national development process, centre-oriented programmes rather than community-based participatory programmes, little attention to human resource development and lack of encouragement to the development and modernization of traditional occupations and skills, lack of effective institutional mechanisms, etc.

Access to Education

The high dropout and lower literacy rates among lower-caste populations have rather simplistically been characterized as the natural consequences of poverty and underdevelopment. Though these rates are partly attributable to the need for low-caste children to supplement their family wages through labour, more subtle and less well-documented is the discriminatory and abusive treatment faced by low-caste children, who attempt to attend school, at the hands of their teachers and fellow students.

Since India's constitutional promise of free, compulsory, primary education for all children up to the age of 14 – with special care and consideration to be given to promote the educational progress of scheduled castes – illiteracy still plagues almost two-thirds of the Dalit population as compared to about one-half of the general population. Most of the government schools – in which Dalit students are enrolled – are deficient in basic infrastructure, classrooms, teachers and teaching aids. Despite state assistance in primary education, Dalits also suffer from an alarming dropout rate. According to the National Commission for Scheduled Castes and Scheduled Tribes' 1996–1997 and 1997–1998 Report, the national dropout rate among Dalit children – who often sit at the back of classrooms – was a staggering 49.35 per cent at the primary level, 67.77 per cent for middle school and 77.65 per cent for secondary school.

Access to Land

Despite decades of land reform legislation, more than 86 per cent of Dalit households today are landless or near landless. Those who own land often own very little. Land is the prime asset in rural areas that determines an individual's standard of living and social status. As with many other low-caste populations, lack of access to land makes Dalits economically vulnerable; their dependence is exploited by upper- and middle-caste landlords and allows for many abuses go unpunished. Many labourers owe debts to their employers or other moneylenders. Indian laws and regulations that prohibit alienation of Dalit lands set ceilings on a single landowner's holdings or allocate surplus government lands to scheduled castes and scheduled tribes. The scheduled castes and scheduled tribes have been largely ignored, or worse, manipulated by upper castes with the help of district administrations.

Socio-economic Exclusion

Dalits are physically abused and threatened with economic and social exclusion from the community for refusing to carry out various caste-based tasks. Any attempt to alter village customs, violate the social order, or to demand land, increased wages or political rights leads to violence and economic retaliation on the part of those most threatened by changes in the status quo. Dalit communities as a whole are immediately punished for individual transgressions; Dalits are cut off from community land and employment during social boycotts; Dalit women bear the brunt of physical attacks, and the law is rarely enforced. Since the early 1990s, violence against Dalits has escalated dramatically in response to growing Dalit rights movements. Between 1995 and 1997, a total of 90,925 cases were registered with the police nationwide as crimes and 'atrocities' against scheduled castes. Of these 1,617 were for murder, 12,591 for hurt, 2,824 for rape and 31,376 for offences listed under the Prevention of Atrocities Act. Dalits are often both reluctant and unable (for lack of police cooperation) to report crimes against them, the actual number of abuses is presumably much higher. India's National Commission for Scheduled Castes and Scheduled Tribes has reported that these cases typically fall into one of three categories: cases relating to the practice of untouchability and attempts to disobey the social order; cases relating to land disputes and demands for minimum wages; and cases of atrocities by police and forest officials. Most of the conflicts take place within very narrow segments of the caste hierarchy, between the poor and the not so poor, the landless labourer and the marginal landowner. The differences lie in the considerable amount of influence that the higher-caste Hindus or non-Dalits are able to wield over local police, district administrations, and even state governments. Even in cases where police are not hostile to Dalits, they are generally not accessible to call upon; most police camps are located in the upper-caste section of the village and Dalits are simply unable to approach them for protection.

Gender Discrimination

Dalit women and girls suffer gender discrimination. The lower-caste women are singularly positioned at the bottom of caste, class and gender hierarchies. Women in Dalit communities are poorly educated and subjected to gruelling labour and many forms of violence, including trafficking and prostitution. Dalit women are consistently subjected to physical abuse and sexual exploitation by higher-caste landlords. Women are raped, mutilated and murdered during caste violence. Lower-caste women also suffer disproportionately in terms of access to health care, education and subsistence wages as compared to women of higher castes. Dalit women in India make up the majority of landless labourers and scavengers.

India has tried to remedy discrimination against women by adopting a constitutional amendment in 1993 that provided for one-third of all panchayat or village council seats and village chief positions to be reserved for women and also reserved a percentage of those for women from the lowest rungs of the caste system.

Failure in the Implementation of Laws

The practice of untouchability, other caste-based discrimination, violence against lower-caste men, women and children, and other abuses violate numerous domestic and international laws. International Human Rights law imposes on governments a duty to guarantee the rights of all people without discrimination and to punish those who engage in caste-based exploitation, violence and discrimination. In its August 2000 resolution, the UN

Sub-commission on the Promotion and Protection of Human Rights urged governments to ensure that 'appropriate legal penalties and sanctions, including criminal sanctions, are prescribed for and applied to all persons or entities within the jurisdiction of the governments concerned who may be found to have engaged in practices of discrimination on the basis of work and descent'. A year later, the sub-commission's working paper on work and descent-based discrimination noted, 'The laws are there, but there is a clear lack of will on the part of law enforcement officers to take action owing to caste prejudice on their part or deference shown to higher-caste perpetrators'.

Though constitutional guarantees and other national legislations banning caste discrimination suggest that government has successfully tackled caste-related violations, much of the legislations remain unenforced. India's own constitutional and statutory bodies, including the National Human Rights Commission and the National Commission for Scheduled Castes and Scheduled Tribes, have repeatedly confirmed and decried the prevalence of the abuses. The potential of the Scheduled Castes and Scheduled Tribes (Prevention of Atrocities) Act enacted in 1989 provides for certain stiffer punishments for abuses against members of scheduled castes and scheduled tribes when committed by non-scheduled caste or non-scheduled tribe members. Its enactment represented an acknowledgment on the part of the government that abuses, in their most degrading and violent forms, were still perpetrated against Dalits despite the constitutional abolition of untouchability. The potential of the Scheduled Castes and Scheduled Tribes (Prevention of Atrocities) Act, 1989, to bring about social change, however, has been hampered by police corruption and caste bias, with the result that many allegations of caste crimes are not recorded in the police records. Ignorance of procedures, lack of knowledge of the act and the dominance of higher castes on state governments have also affected its implementation.

Hidden Apartheid: Caste Discrimination Against India's 'Untouchables': A Review

India has consistently failed to uphold its international legal obligations to ensure the fundamental human rights of Dalits despite laws and policies against caste discrimination, the Center for Human Rights and Global Justice and Human Rights Watch said in its new report. More than 165 million Dalits in India are condemned to a lifetime of abuse simply because of their caste. The 113-page report, *Hidden Apartheid: Caste Discrimination Against India's 'Untouchables'*, was produced as a 'shadow report' in response to India's submission to the United Nations Committee on the Elimination of Racial Discrimination (CERD), which monitors implementation of the International Convention on the Elimination of All Forms of Racial Discrimination (ICERD). On 27 December 2006, Mr Manmohan Singh became the first sitting Indian Prime Minister to openly acknowledge the parallel between the practice of untouchability and the crime of apartheid. Prime Minister Mr Manmohan Singh described 'untouchability' as a 'blot on humanity' adding that 'even after 60 years of constitutional and legal protection and state support, there is still social discrimination against Dalits in many parts of our country'.

Indian Government can no longer deny its collusion in maintaining a system of entrenched social and economic segregation. Entrenched discrimination violates Dalits' rights to education, health, housing, property, freedom of religion, free choice of employment and equal treatment before the law. Dalits also suffer routine violations of their right to life and security of person through state-sponsored or state-sanctioned acts of violence, including torture.

Caste-motivated killings, rapes and other abuses are a daily occurrence in India. Between 2001 and 2002, approximately 58,000 cases were registered under the Scheduled Castes and Scheduled Tribes (Prevention of Atrocities) Act – legislation that criminalizes particularly egregious abuses against Dalits and tribal community members. These figures represent only a fraction of actual incidents since many Dalits do not register cases for fear of retaliation by the police and upper-caste individuals.

According to unofficial estimates, more than 1.3 million Dalits – mostly women – are employed as manual scavengers to clear human waste from dry pit latrines. In several cities, Dalits are lowered into manholes without protection to clear sewage blockages, resulting in more than 100 deaths each year from inhalation of toxic gases or from drowning in excrement. Dalits comprise the majority of agricultural, bonded and child labourers in the country. Many survive on less than US$1 per day.

In January 2007, the United Nations Committee on the Elimination of Discrimination against Women concluded that Dalit women in India suffer from 'deeply rooted structural discrimination'. 'Hidden Apartheid' records the plight of Dalit women and the multiple forms of discrimination they face. Abuses documented in the report include sexual abuse by the police and upper-caste men, forced prostitution and discrimination in employment and the payment of wages.

The Center for Human Rights and Global Justice and Human Rights Watch call on CERD to scrutinize the gap between India's human rights commitments and the daily reality faced by Dalits. In particular, CERD should request that the Indian Government:

- Identify measures taken to ensure appropriate reforms to eliminate police abuses against Dalits and other marginalized communities;
- Provide concrete plans to implement laws and government policies to protect Dalits, and Dalit women in particular, from physical and sexual violence;
- Identify steps taken to eradicate caste-based segregation in residential areas and schools, and in access to public services;
- Outline plans to ensure the effective eradication of exploitative labour arrangements and effective implementation of rehabilitation schemes for Dalit bonded and child labourers, manual scavengers and for Dalit women forced into prostitution; and
- Mobilize the entire government and make good on its paper commitments to end caste abuses.

Consequences of Casteism

Obstacle in Development of Nation and Nationalism

Casteism divides a country into various small parts or sections that is not beneficial to the nation. As a result, every caste demands individual benefits and privileges that give rise to communal tensions and conflicts.

The appointments to various government and private services are done on the basis of caste; there seems to be a fear of inefficient and worthless professionals who do no good during their service period but causing more troubles and create problems for the people.

Hurdle to Democracy

Many political parties have been asking for more votes on communal considerations and they mostly succeed in their evil desires. This also results sometimes in wrong selection of leaders of our country who play ridiculous games with rights and interests of the people to gain more and more power.

Casteism today helps promote contempt and disapproval among the people of different castes. The result of this has been social disharmony. In reality, casteism is killing Indian culture.

Recommendations

The government must act to uphold its own constitutional principles and work towards the full enjoyment of rights by all citizens, regardless of caste or descent. The government should:

- Ensure that all necessary constitutional, legislative and administrative measures, including appropriate forms of affirmative action, are in place to prohibit and redress discrimination on the basis of caste and that such measures are continued until discrimination is eliminated.
- Enforce and implement an effective and time-bound programme to abolish untouchability and similar practices in all spheres.
- Enact and enforce laws related to compulsory primary education and the elimination of child labour, bonded labour, manual scavenging, caste-bound free labour, the *devadasi* system or temple prostitution and other similar practices.
- Monitor and publicize the extent to which existing laws apply to end caste discrimination have been implemented.
- Monitor and analyse educational syllabi and textbooks that perpetrate caste-based oppressions and exclusion, and glorify worldviews that have contributed to the continued existence of a system of hidden apartheid. Implement alternatives that emphasize human rights education at the school and university levels.
- Allocate adequate funds for programmes for the socio-economic and educational support of communities that have faced discrimination on the basis of caste or descent.
- Ensure greater participation by the affected communities in civil administration, especially the administration of justice, including in key institutions such as the police and judiciary.

- Launch nationwide public awareness campaigns regarding legal prohibitions on discrimination on the basis of caste or descent. This campaign should explain in simple terms what actions are legally prohibited and what alternative is available to the victims of discrimination and abuse.

Conclusion

As is evident from the above discussion, casteism is a social evil in our country and we, as the people of this country, are solely responsible for providing the routes and the roots to this problem. But, we have the power to eradicate the same, the only requirement is to open our minds and think before reacting. Almost all of us are heard to be using the word Caste while discussing any national matter. If all of us avoid doing this, we can certainly help rout out this evil from our minds leaving no traces behind.

Though we often talk about unity of various religions in India and various social reforms have brought great changes in the social environment of our country, still we see casteism as an obstacle or major hindrance in the way of national integration in India. We need to develop such a peaceful environment in our country where there is no distinction among people on the grounds of caste and religion. The upcoming generation must not be encouraged to follow the regulations passed for different castes. It can be destroyed only by development of new psychological tendencies and behaviour patterns and this can be done only by adequate education.

It is also the responsibility of the respective states to endeavour, not merely the passing of remedial laws, but by positive state action, to ensure that violation of laws does not go unpunished. The strict enforcement of the law can assist the other ongoing educational processes in society to bring about attitudinal changes in the direction of tolerance, compassion and justice.

Suggested Readings

Atal, Yogesh, 1968, *The Changing Frontiers of Caste*, National Publishing House, Delhi.

——, 2006, *Changing Indian Society*, Rawat Publications, Jaipur.

Bayly, Susan, 1999, *Caste, Society and Politics in India from the Eighteenth Century to the Modern Age*, Cambridge University Press, New Delhi.

Béteille, André, 1981, *Backward Classes and the New Social Order*, Oxford University Press, Delhi.

——, 1992, *The Backward Classes in Contemporary India*, Oxford University Press, Delhi.

Charsley, S.R. and G.K. Karanth (eds.), 1998, *Challenging Untouchability*, Sage Publications, Delhi.

Chaudhuri, S.N., 1988, *Changing Status of Depressed Castes in Contemporary India*, Daya Publishing House, Delhi.

Ghurye, G.S., 1969, *Caste and Race in India*, Popular Prakashan, Bombay.

Gupta, Dipankar, 1991, *Social Stratification*, Oxford University Press, New Delhi.

Jogdand, P.G., 2000, *New Economic Policy and Dalits*, Rawat Publications, Jaipur.

Kothari, Rajani (ed.), 1973, *Caste in Indian Politics*, Orient Longman, New Delhi.

National Commission for Scheduled Castes and Scheduled Tribes, 1999, *Highlights of the Report, 1996–97 and 1997–98*, Government of India, New Delhi.

Omvedt, Gail, 1995, *Dalit Visions: the Anti-caste Movement and the Construction of an Indian Identity*, Orient Longman, New Delhi.

——, 1999, *Dalits and the Democratic Revolution*, Sage Publications, New Delhi.

Sathyamurthy, T.V., 1996, *Region, Religion, Caste, Gender and Culture in Contemporary India*, Oxford University Press, New Delhi.

Silverberg, James, 1969, 'Social Mobility in the Caste System in India: An Interdisciplinary Symposium'. *The American Journal of Sociology*, 75(3), November, pp. 443–444.

Zelliot, Eleanor, 1995, *From Untouchable to Dalit: Essays on the Ambedkar Movement*, Manohar Publisher, New Delhi.

3

Hidden Casteism in Education in India

M.S. Wankhede

Background of the Caste in India

Theoretically as well as practically caste is the one of biggest problems in India, which has created too much of nuisance in Indian society and culture. It is the problem that has put India on the second partition into the several cultural groups such as *Khalistan* and *Dalitstan*. It is a unique problem in the world and has created too many barriers, for 'as long as caste in India exists, Hindus will hardly inter-marry or have any social intercourse with outsiders; and if Hindus migrate to other regions on earth, Indian caste would become a world problem'.[1] It is indicative of the fact that caste problem is extremely dangerous to the human world. Anthropologists, ethnologists and historians agree that the population of India is a mixture of Aryans, Dravidians, Mongolians and Scythians who came to India from various directions centuries ago. They were in a tribal state when they stepped in India and had different cultures.[2] It is these different cultures that have posed great problems to Indian society.

Nowhere in the world we find the hierarchy of 'castes' originated in the four *varnas* – *Brahmin, Kshatriya, Vaishya* and *Shudra* – of which the first three *varnas* are considered 'twice-born' and the last one as 'unclean caste'. But it is a fact that we can find 'no universally accepted theory about the origin of the Indian caste system'.[3] Even when no one knows the universally accepted theory of the origin of the caste system it has stuck very deep into the Indian society and has made every Indian mentally a slave. 'A caste is a combined social system of occupation, endogamy, culture, social class and political power'.[4] 'Social stratification' and 'social restrictions' are at the forefront of the Indian caste system. The social classes in the Indian caste system are based on thousands of endogamous hereditary groups called jatis or castes and within a *jati*; there exist exogamous groups known as *gotras*, the lineage or clan of an individual.[5] It is obvious that the Indian castes are not limited to only four *varnas* referred above but are subdivided into several subcastes and *gotras*. The most neglected and sufferer group of the Indian caste system is the untouchables or the Dalits. This group was considered either the lowest among the *Shudra* or outside the *varna* system altogether. This might have been because of their fighting spirit against injustice.

It would be quite appropriate here to see a few definitions of caste. Nesfield defines a caste as 'a class of the community which disowns any connection with any other class and can neither intermarry nor eat nor drink with any but persons of their own community'.[6] Dr Ketkar defines caste as 'a social group having two characteristics: (i) membership is confined to those who are born of members and includes all persons so born; (ii) the members are forbidden by an inexorable social law to marry outside the group'.[7] No definition is complete or correct by itself as several dimensions are not covered by these definitions. This chapter does not concentrate on the caste system in India and the origin of castes or *varnas* but how they are the sources of deprivation for many lower castes such as scheduled castes and scheduled tribes; so attempts are made to see the roots of this evil called casteism and untouchability.

There is social inequality in many nations of the world but we do not get any example in the world where inequality is based on caste system as in the Indian institution of caste. Caste is the point of criticism for both Indian and foreign observers. It is point of view of some educated Indians to address non-Indians that caste has been abolished or that 'no one pays attention to caste anymore'.[8] But such statements are far from reality. In fact, the barriers of caste have been destroying the harmony and integrity of India. Since independence, a significant change, without doubt, has taken place in the caste system, but it has not been eradicated nor has it provided any opportunity to the untouchables for any kind of upliftment, development and progress in life. The problem of caste and untouchability has not been solved even after the 63 years of the enforcement of the Indian Constitution in 1950, which has forbidden the discrimination on the basis of caste. Many critics of Hinduism find the roots of caste system in the *varna* system. We find the controversies in many Hindu scriptures. On the one hand, they contain passages sanctioning the caste system, and on the other hand, they give indications that the caste system is not an essential part of Hinduism. This makes evident that there is no solid proof when and how the castes in India came into existence. Even most of the Vedic scholars believe caste system to be a subsequent and artificial insertion. But Dr B.R. Ambedkar concluded after a thorough study that this is a much later interpolation and gave strong evidence to support his conclusion.[9]

Buddha, Mahavira and others challenged caste system. Many saints including Nanak, Kabir, Eknath, Ramanuja, Tukaram and others rejected the caste discriminations during their respective periods. The efforts of various social reform movements such as Brahmo Samaj, Arya Samaj, Ramakrishna Mission, etc. and social reformers such as Raja Ram Mohan Roy, Swami Dayanand Saraswati, Sri Ramakrishna Paramahamsa, Swami Vivekananda, etc. could not prove to be fruitful to eradicate untouchability and casteism. Narayana Guru, a pious Hindu and an authority on the *Vedas*, also criticized casteism and campaigned for the rights of lower-caste Hindus within the context of Hinduism but his efforts also went in vain. Swami Vivekananda declared that there is no place for caste system in Hinduism but his followers gave no concrete form to the declaration of Vivekananda. In spite of positive practical efforts Mahatma Phule's Satyashodhak Samaj also failed to eradicate casteism and bring about equality among all Indians.

The renaming of the Dalit (downtrodden/untouchables) by Mahatma Gandhi as *Harijans* (children of God) could not help in the eradication of untouchability. Rather, I feel, it helped the problem of casteism and untouchability making it a stronghold in the Indian society and in the hearts and minds of Indian people. Therefore, Gandhi's contribution towards the emancipation of the untouchables is debated and questioned even today. The Constitution of India outlawed the practice of untouchability but not with full control. Mr K.R. Narayanan's taking office in 1997 as the President of India and Mr K.G. Balakrishnan's becoming the Chief Justice of India do not and cannot prove that casteism in India has been abolished. In order to have positive steps towards the eradication of caste and untouchability, the Government of India promised, through the Indian Constitution, reservations in education and jobs for the lower and deprived castes in India but the Indian reservation system could not fulfil its promise as this has limited its scope entirely on quotas. Since the 1980s, caste has become a major issue in the politics of India and almost all the Indian political parties are playing a 'politics' of caste. The relevant things to the caste system in India, untouchability, casteism, inequality on the basis of caste and discrimination have been discussed here for the better understanding of the topic but this is not the aim of this chapter. This chapter focuses its attention on hidden casteism in education in India.

Education and Caste Discrimination

Education is a larger field and it is the most important instrument for bright future of human beings. We have pre-primary, primary, middle or intermediate, secondary or high school, and higher levels of education. No level of education is sans discrimination based on caste. An amendment of the Constitution made in 1976 is Article 42, which has transferred education from the state list of responsibilities to the central government but this transfer of responsibility, which might have been done for the proper implementation of education policies, could not do, I feel, much in that direction. Article 43 of the Constitution provides an opportunity to all children through age 14 to get free and compulsory education.[10] It has also given the states the power to set standards for education within their jurisdictions. National Policy on Education in 1986 implemented a long-term series of programmes to improve India's education system. The policy allowed all children through the primary level to have access to education of comparable quality irrespective of caste, creed, location or sex. Urban schools are supervised by the state education ministry and the municipal government while the schools in rural areas are controlled by either the district board or the panchayat. The panchayats play a significant role in education in rural areas as the appointment and transfer of teachers come within their jurisdiction and this role of the panchayats paves the way for corruption and discrimination on the basis of caste. India spends an average 3 per cent of its GNP on education to have equality of education for all without any kind of discrimination based on caste, language, religion or gender. But nowhere have we found proper implementation of educational policies.

Though primary and middle school education is compulsory, only slightly more than 50 per cent of children between the ages of 6 and 14 actually attend school; the attendance of the students varies from region to region and according to gender. The non-attendance of the students between the ages of 6 and 14 is only from the lower castes called scheduled castes, scheduled tribes and other backward classes. A 1985 report by the Ministry of Education shows that nearly 60 per cent of children drop out between grades 1 and 5 and, I feel, this dropout is from the lower castes such as scheduled castes, scheduled tribes and other backward classes. In India many schools are private, while others are run on government grants-in-aid. Private schools are run by the Church and missionary societies in India. The middle-class families send their children to private schools and lower-class families send their children to under-financed and under-equipped municipal or village schools. To get higher education is the matter of wealthy and privileged class. Today education serves a purpose to achieve progress and development in life but education is becoming more 'cost-base' than 'caste-base'. So it is possible for few who have sufficient resources of income to make it a source of upward mobility and even to control the process of admission and jobs. This is a common practice today and the result of this practice is the discrimination based on castes, which shows hidden casteism.

Experiences of Education and Hidden Casteism

There are three kinds of colleges in India – government colleges, colleges managed by religious organizations and the private sector and the professional colleges. The government colleges are managed by the government and the number of such colleges is more than 50 per cent; the colleges run by the private managements have their own criteria for fees. Today there is Shikshan Shulk Samiti that is also under the control of the government but the unity of management authorities compel the government to take the decision favourable to them only and the result is that private colleges charge 15–20 times the fees of the government colleges. Political considerations and political patronage play a significant role in the admissions and appointments in these colleges. Through the governor as the university chancellor, the state controls education in colleges and universities but indirectly it is under the control of the politicians as the vice chancellor is a sheer political appointee. The appointment of vice chancellor is made only by the recommendation of the ruling political party and considering it an isolated post, though many qualified candidates from scheduled castes apply for the post, no one gets appointment as a vice chancellor. Only persons involved in power game get appointed. This can be verified from the appointments of the vice chancellors in the universities of Maharashtra. It would be suggested here that there is a need for reconsidering the definition of the isolated post.

In the colleges and universities, certain number of seats in admission and jobs are reserved for scheduled castes and scheduled tribes as well so that counterbalance would be maintained to avoid inequalities in education and jobs in these places. The government has been playing a double game. On the one hand, the provision for reservation in education and in jobs is made, and on the other hand, permanent non-grant colleges are sanctioned such as the sanctioning of the liquor shops without any master plan and thinkable logical policy for the permanent non-grant colleges. The dropout rates of the scheduled castes and schedule tribes are high in the primary schools; few students from these communities somehow come to the colleges for higher education and the rarest achieve the highest degrees in education resulting in very small number of candidates to secure higher posts in the government, semi-government and public sectors. If the non-grant and autonomous private colleges are continued to be sanctioned by the government, a day will come when all the government colleges would be deserted and private colleges would be full, for 'higher the cost, higher the quality' is the mentality of the Indians. These private colleges would be charging higher fees and the backward classes would not be in the position to pay the fees to get the degrees despite the reservations in education, and they would never get any jobs in the nearest future for two reasons: first they are not educated or have any degrees, and the second, there would be no provision for reservation in jobs in the private institutions. And one more reason can be added, that is, the sumptuous donations to get appointment. This is a new policy to prevent the lower classes to get education and jobs, which may be termed as 'a new law of modern *Manu*' or knowingly or unknowingly the practice of implementation of Hinduism. The tactics followed by the government is certainly an example of hidden casteism and this is against the Indian Constitution. Liberalization, privatization and globalization are the brakes for the lower castes such as scheduled castes and scheduled tribes to get education and jobs as well. The international universities are coming into India, and they would charge higher fees and would give no reservations to any category. This will result in the prevention of backward classes to be educated and get ready for jobs.

It has been said that 'education can be seen as a tool that one social class uses to prevent the rise of another'.[11] The inequality and differentiation can be seen from the middle-class thinking:

> Middle-class Indians frequently distinguish between the children of the poor as 'hands', or children who must be taught to work, and their own children as 'minds', or children who must be taught to learn.[12]

The statement clearly indicates the distinction between children of the poor and children of the middle class. We know well that the efforts of the government for the provision of physical facilities for the primary schools in the country through 'Operation Blackboard'. The purpose of the 'Operation Blackboard' was to make the basic amenities available for village schools and for that, in 1987, 1 billion rupees were sanctioned but not spent. When we look at the dropouts in the primary schools, it comes to our notice that the dropouts are very high from the backward classes such as scheduled castes and scheduled tribes, for they live in utter poverty and our below poverty line scheme can confirm this. In 1979, in order to reduce the dropouts, the government had implemented the non-formal education system so that dropouts would be lessened and other un-enrolled children could be educated. To this non-formal education system, National Policy on Education (1986) gave a new momentum. But all these efforts of the government could not give the expected fruit. This is the indication that the authorities are not in position to perform their responsibilities morally. Moreover, they might be reluctant because their children are not a part and parcel of those rural/government schools; and this will not affect education of their children. Isn't it the hidden casteism in education? The answer to this question has to be positive. The government employees appointed for this purpose do not work sincerely, honestly and morally, though it is their moral responsibility to work for the implementation of the government educational policies. The things for the scheduled castes and scheduled tribes are not just, though various provisions of reservations for them are made to provide them opportunities in education and jobs.

Article 46 of the Constitution states that 'The State shall promote, with special care, the education and economic interests of the weaker sections of the people, and, in particular of the scheduled castes and scheduled tribes, and shall protect them from social injustice and all forms of social exploitation'. Articles 330, 332, 335, 338 to 342 and the entire Fifth and Sixth Schedules of the Constitution deal with special provisions for implementation of the objectives set forth in Article 46. These provisions need to be fully utilized for the benefit of these weaker sections in our society.[13]

Apparently, Article 46 gives the guarantee of special care to be taken for the scheduled castes and scheduled tribes in education and economic development and solidarity. The moral responsibility of the government is to protect the weaker section from social injustice and social exploitation. This sounds well on paper but in practice it is the opposite and the darker side of this commitment and guarantee, given in the Constitution, come to fore. We feel that governing class has no foresight and they do not have any concern with the guarantee promised in the Indian Constitution. Either they are there to govern for their own selfish motive or for the benefits of their people and not for utilizing the provisions of various articles of the Constitution for the benefit of the weaker sections in the society. This example would make this point clear. Private colleges and schools are run mostly by the politicians. They run these institutions as a means of their source of earning and also as a means to protect the benefits of their near and dear ones because these institutions serve the purpose of guaranteed source of jobs for them. To have an appointment for the post of a lecturer or an assistant professor in the colleges, today, a candidate has to pay 15–20 lakhs of rupees, for the non-teaching post 5–10 lakhs and for the post of a teacher in a school or in a junior college, any candidate has to pay 10–15 lakhs.

University Grants Commission has laid down certain norms for the appointment of assistant professors. For the appointment of the assistant professor, National Eligible Test/State Eligible Test has been made a required qualification. But there are several examples, wherein despite the availability of the qualified candidates, only postgraduate candidates have been appointed in the last two decades. Politicians force government to regularize the services of such candidates and government had to issue several regulations for the protection of these candidates. When the candidates from backward classes were not available, they were happy to remark 'candidates are not available' and appoint their relatives and near and dear ones for the post. When the candidates from these weaker sections, following the reservation in education, were able to secure degrees, the remark was changed to 'suitable candidates are not available' or sometimes applications of these candidates were not entertained and thrown into the dustbin so that they could make a show that no candidate from these categories was available. They followed this practice for some years and managed to de-reserve the post to provide an opportunity to their own candidates. There are several examples of such kind at college levels. If an honest survey is made in this direction, a number of examples would come to light. 'University Grants Commission provides relaxation of 5 per cent from 55 per cent to 50 per cent at the Master's level for appointment as Lecturer from scheduled castes/scheduled tribes'.[14] Even they are given 5 per cent relaxation in the passing of NET/SET examination. This is an example of a policy of positive discrimination towards the backward classes. But what is the use of this relaxation when they are not getting jobs on passing NET/SET examination. That becomes a piece of paper in addition to other degrees. Moreover such certificate holders wander in search of jobs and non-certificate holders enjoy drawing sumptuous salaries. 'UGC has established SC/ST Cells in 113 Universities including Central Universities to ensure proper implementation of the reservation policy'.[15] But this is my practical experience that no university including any of the central universities is ensuring proper implementation of the reservation.

The following examples will speak the truth. Dr P.D. Nimsarkar, Reader and Head, Department of Linguistics, Foreign and Indian Languages, attended an interview for the post of professor in the Department of Phonetics in the English and Foreign Languages University, Hyderabad (a central university). He was the only fully qualified candidate among the others for the post but he was not selected for the post and the committee remarked 'not found suitable'. Other example is from Rashtrasant Tukadoji Maharaj, Nagpur University, Nagpur. Dr Ramteke, having fully qualified, was declined the appointment as a reader in the Department of Computer Science and other non-qualified candidate was appointed. His case was settled by the High Court and the chancellor directed the university authorities to discontinue services of Mr Bute who was appointed for the post. High Court order was implemented but Dr Ramteke could not get the post even today. This has been done deliberately by all concerned to protect the political relationships at the cost of hidden casteism. The interviews for the post of librarian in the Nagpur University were not held for reasons better known to the authorities. But it has come to light that the qualified applicants for the post were only from the scheduled castes and the post is unreserved, so the authorities were reluctant to hold the interviews. Some employees from scheduled castes working in the universities have launched complaints under atrocities against the then vice chancellor and pro-vice chancellor for the injustice done to them and the enquiries are going on in the matter. These acts are deliberate and proof of hidden casteism. One example from the institute of the ex-MP and Finance Minister for states Mr Shantaram Potdukhe, who runs a college named as Sardar Patel Mahavidyalaya, Chandrapur, under Sarvodaya Shikshan Mandal, will also speak the truth. The advertisement regarding the post of assistant professor of political science was advertise twice but not a single applicant was selected for the post, though there were around fully qualified 18–20 candidates present for the post but all of them were from scheduled castes and the post is not meant for them. A scheduled caste principal in this college at Aheri was terminated before the completion of the probation period. If such condition is found in the institutions of the public servants like Shantaram Potdukhe, who would care for the lower classes such as scheduled castes and scheduled tribes. These people enjoy the benefits of the government but neglect the policy of 'positive discrimination'.

The basic principle of National Common Minimum Programme (here after NCMP) (2004–2005) was 'To provide for full equality of opportunity, particularly in education and employment for scheduled castes, scheduled tribes, other backward classes and religious minorities'.[16] But NCMP could not succeed in protecting these weaker sections. With a goal of Universalization of Elementary Education, Sarva Shiksha Abhiyan (SSA) was implemented and it promised 'to change the face of elementary education sector of the country'[17] and its target was 'to provide useful and quality elementary education to all children in the 6–14 age groups by 2010'.[18] This scheme of the government also failed and the reasons are obvious because: 'The thrust of the scheme is on disadvantaged groups like girls, scheduled castes/scheduled tribes, working children, urban deprived children, disabled children, etc.'[19] Until and unless there are morals among the policy makers, implementers and the concerned authorities, no scheme of the government is going to be successful. The reservations for the scheduled castes and scheduled tribes in the government jobs and education are given because of 'a policy of positive discrimination towards the Backward Classes'.[20] But no one is in the position to understand this 'positive discrimination'. Though there has been positive discrimination in education, yet several scheduled caste families are not in the position to utilize education facilities because of poverty. This also results in the non-utilization of the policy of 'positive discrimination' in government jobs. Moreover, the high-caste communities are creating tension among the younger generations to arm against the weaker sections of the society on the point of reservations and the very obvious example is the riots after implementation of Mandal Commission in the 1990s. Today, the high-caste communities are playing a politics of reservation.

Discrimination within Scheduled Castes

The 83rd Amendment of the Indian Constitution recognizes education as a fundamental right of all Indian citizens. But it has not reduced disparities between the various castes. The Scheduled Caste is the most disadvantaged community. Particularly previously Mahar and today's Buddhist community is at tremendous loss. In the government-aided schools, the authorities are ready to follow reservation policies with heavy heart but with discrimination among the castes in 'scheduled castes'. They openly speak out that they would appoint a candidate from scheduled caste except from Mahar community. They are ready to appoint the candidates from the scheduled caste but they do not want to appoint Mahar or Buddhist. Instead, they prefer any other castes from the scheduled castes. This is an example of social exclusion and targeting of the Buddhist community. Buddhists are being isolated by the high-caste communities, authorities in the field of education and even from the other castes from the scheduled castes. For the maintenance of castes in the Indian society, I feel, Mahatma Gandhi is to be blamed. It was Mahatma whose aim was to liberate India from the British Rule; he also showed his interest to abolish untouchability and he believed in raising the status of 'untouchables'. He wanted to remove the disgrace and practice of untouchability, but at the same time he wanted to retain the elements of traditional caste system. This shows his dual policy, and hence he is to be blamed for this. On the other hand Dr Babasaheb Ambedkar, the chief spokesperson for scheduled castes, wanted to destroy the caste system honestly so that untouchability could be destroyed. It was his motif that until and unless the Indian caste system is abolished, untouchability could not be abolished. He demanded separate electorate for the scheduled castes similar to that of Muslims, Sikhs and Christians in order to uplift the status of the lower class that had been crushed under the deprivation and discrimination of the casteism and untouchability for ages. But he had to drop his demand of the separate electorate because Mahatma Gandhi had threatened a hunger strike till death and the result was the Poona Pact, which is still a matter of intense debate.

Article 341 of the Indian Constitution empowers the President of India to specify 'castes, races or tribes which shall for the purposes of this constitution be deemed to be scheduled castes'.[21] The First Amendment (1951) of the Constitution allowed the state to make special provision for advancement of socially and educationally backward classes such as scheduled castes and scheduled tribes. But this has proved only an amendment on paper and practically the backward classes could get no benefit.

I have already discussed the point of scheduled castes, particularly Mahars in Maharashtra, being targeted and isolated not only by the caste Hindus but also by the other castes under the scheduled castes. Even after six decades of independence there is not any change in the social and economic position of the scheduled castes. Major portion of the scheduled castes is still the victim of economic exploitation. The picture of rural India is very horrible. If we look at the scheduled caste citizens of India living in the rural areas we can witness their very pitiable condition as almost 90 per cent of the scheduled castes still live in rural areas. Their state is like that of the marginal farmers or landless labourers in the villages. Following the advice of Dr Babasaheb Ambedkar, some of the scheduled caste families left rural areas and came to settle in cities and towns. Here, in cities, they could find no better residence and settled in slums and on the pavements. Here too they could not get relief from the utmost poverty and victimization of the caste discrimination. They became the lowest paid wage workers for the worst jobs. They have to toil and moil to make both ends meet. Though the place has been changed, the work and working conditions for them remained the same. They hopefully came to the cities to be prosperous in life but found themselves lost in the depth of their poverty. They are not in a position to send their children to the private schools to get education due to sheer poverty. Poverty is such a burden on the shoulders of the scheduled castes that they do not think of sending their children to the government and corporation schools as they feel, under the burden of poverty, that their children can share the responsibility of earning some money to add to the family income by doing some physical work in the factories, hotels or at some construction sites. Thus, the insecurity of insufficient economic sources leads to the great problem of child labour and the result is the dropouts of the scheduled caste children from the primary schools.

The scheduled caste people are still engaged in traditional occupations such as sweeping and cleaning of the latrines. Mostly, the scheduled caste workers are casual labourers, in small factories, excavations and brick kilns or on construction sites. Some of them are cycle rickshaw pullers or engaged in paltry trades. Women, children and some men work for lower wages. The position of all scheduled castes is not the same and pitiable as narrated here. There are scheduled castes in secure jobs such as the public service, banking and railways and sometimes in private industry. But though this number is very low, in the case of case of the city dwellers-scheduled castes that can be taken positively and these people have got greater access to secondary and higher education for their children. One negative thing has also been observed with the settlement of scheduled castes in the cities, that is, within the scheduled caste community a growing middle class has emerged. One more very positive thing in the case of the city dwellers belonging to scheduled castes is that there is less caste-based discrimination in the urban areas but caste basis has not left them fully as the residential patterns in poorer areas indicate it. Scheduled castes people are living in similar urban areas.

The official policy of positive discrimination in favour of the scheduled castes in the civil service resulted in growing number of scheduled caste public servants. This is because of Dr B.R. Ambedkar's conversion to Buddhism, which brought awareness among the scheduled caste people. No doubt, the levels of scheduled caste recruitment in the central civil service have been increased but cannot be termed satisfactory: 'From 1949 to 1979, this rose from 0.71 per cent to 4.5 per cent in Class I posts, from 2.01 per cent to 7.3 per cent in Class II posts, and from 7.03 per cent to 12.35 per cent in Class III posts'.[22] Would we call it a satisfactory change? In the last three decades, not a single sector has been filled with 15 per cent reservation of the scheduled caste sanctioned by the Indian Constitution. On the contrary, we find over-representation in the lower Class IV posts and the scheduled castes occupy almost all Class V posts – the posts of sweepers, which are the traditional occupations for the scheduled castes. The same has happened in the posts for public sector and nationalized industry though the positive discrimination began late in the 1970s. For the reservation policy, privatization is most dangerous. As in the private sector, there is no provision of positive discrimination. There is no ray of hope for progress of the lower classes such as scheduled castes and scheduled tribes, as they are going to get no jobs in the private sector. Fighting against all odds former untouchables are gaining increasing access to education and jobs. Due the efforts of to Dr Babasaheb Ambedkar for the tremendous foresight in initiating reservations in the Indian Constitution for the backward classes such as scheduled castes and scheduled tribes.

As suggested by the University Grants Commission Chairman, Padmashree Dr Sukhadeo Thorat, the government should form policies for all sectors – public and private – to end the hidden caste-based discrimination. He lamented that over the six decades of implementation of the Indian Constitution, the worst forms of caste discrimination are still observed in the Indian society. On the occasion of the release of his latest book *Blocked by Castes: Discrimination in Modern India*, Dr Thorat asserted, 'Though reservation is criticized, it gives jobs in public sector which is not more than 10 per cent of total job providers. The other sectors offer 90 per cent of jobs. There is uncontrolled discrimination in non-public sectors'. Further he added, 'The benefits of India's economic growth haven't trickled down. Government data show, formerly untouchable castes were still poorer, more illiterate, and having worse wealth'. His book is the result of his series of researches and studies across the country.

Conclusion

In order to have proper implementation of the government policies in education and jobs to protect the interests of the lower classes such as Scheduled castes and scheduled tribes, all private educational institutions should be taken over by the government. Second, to monitor the policy of 'positive discrimination' in favour of scheduled castes and scheduled tribes, a vigilance committee should be formed under the control of the Ministry of Education, and the members of the committee should be from the backward classes to watch the implementation of government policies in favour of scheduled castes and scheduled tribes. The government policy of privatization should be abandoned as early as possible. Provisions for the punishment for those officials who neglect their responsibility towards the lower classes should be implemented and tightened so that no officials would dare neglect their duties and responsibilities. To decide the cases of atrocities fast-track court should be set up immediately and all the offenders should be severely punished. The sooner the better, the nationalization of education should be done. For the eradication of the hidden casteism, all these steps, I feel, are absolutely necessary.

Notes

1. www.columbia.edu/itc/mealac/pritchett/00ambedkar/txt_ambedkar_castes.html
2. www.columbia.edu/itc/mealac/pritchett/00ambedkar/txt_ambedkar_castes.html
3. http://en.wikipedia.org/wiki/Caste_system_in_India
4. http://en.wikipedia.org/wiki/Caste
5. http://en.wikipedia.org/wiki/Caste_system_in_India
6. www.columbia.edu/itc/mealac/pritchett/00ambedkar/txt_ambedkar_castes.html
7. www.columbia.edu/itc/mealac/pritchett/00ambedkar/txt_ambedkar_castes.html
8. http://www.indianchild.com/caste_system_india.htm
9. http://en.wikipedia.org/wiki/Caste_system_in_India
10. http://countrystudies.us/india/37.htm
11. http://countrystudies.us/india/37.htm
12. http://countrystudies.us/india/37.htm
13. http://india.gov.in/sectors/education/edu_scheduled_castes.php
14. http://www.unicef.org/files/Social_Exclusion_of_Scheduled_Caste_Children_from_Primary_Education_in_India.pdf
15. http://www.unicef.org/files/Social_Exclusion_of_Scheduled_Caste_Children_from_Primary_Education_in_India.pdf
16. http://india.gov.in/sectors/education/edu_scheduled_castes.php
17. http://india.gov.in/sectors/education/edu_scheduled_castes.php
18. http://india.gov.in/sectors/education/edu_scheduled_castes.php
19. http://india.gov.in/sectors/education/edu_scheduled_castes.php
20. http://india.mapsofindia.com/india-forum/races-and-castes.html
21. http://www.faqs.org/minorities/South-Asia/Scheduled-Castes-of-India.html
22. http://www.faqs.org/minorities/South-Asia/Scheduled-Castes-of-India.html

Suggested Readings

Ambedkar, B.R. (Pradeep Gaikwad, editor), 2008, *Buddha and His Dhamma*, Samta Sainik Dal Publication, Nagpur.

Byrne, David, 2009, *Social Exclusion*, Rawat Publications, Jaipur (Indian reprint).

Ellwood, Wayne, 2005, *The Non-sense Guide to Globalization*, Rawat Publications, Jaipur.

Klasing, Insa, 2007, *Disability and Social Exclusion in Rural India*, Rawat Publications, Jaipur.

Moon, Vasant (Compiler), 1979, *Dr Babasaheb Ambedkar, Writings and Speeches*, Vol. 1, Education Department, Government of Maharashtra, Bombay, October.

——, 1987, *Dr Babasaheb Ambedkar, Writings and Speeches*, Vol. 3, Education Department, Government of Maharashtra, Bombay, April.

——, 1989, *Dr Babasaheb Ambedkar, Writings and Speeches*, Vol. 5. Education Department, Government of Maharashtra, Bombay, April.

Rao, Yagati Chinna (Ed.), 2009, *Dividing Dalits*, Rawat Publications, Jaipur.

Singh, Yogendra, 2009, *Modernization of Indian Tradition*, Rawat Publications, Jaipur.

Thorat, Sukhadeo and Katherine S. Newman, 2010, *Blocked By Caste: Economic Discrimination in Modern India*, OUP, New York.

4

Poverty Alleviation Measures and Dalits of Eastern Uttar Pradesh

The Need for Structural Transformation

Bibhuti Bhushan Malik

Nowadays issue of Dalits and their caste-based exclusion is widely debated in academic circles. Sociologists view it from structural perspective and envisage upon structural reality around which issues of cultural subjugation and deprivation; educational backwardness; economic disadvantage and political negligence are revolving. Basic facilities such as housing, drinking water, food availability, education and health service are inaccessible to most Dalits owing to intensity of deprivation and magnitude of poverty. Anti-poverty programmes are major government initiatives in rural pockets with special provision for Dalits. Such provisions are continuously reviewed to strengthen in successive years in order to sharpen their focus on reduction of rural poverty especially among Dalits. In this backdrop, the study is being undertaken to explore food availability and impact of poverty alleviation programme among Dalits in eastern Uttar Pradesh (UP). The study explores to understand extent of successiveness of such programmes through assessment of impact and further suggests how structural transformation implementation of anti-poverty programmes help to yield a desired change in socio-economic life of Dalits. Moreover, it also investigates significant change these programmes brought in life of Dalits in the study area.

Objectives

Main objectives of the study are threefold: first, to study the concept of Dalits and its definition; second, to know about food availability and lean period of food scarcity prevalent in the area; and third, strategy of government to counter deprivation through anti-poverty measures, how its operation and successful implementation at local level be explored to generalise significant change in life of the target group, resulting into community development.

Methodology

Primary data are collected through intensive fieldwork by administering interview schedule, focused interview and quasi-participatory observation method. Secondary and documentary data are used to explain magnitude of servitude and level of poverty persistence among Dalits of Uttar Pradesh. It also ascertains nature and extent of change brought about by such measures in life of Dalits. The study is undertaken in the most backward region of eastern UP especially in two selected blocks under Varanasi district. Respondents are village-level Dalit worker, labourer and small farmer and most of them are beneficiary of anti-poverty programmes. Beneficiary list is collected from block office. There are eight blocks in Varanasi district, out of which one-fourth blocks are selected purposely: *Kashi Vidyapeeth* and *Pindra*. Mostly, six villages of three different types are selected from each block. Type of village is selected on basis of following criteria: (1) village of high incidence and magnitude of poverty, (2) village of middle incidence and magnitude of poverty and (3) village of lowest incidence and magnitude of poverty.

In these blocks, there are around 312 villages, out of which 12 villages are selected for the study. Random sampling is used among 441 households from 12 villages of Varanasi district. Household respondents are interviewed through interview schedule. The villages and the respondents are presented in Table 1. To explore a sociological perspective qualitative analysis of data is made. This is done by understanding and involving interactive process.

Table 1
Sample Village and Number of Respondents

Block	*Name of the Village*	*Number of Respondents*	*Percentage of Respondents*
Kashi Vidyapeeth	Pahadi	35	7.94
	Bachhav	38	8.62
	Tengra	37	8.39
	Anantpur	40	9.07
	Harpalpur	35	7.94
	Narottam Kala	37	8.39
Pindra	Katauna	39	8.84
	Thana	36	8.16
	Rasoolpur	37	8.39
	Muroi	34	7.71
	Murdi	37	8.39
	Tiwaripur	36	8.16
	Total	441	100.00

Concept of Dalit and its Definition

The term Dalit denominates a symbol of revolution and rejects oppression and depression. Indeed Dalit and its origin need to be located in historicity. Traditionally, the people were known as *Chandal, Avarna, Acchut, Asprushya,* depressed class, *Harijan* or untouchable; because they were born in a *Shudra* or *Ati-Shudra* family and were in bottom most position in hierarchical order of *Varna Vyavastha*; in today's context they call themselves Dalit. However, these nomenclatures were challenged and defined and redefined in different periods of time. The term Dalit has come into practice after Dalit Panther movement in 1970 in Maharashtra. Definition propounded by Dalit Panthers include members of Scheduled Castes (SCs), Scheduled Tribes (STs), landless and poor peasant, women and all those who were exploited economically and politically in name of religion (Murugkar, 1991: 237). Above definition of Dalit suggest a class connotation, which is far difficult to agree with.

The definition propounded by Dalit Panthers gives a very inclusive notion of Dalits, which includes tribe, peasant and women. Moreover, it cannot be defined in above class manner because all these categories are not homogenous in sociological sense. Hence, it can not be clubbed together. This is because Dalits in India have a different history of suffering in so called modern, democratic and globalized world. Caste and caste identity exist and determine mode of social interaction even after seven decades of independence. Therefore, Dalits can not be categorized and put together with others. This can be said that persons, who are untouchables and victim of *asprushyata*, also suffer from discrimination due to Hindu hierarchical order, are called as Dalits. In this context, definition given by Gangadhar Pantawane is appropriate, 'Dalit is not a caste. Dalit is a symbol of change and revolution. Dalits believe in humanism. Dalit rejects existence of God, rebirth, soul, sacred book that teaches discrimination, fate and heaven, because these made him a slave. He represents exploited in his country. In other words, they are also known as depressed class. These people therefore are constitutionally defined and known as Scheduled Castes'.

In the study, the term Dalits is not used in a comprehensive sense and does not include all depressed and disadvantaged people of India. Here the term is used in context of person – those who suffer stigma of untouchability and engage in unclean/polluted occupation and mainly reside in rural Uttar Pradesh. Generally in rural India, condition of Dalits is the worst in terms of their life and livelihood. P. Sainath (1999) argues that 'half a century after independence, Dalits still live in segregated section of overwhelming majority of Indian villages. In several parts of country, it is risky for them to even walk through upper caste *bastis*. They have no access to burial ground/burning *ghat* in many villages'. This depicts real picture of Dalits in rural India. Other aspect of rural India is poverty, hunger and malnutrition.

After independence, a systematic effort is being made by successive governments to bring desired change in live of disadvantaged people. Plethora of policies and programmes are framed and implemented for welfare of people in general and Dalits in particular. Government of India's anti-poverty programmes are a few of such notable policies and programmes initiated in rural areas.

Programmes are reviewed and strengthened in successive years in order to sharpen their focus on reduction of rural poverty. Planning commission data reveal that combined ratio of poverty was 54.9 in 1973-74, which declined to 19.3 in 2001–02. Likewise, number of poor was 321.3 million in 1973–74 which declined to 220 million by 2007. Poverty ratio (people below poverty line) estimated by planning commission at national level came down from 36.0 per cent in 1993–94 to 26.1 per cent in 1999–2000 (Malik, 2009: 48). However, number of rural poor is still very high, which requires further review and restructure of anti-poverty programmes. These policies always have a community development perspective in their focus. In next section, poverty alleviation measures are discussed to highlight features of these programmes to provide a background to the study.

Poverty Alleviation Measures in India: A Review

Traditionally, concept of welfare originated in compassion for less fortunate whose deficiency was in physical, mental or material form. However, modern view of welfare and poverty alleviation is non-religious and driven by logico-rational methods. It stands in contrast to old-world concept of charity. It recognises right of every individual to gain knowledge, to work and earn, to be self-supporting and to live with dignity and self-respect. State and society as a whole should provide programme for removal of its disability through opportunity to gain and use knowledge, skill and facility in order to exercise right and responsibility of citizens on an equal footing with everyone else in society. Modern state ensures this through constitutional provision on which governmental programmes can be legally based and sustained.

Western scholars such as Ragnar Nurkse explain problem of poverty by the concept of vicious circle of poverty. He wrote, 'The concept implies a circular constellation of forces tending to act and react upon another in such a way as to keep a poor country in a state of poverty'. That means poverty tends to poverty. To break this circle, a number of poverty alleviation programmes have been launched in India. Basic objective of development planning of government of India is to ensure growth with social justice.

As part of such broader objective, the government has set for itself the goal of reduction in incidence of poverty and its ultimate eradication within a time frame. To achieve such a goal, it evolves appropriate policy, strategy and programme. These policies initially started with community development programmes (CDP) in 1952, modified and changed in different nomenclatures and today Mahatma Gandhi National Rural Employment Guarantee

Act is in operation. Till today, as many as 40 rural development programmes are planned and implemented. However, out of these programmes only a few important poverty alleviation programmes are considered for discussion which have, in some or other way, helped to improve standard of living of rural poor and reduce poverty to a certain extent among them too.

Community Development Programme: First and the foremost rural development programme initiated in Independent India. The programme was launched on 2 October 1952 with 55 pilot projects on an experimental basis. However, in a short span of four years, it was extended to 114 blocks by 1956 and by early 1960 the programme was extended to almost all 5,011 community development blocks in the country. But, due to rapid expansion of the programme in a short-span of time, lack of effective participation of people, unqualified extension workers and lack of functional responsibility and coordination on part of administration, CD programme could not attain the intended results.

Agricultural Development Programme: Due to failure of monsoon, neglect of agricultural sector and withdrawal of US assistance under PL-480, Indian planners concentrated much on programmes for rapid increase in agricultural production, specifically food grain production. Thus, in early phase of Third Five-Year Plan, Intensive Agricultural District Programme (IADP) was launched in seven districts of seven states with technical assistance from Ford Foundation. Districts were selected with an objective of integrated and intensified approach to problem of agricultural production in areas that were more responsive to such productive efforts. Later on, nine more districts were added.

Area Development Programme: Along with these (SFDA and MFAL), target-oriented beneficiary programmes in the Fourth Plan had also been introduced as Drought Prone Area Programmes (DPAP) and Desert Development Programme (DDP) with a view to increase employment and income of poor. In order to supplement these special programmes, it also introduced Cash Scheme for Rural Employment (CSRE).

Wage Employment Scheme: In 1981, earlier Food for Work Programme (FWP) launched in 1977 was redesigned as National Rural Employment Programme (NREP), mainly to generate additional employment avenues and to create durable assets.

Redesigning of the programme was quite imperative to strengthen rural infrastructure resulting in higher production. In 1983, *Rural Landless Employment Guarantee Programme* (RLEGP) was introduced with an objective to expand employment opportunities in rural area and to provide guaranteed employment to at least one member of every landless labour households up to 100 day in a year. These two programmes were later merged and *Jawahar Rozgar Yojana* (JRY) was launched as a centrally sponsored scheme in April 1989. Main objective of JRY was generation of additional gainful employment for unemployed and underemployed people in rural area through creation of rural economic infrastructure, community and social asset with an aim to improve quality of life of rural poor. The programme, however, suffered from several weaknesses (Sharma, 2000). The JRY meant for wage employment also helps build rural infrastructure and community assets, thus investing in overall development. In this scheme, central and state share is 80:20 respectively. Under JRY, there are two sub-schemes: (a) Indira Awas Yojana (IAY) and (b) Million Wells Scheme (MWS) with emphasis on SC/ST population. District administration selects backward groups and passes 80 per cent fund to panchayats while retaining 20 per cent for inter-block or inter-village work. Along with employment schemes, there are four newly formulated welfare schemes directed toward poor in the country. These are (a) National Social Assistance Programme (NSAP), (b) National Programme of Nutritional Support to Primary Education (NPNSPE), (c) Indira Mahila Yojana (IMY) and (d) Rural Group Life Insurance Scheme (RGLIS).

National Social Assistance Programme (NSAP): The programme has following three components: (i) National Old Age Pension Scheme is applicable to destitute persons aged 65 and older. Beneficiary receives ₹ 75 per month. The programme was renamed as Indira Gandhi National Old Age Pension Scheme (IGNOAPS) on 15th August, 2007 and amount of benefits was revised from ₹ 75 pm to ₹ 200 pm. In April, 2011 eligibility criteria of IGNOAPS was further reduced from 65 years to 60 years. Further pension amount was also increased to ₹ 500 pm among beneficiaries aged 80 and above year. (ii) National Family Benefit Scheme (NFBS) provides a lump sum benefit to bereaved family on death of primary breadwinner of a family. The scheme is applicable to persons in age group of 18–64. An amount of ₹ 5000 is provided in case of death due to natural cause and ₹ 10,000 in case of accidental death. In the year 1998, the amount of benefit increased to ₹ 10,000 in case of death due to natural illness. (iii) National Maternity Benefit Scheme (NMBS) has a provision of ₹ 300 per pregnancy for pre-natal and post-natal maternity care up to first two live birth of women belonging to poor household. Women of age 19 year and older are eligible to receive such financial benefit. These schemes are implemented through local bodies that are panchayats and municipalities. Major central interventions in such direction are Integrated Rural Development Programme (IRDP), Jawahar Rozgar Yojana (JRY) and Employment Assurance Scheme (EAS). The EAS was launched in 1993 with an objective to provide gainful employment during lean agricultural period in manual work to all able bodied adults in rural area who are in need of work but cannot find it. Secondary objective is creation of economic infrastructure and community asset for sustained employment and development.

Million Wells Scheme (MWS) was launched in year 1996 with following objectives: (i) creation of assets in favour of rural poor particularly SCs and STs for their direct and continuous benefit by providing open irrigation wells free of cost, (ii) generation of additional gainful employment for target group and improvement in overall quality of life in rural area. The scheme is for small and marginal farmers (belonging to SC/ST, non-SC/ST) who are below poverty line and free bonded labourers.

Indira Awas Yojana (IAY) became an independent scheme on 1 January 1996 under 'Rural Housing' Scheme, to provide assistance for construction of dwelling unit to members of SCs, STs and non-SC/ST rural poor subject to condition that benefit to non-SC/ST would not be more than 40 per cent of the scheme of allocation.

Self-employment Programme encapsulates Integrated Rural Development Programme (IRDP) as the only self-employment programme. Over the years, a number of programmes are added such as Training of Rural Youth for Self-Employment (TRYSEM), Development of Women and Children in Rural Area (DWCRA), Supply of Improved Tool Kits to Rural Artisans (SITRA) and Ganga Kalyan Yojana (GKY).

Swarna Jayanti Gram Swarozgar Yojana (SGSY): Under this all above programmes are merged into a new scheme called Swarna Jayanti Gram Swarozgar Yojana (SGSY) since April 1999 having following objectives: (i) bring each assisted poor family above poverty line in three year, (ii) ensure each household to earn at least ₹ 2,000/- net income per month after repayment of loan to bank. On 25 September 2001, the Sampoorn Grameen Rozgar Yojana (SGRY) was launched to attain these objectives.

Mahatma Gandhi National Rural Employment Guarantee Act (MGNREGA) was launched in 2005. The scheme is part of central government National Rural Employment Guarantee Act of 23 August 2005. Initially it was implemented on 2 February 2006 in 200 districts. Later in year 2009, it was renamed as MGNREGA. Main aim of this scheme was to give guarantee to provide 100 day work to poor labourer families at village level.

Presenting all these policy measures in a nutshell it may be said that ultimate aim of various rural development programmes are to alleviate poverty and improve socio-economic condition of people. However, in following section it is being discussed about impact of all these programmes in a micro context by exploring significant dent it made or not on life and livelihood of Dalits in Uttar Pradesh. This micro study is based on an interview of 441 Dalit households in eastern Uttar Pradesh and further examines their situation and sufficiency of food availability in a year on daily requirement basis.

Status of Food Availability and Lean Period Food Scarcity

Food is prime concern of human being for active and healthy life. A human or any living being can live without luxury, but cannot survive without food.

Hunger is first and most tenacious enemy of people. Communities can be divided into fed and unfed, rich and poor and likewise. A society or nation, just cannot flourish without food security. The study reveals 10.88 per cent people suffer from chronic hunger throughout the year and 27.89 per cent of people do not get sufficient food during some periods of the year. But positive aspect is that 61.22 per cent of Dalits get sufficient food round the year. Sub-caste wise analysis shows magnitude of food shortage among 71.1 per cent of *Chamar's* is very acute, whereas food scarcity among *Khatiks* is nil during all seasons.

Table 2
Availability of Food

Status of Food Availability	*Percentage*
Availability of food in a year	61.22
Availability of food during some month in a year	27.89
No food in a year	10.88

Moreover, during lean period in month of July, August and September food scarcity becomes more acute and severe for large number of Dalits every year. It was astonishing to find that Supreme Court of India ordered on 30 August 2010 free distribution of food grains to poor as large quantity of food grains were getting rotten in godowns. On the contrary it is understood for government that such order is a 'suggestion' and not possible to implement in totality (*ToI*: 2010: 8). This example shows that our government is careless and callous towards mitigating hunger and even trying to mislead people.

Government Strategy to Counter Deprivation through Anti-poverty Measures

To alleviate poverty successive governments introduced a number of anti-poverty programmes since independence. These include various social welfare programmes and employment generation programmes such as National Rural Employment Programme. MGNREGA is considered as a landmark and the latest programme in poverty alleviation measure. The philosophy underlying the poverty alleviation programmes is to tackle rural poverty by endowing poor with productive asset and train them for raising their skill, so that they can be assured of income source. *Garibi hatao* (eradicate poverty) slogan was announced during 1971 general election. Since then plethora of welfare programmes and policies are formulated and implemented by central as well as state governments to address poverty. Apart from state and central government, stupendous efforts are being made by several international bodies for this purpose too, and worldwide consensus is being made to help underdeveloped and poor people. The year 1996 was observed as International Year for eradication of poverty. But unfortunately the result (refer Table 3) is quite dissatisfactory as about 62.36 per cent Dalits in eastern UP do not know what kind of poverty alleviation measures are in vogue. Only 37.64 per cent know about these programmes. This data point towards failure of poverty alleviation programmes in the area. Further Table 4 reveals that among 16 mega poverty alleviation programmes, 27.43 per cent Dalit are informed and aware about MGNREGA, 12.01 per cent are aware about availability of food item in BPL card, 10.45 per cent know IAY scheme; 6.57 per cent understood about Antyodaya Anna Yojana (AAY) and 1.36 per cent are aware about midday meals and food for work scheme. Other programmes are not known to people. Almost every programme is in operation in pen and paper but only 25.17 per cent are beneficiaries of it; 12.24 per cent households are deprived of any benefit from any such programme (refer Table 5).

Information and dissemination regarding each and every programme is very meagre, that is 62.36 per cent hardly know about existing programmes. Breman (2007:1) also point out that in poverty regime in village India focuses sharply on question whether rural poor are able to share meaningfully in process of development. Job card is necessary to get work in MGNREGA scheme, where 100 day job guarantee is given to people in a year, but only half of the household possess job card. From several beneficiary assistance programme, 90.70 per cent households get kerosene oil, 39.22 per cent households get rice and wheat at subsidized rate and 34.69 per cent households avail AAY facility. The IAY is centrally assisted programme aimed to construct dwelling unit, which is provided free of cost to the poorest of the poor people belonging to SC/ST and bonded labour communities. But this study reveals that only 22.67 per cent households are benefited from it (refer Table 6).

Table 3

Level of Awareness of Poverty Alleviation Programmes

Response	*Frequency*	*Percentage*
Aware	166	37.64
Not aware	275	62.36
Total	441	100

Table 4

Programme and Scheme wise Level of Awareness

Name of the Schemes	*Response*							
	Yes		*No*		*Not Applicable*		*Total*	
	Frequency	*%*	*Frequency*	*%*	*Frequency*	*%*	*Frequency*	*%*
Food for work	6	1.36	160	36.28	275	62.35	441	100
Food items in BPL card	53	12.00	113	25.62	275	62.35	441	100
Food items in Antoday Anna Yojna	29	6.57	137	31.06	275	62.35	441	100
Midday meal	6	1.36	160	36.48	275	62.35	441	100
MGNREGA	121	27.43	45	10.2	275	62.35	441	100
Old Age Pension	29	6.57	137	31.06	275	62.35	441	100
Widow Pension	11	2.49	155	35.14	275	62.35	441	100
Indra Awas Yojna	47	10.45	119	9.98	275	62.35	441	100
Mahamaya Awas Yojna	4	0.91	162	36.73	275	62.35	441	100
Jalnidhi Yojna	11	2.79	155	35.14	275	62.35	441	100
SC/ST Marriage Scheme	3	0.68	163	36.96	275	62.35	441	100
SYGSRY	14	3.17	1.52	34.46	275	62.35	441	100
Savitri Bai Fule Balika Samrudhi Yojna	5	1.13	161	36.5	275	62.35	441	100
Physically Challenged Pension	2	0.45	164	37.18	275	62.35	441	100
Clean Toilet	17	3.85	149	33.78	275	62.35	441	100
Kerosene on APL Card	1	0.23	165	37.41	275	62.35	441	100

Table 5

Beneficiary of Poverty Alleviation Programme

Response	*Frequency*	*Percentage*
Not applicable	275	62.36
Yes	111	25.17
No	54	12.24
Unable to answer	1	0.23
Total	441	100

Table 6

Number of Beneficiaries of Poverty Alleviation Measures

What are Provided as a Beneficiary of such Programmes?

Name of the Schemes	*Response*					
	Yes		*No*		*Total*	
	Freq-uency	*%*	*Freq-uency*	*%*	*Freq-uency*	*%*
Money to construct the house under Indira Awas Yojna	100	22.67	341	77.33	441	100
Mahamaya Awas Yojna	23	5.21	418	94.79	441	100
Rice in Rs. 3 per Kg. and Wheat Rs 4.85 per Kg. (Antodaya)	153	34.69	288	65.31	441	100
Drinking water (hand pipe) (Jan Nidhi Yojna)	40	9.07	401	90.93	441	100
Rice in Rs. 6.15 per Kg. and Wheat Rs. 4.85 per Kg. (BPL)	173	39.22	268	60.78	441	100
Financial assistance for construction of toilets	51	11.56	390	88.44	441	100
Kerosene	400	90.70	41	9.30	441	100
MGNREGA	57	12.92	384	87.08	441	100
Old age/widow pension	21	4.7	420	95.24	441	100

Anti-poverty Strategies and Dalits: A Gap between Policy Formulation and Implementation

Despite anti-poverty measures, still 45.12 per cent of Dalit households' condition has not improved; 37.87 per cent said their situation improved to some extent after availing support and only 14.29 per cent people said that they are relatively better availing such support (refer Table 7). Answer to the question of where problem lies and why their overall condition has not been improved despite several efforts by government, (as stated in Table 8) 19.04 per cent people agreed that problem remains in implementation of policies and also lack of on time dissemination of information about welfare policies and programmes. Insufficient money and lack of income are major constrains for socio-economic backwardness of people. Households (11.79%) are denied to have proper and suitable kind of income and employment opportunity by village Pradhans; as a result their situation is not improving. Among these households (as presented in Table 9) 38.78 per cent have BPL card, 34.69 per cent households have AAY card and 21.09 per cent have above poverty line (APL) card. Almost 96.15 per cent households do have ration card. Presently central government is trying to curb poverty by providing at least 100 day work in a year for which job card is necessary to get work under MGNREGA but the study reveals that only 50 per cent of the households possess job card (refer Table 10). Not only this but also other irregularities are noticed as some families do not possess job cards while grampradhan enjoyed certain status by controlling the card and pay less wage in most cases. The Hindu (2009) in its report also supplements the similar view that 'there are many states where large number of people demanded, but did not receive job cards. In many panchayats, job cards are in the control of implementing agencies. Possessing job card as a record of individual entitlement, to be updated by authorities, and kept in possession of workers, would ensure MGNREGA is monitored by its workers'.

Table 7

Impact of Anti Poverty Strategy

Do you think after such help you economic situation has improved?

Response	*Frequency*	*Percentage*
Yes	93	14.29
No	199	45.12
Improved to some extent	167	37.87
Unable to answer	12	2.72
Total	441	100

Table 8

Causes for Not Improving Overall Condition of Dalits

Name of the Schemes	*Response*					
	Yes		*No*		*Total*	
	Frequency	*%*	*Frequency*	*%*	*Frequency*	*%*
Insufficiency of money and lack of income and employment	52	11.79	389	88.21	441	100
Deliberate denial of basic benefits of programmes by the village *Pradhan*	21	7.02	410	92.98	441	100
Income is less but number of family members are more	11	2.49	430	97.51	441	100
Not getting work regularly	14	3.17	427	96.83	441	100
Given benefits are not sufficient	24	5.44	417	94.56	441	100
Illness and old age	5	1.113	336	98.87	441	100
Poor Implementation of government policies/not properly informed regarding government schemes	84	19.04	357	80.96	441	100
Lack of good agricultural land	7	1.58	434	98.42	441	100
Unable to answer	162	36.73	279	63.27	441	100

Table 9

Type of Ration Card

Response	*Frequency*	*Percentage*
Not Applicable	17	3.85
Antodaya	153	34.69
BPL	171	38.78
APL	93	21.09
Anapurna	7	1.59
Total	441	100

Table 10

Possession of Job Card

Response	*Frequency*	*Per cent*
Yes	222	50.34
No	219	49.66
Total	441	100

The study area is lagging beyond configuration of development and is regarded as the most backward area in the region. It shows huge cleavage exists between policy formulation and implementation in a committed sense. Major problems and drawbacks with poverty alleviation programme are their improper implementation, leakage of fund and rampant corruption. These are major weaknesses of poverty alleviation measures. Other studies also come up with such kind of findings that despite array of developmental programmes on a large scale, extent of their impact to reduce poverty in India is not established. Expenditure on poverty reduction programmes in India are stepped up since Fifth Five-Year Plan and subsequent period, (till 1989–1990) also witnessed a declining trend in poverty. But studies on poverty confirm significant role of other factors (such as agricultural growth, non-farm employment and inflation) or of broader categories of public expenditure through their impact on aggregate demand (Datta and Ravallion, 1996; Sen, 1996; Srivastava, 1997). The NSS 50th Round (1993–1994) also gathered some information on incidence of a few programmes (IRDP, Public Works Employment and PDS). These results are analysed in detail in a report (World Bank, 1998) that suggested very low incidence with some variation between states in consumption quintiles. At a more disaggregate level, micro studies are fairly successful in assessing impact of these poverty alleviation programmes. A detail evaluation of the anti-poverty programmes, based on existing evidence, is attempted by Srivastava (1997), and he concludes that 'while impact of the programme is generally positive, their effectiveness is quite low and considerably below official estimates'. Hence, anti-poverty measures are neither bringing any desired result nor it can enhance the socio-economic condition of people in true sense of empowerment and building capabilities.

Finding and Conclusion

Poverty and hunger are intertwined and many philanthropists and researchers are working to find out genesis and causes of growth of poverty. Nobel laureate economist Amartya Sen suggests hunger has less to do with shortage of food than with a shortage of affordable or accessible food (www.wfp.org). United Nations World Food Programmes (WFP) points out that more than 27 per cent of world's under nourished population lives in India, while 43 per cent children (younger than 5 year) are underweight. It is a serious concern that many people are living with absolute poverty and hunger in India. 'Absolute poverty is a condition characterized by severe deprivation of basic human need, including food, safe drinking water, sanitation, health, education and information' (UN Copenhagen Declaration and Programme of Action 1995).

As per the study, 10.88 per cent people suffer from absolute poverty but if one takes composite criteria of poverty, number goes up to more than 60 per cent. It depends not only on income but also access to service such as health care, education and safe drinking water. Dalits in India have a history of suffering, deprivation and destitution, which prevails even in modern, democratic and globalized world despite several efforts by governments through policies and programmes. It is unfortunate that these programmes have become a lip service to Dalits without making any significant dent in their life. What needs to be done is to create a true society based on democratic and egalitarian principles with requisite basic amenities to lead a dignified life irrespective of caste, creed, sex, religion and ethnicity.

By reviewing all these programmes and their performance at grassroots level, it can be said that ultimate aim of various rural development programmes is to alleviate poverty, enhance standard of living and capacity building of the poorest of the poor. However, it is necessary to mention that there is a qualitative difference between people-oriented economic policy verses populist economic policy. It can be suggested that governments need to shun populist policies and opt for a policy of empowerment of people, particularly for poor and helpless, through redistribution of land, access to credit, provision of primary education and vocational training, creation of productive employment and basic infrastructural facilities.

Further, mere pumping of more funds is not enough. Structural change of fundamental nature is needed to achieve better result. Identification of eligible beneficiaries is of utmost importance. More important than those is creation of awareness among people about various programmes launched for their benefit, so that they can avail these facilities. Poverty alleviation cannot be achieved without participation of people in understanding and solving poverty-related problems. Stimulation of people's ideas for a better life and building up their capabilities for planning for local development is best way to ensure development in life of people. In this process, voluntary agencies need to play important role. There are a number of success programmes in rural development with active involvement of non-governmental organisations. These have to be replicated and made widespread instead of remaining scattered in a few pockets. Moreover, many government efforts for rural poverty alleviation have to contend with many adverse factors such as rapid population growth, lack of education and infrastructure and anachronistic administrative and financial procedures. Attacking these obstructions become important to spearhead poverty alleviation programmes. Further poverty alleviation programmes also need to be supported by other agencies having adequate measures for rural development viz. (a) infrastructural development, (b) better communication (c) provision of electricity for increasing productivity input, (d) environment protection, (e) planned use of natural resource, (f) strengthening of human resource, (g) education and skill acquisition and (h) adequate primary health service, (i) taking science and technology to grassroots level and with help of people themselves, to control population growth.

Moreover, a 'Mission Mode' approach to poverty alleviation is a demand of the day. It requires a well-designed collaborative and concerted effort by government, voluntary agencies, social and natural scientists and people's organization. Such a participatory movement has to be encouraged by government. In addition, rural communities must be helped to evolve their own alternative model for rural development. Such type of localized approach is essential because socio-economic fabric of India is made up of different local combinations of historical event, cultural stream, geographical condition and population group.

Poverty alleviation efforts have, therefore, to accept urgency of decentralized programmes, which can readily respond to such diversity and leave control of local action with intended beneficiaries.

References

Breman, Jan, 2007, *The Poverty Regime in Village India: Half a Century of Work an Life at the Bottom of the Rural Economy in South Gujarat*, Oxford University Press, New Delhi.

Datt and Ravallion 1996, 'India's Checkered History in Fight against Poverty: Are there Lessons for the Future?' *Economic and Political Weekly,* Special Number, Vol. XXXI Nos, 35, 36 and 37, September.

Malik, B.B., 2009, *Poverty in India: Fundamental issues-A Social Science Perspective,* Mittal Publications, New Delhi.

Murugkar, Lata, 1991, *Dalit Panthars Movement: A Sociological Appraisal,* Popular Prakashan, Bombay.

NSS 50th Round, 1993-94, Department of Statistics, Government of India (1996a) *Level and Pattern of Consumer Expenditure: Fifth Quinquennial Survey,* NSS 50th Round, 1993-94. Report No. 402.

Nurkse, Ragnar 1953, *Problem of Capital Formation in Under Developed Countries,* Basil black- well, Oxford.

Sainath, P, 1999, 'Dalits and Human Rights: The Battles Ahead-I', *PUCL Bulletin,* July, New Delhi.

Sen, Abhijit 1996, 'Economic Reforms, Employment and Poverty: Trends and Options' *Economic and Political Weekly,* Special Number, Vol. XXXI.

Sharma, P. Kumar, 2000, 'Unemployment and Poverty in Rural Areas', *Kurukshetra,* Vol. 48, No. 7.

Srivastava, Ravi S., 1997, *Poverty in India: A Review of Nature, Trends and Eradication Strategies,* Status Paper Commissioned by the Center for Development Research, Copenhagen, for the European Union Research Project on Poverty Reduction in India.

The Hindu, 2009, 'NAREGA: Breaking New Ground', Sunday, June 21 Weekly Edition.

The Times of India, 2010, (1 September), New Delhi Edition.

The Times of India, 2010 'A Job Not Done Well' Sunday, August 29, New Delhi Edition.

World Bank, 1998, *Reducing Poverty in India: Options for More Effective Public Services,* Report No. 17881-IN, Poverty Reduction and Economic Management Unit, South Asia Region, The World Bank Washington D.C.

World Food Programmes (WFP) (http://en.wikipedia.org/wiki/World_Food_Programme)

5

Hidden Caste Discrimination in Panchayat Raj

A Study of Scheduled Caste Women

Sujata Karade

No country or society can prosper without equal opportunities to its citizens, but in India, two categories of people are kept away from nation-building activities. They are Dalits and women. Nowhere do women have equal rights and status with men. Although the United Nations recognizes equality of women, there is a lot of discrimination on the basis of sex, crushing poverty overlaid with longstanding patterns of discrimination create condition for women, which threaten their well-being, deny them choice of child bearing, limit opportunities for education and training and restrict economic participation and cultural, social, political and economic rights. Women are not only economically dependent but also politically and legally powerless. As daughters, wives, mothers and sisters, they are caught in a life cycle that brings unequal treatment to their share. In India *Matru devo bhava* is a saying in Sanskrit that equals mother to God. It represents the Indian sentiment, which places the mother above every one; however, it has only been a lip service. In reality, it exists only in books.

Before 300 B.C. women enjoyed a high status. The position of Hindu women, however, was very different from the lower status; they were graded after about 300 B.C. It appears as if several drastic social changes took place in the Indian society, which led to the curtailment of the freedom to women. Significant changes occurred in the social, economic and political status of women during the nineteenth century in India. There were three main reasons responsible for bringing virtual difference in the position of women in the society. First, the change in the outlook that was the result of the acceptance of tenets of liberal philosophy from the West, which emphasized the principle of contract rather than status. It was a rational outlook of life and its problems. Second, the great social reformers such as Raja Ram Mohan Roy, Ishwar Chandra Vidya Sagar, Jyotiba Phule, Dayanand Saraswati and Keshav Chandra Sen worked for the upliftment of women. These are the deeds of service for the cause of women in India. Third, there was firm faith in Mahatma Gandhi and the leaders of the national movement that the liberation of the country from the bondage of imperialism was possible without the active participation of women who were constitutional half of the population of the country. A lot has also been written on Indian women. In the last three decades, women's studies centre has appeared in many Indian and foreign languages with the focal points ranging from abortions of female foetus to bride-burning and the ideology of sati. But amazingly there is little interest in Dalit women. Most of women's studies concentrated on middle class women, among whom very few are Dalits, because only an estimated 5 to 10 per cent of Dalit women are able to lead a middle class life. On the other hand, in the general literature of Dalits, usually no special attention is paid to Dalit women and their specific problems.

History of the Scheduled Castes

The term 'scheduled caste' has been applied to such of those castes and communities, which have been listed in the Schedule by the Government of India. The scheduled castes were the former untouchable castes of the Hindu religion. Beside the four traditional castes, there was another group of persons even during the early days of *chaturvarnya* who came to be described as untouchables because they were of darker skin and were engaged in unclean occupations. They were referred in earlier times as *Anatyajas, Pariahs, Ati-Shudras*, etc. and in the modern context as depressed classes and scheduled castes. These people were the outcastes and as such were socially ostracized by caste Hindus. As a part of the lowest strata in the society, the untouchables formed the fifth *varna* (*panchamas*) or the fifth caste. They were assigned a position much lower than that of the *Shudras*. They were expected to do all the dirty jobs in society. As untouchables, this group was denied the right to: (1) enter the temple and worship with other Hindus, (2) send their children to school, (3) draw water from public wells, (4) improve their economic and educational condition and (5) be treated civilly as self-respected members of the community on par with caste Hindus.

In different parts of India, a large majority of the untouchables were farm workers, who were hereditary serfs attached to agricultural holdings, while the exact position of the untouchables carried from region to region, the general characteristics observed were as follows:

1. The untouchables were to live outside of the village inhabited by caste Hindus.
2. They were not to pollute these communities buy physical contact or use of public premises including wells and tanks.
3. They were not to use clothes and ornaments, which will mark them off as upper caste people.
4. They were not to acquire education or training, which will equip them for performance of better jobs or callings.
5. They were to engage in occupations such as menial jobs, agricultural work and so on.

Dr B.R. Ambedkar argued that the depressed classes should be entitled to special protection more than any other religious majority in the country, while framing the Constitution of India. Dr Ambedkar who was one of its architects secured necessary constitutional guarantees for the upliftment of the Dalits. Before independence, Dr Ambedkar organized many women conferences at places such as Mahad (1930), Nagpur (1931), Koregaon (1934), Tumsar (1939) and Nagpur (1938). Therefore, many Dalit women were aware of their education and rights.

The Government of India, for the first time in its history, took up the removal of untouchability as one of its main and important tasks. The state legislations passed certain measures for the removal of untouchability after independence. The schemes included socio-economic upliftment, health, and housing schemes. Many scheduled caste people have sought urban upliftment. Therefore, if the members of scheduled castes communities are in a position to seek entry into urban settlement, a change in their life pattern was expected.

The Problem

India has ensured equal status to women under its Constitution under Article No. 14, which provides that 'The State shall not deny to any person equality before the law or the equal protection of the laws within the territory of India'. This provision clearly shows that women in India enjoy right to equality; any type of discrimination against them shall be violations of equality of right and respect for human dignity. The Constitution also provides under Article No. 15 that every female citizen has a right to access to the use of wells, tanks, bathing ghats, roads and places of public resort maintained wholly or partly by public funds.

Since the Constitution of India stresses the need for promoting with special care the educational and economic interests of the weaker sections of the people, the welfare and development of women received particular attention from the beginning of independence. The problem of SCs has been universally acknowledged to be a major social problem. They have been facing dual problems such as gender and caste problem. Therefore, central and state governments have been implementing various development programmes for the upliftment of SCs, especially reservation in education, service and political participation.

The Community Development Programme (CDP) and the National Extension Service Programme (NESP) were the two major development programmes launched in 1952 and 1953, respectively. The First Five-Year Plan for rural development was to be implemented with the help of village panchayats and by involving the entire community. The idea was to have people's participation in the programmes meant for them through cooperation of local bodies. But in every society following patriarchy, women are depressed in the society. In 1974, Vina Mujumdar make report and argued for women's representation on the ground that such a move would take up the cause of other disadvantaged women. An election commissioner T.N. Seshan also felt that the absence of women from political decision-making process made the drafted laws and regulations discriminatory against them.

Before the 73rd Amendment, there were certain drawbacks leading to ineffective implementation, insufficient representation of the weaker sections, including scheduled castes, scheduled tribes, other backward castes and women, or lack of political will to share power, as well as absence to peoples' participation in Panchayat Raj Institution (hereafter PRI). Therefore, Rajiv Gandhi government introduced the 64th Constitutional Amendment Bill in 1989 seeking to strengthen PRI. This bill was criticized on various grounds. Finally in 1992, the bill was reintroduced and passed as the 73rd Constitutional Amendment. On 24 April 1993, the structural framework of the amendment was prepared keeping in view the past experiences of the local government bodies (hereafter LGB). In this bill, a salient feature is the reservation of one-third of seats both in reserved and unreserved categories for women at every level of LGB. One-third of the posts of the chairpersons at each level also were to be reserved for women.

As a result, a large number of women came in the decision-making positions at the local level from among the 15–20 lakhs contesting the polls, 7–8 lakhs women and about 75,000 women as office bearers at all levels of panchayat share the responsibility in the development process. But those scheduled caste women who have come to PRI level are facing all sorts of problems. Women from general category are facing gender problem. But scheduled caste women are facing gender, class and caste problem as the upper castes used them as rubber stamp.

The Maharashtra State Government has made many attempts in evolving multidimensional social policies with high hopes of bringing about radical changes in the condition of the SC women. Some questions that came up are as follows: What is the impact of government welfare programmes on SC women? How far are they benefited from these policies and Why? What is the relation between achievements and political participation of the SC women?

Objectives of the Study

The present study has been undertaken with the following objectives:

1. To understand the family, political, educational background of SC women who are politically representing local government bodies.
2. To find out how SC women are being dominated by the patriarchy.

3. To account of SC women's work in the local government bodies.
4. To find out, the problems faced by the SC women in the work of government and non-government level.

The Study Area

For the present study, the researcher has selected the area of Sangli District. In this district, many villages have received various awards for being ideal villages, Tanta Mukti Gaon. This district is also well known for cooperative movement and many SC political leaders have come from this district. Therefore, this district has been selected for the present study.

Sampling Design

This district is divided into 10 tehsils for administrative work namely *Khanapur, Jat, Kavathe Mahankal, Palus, Tasgaon, Shiral, Walwa, Vita* and *Miraj*. The researcher has selected the whole district for the research. A total of 184 SC women have been elected on reserved posts and 22 on open posts. The total of SC women is 206. These women represent SC women in PRI.

Selection of the Respondents

The researcher used census study method for the present study. The SC women members of PRI are respondents of this study. The information of family background, educational status, migration and impact of governmental welfare policies and related information have been collected from the respondents.

After independence, the government has drafted policies regarding women's empowerment. 73rd Amendment relates to PRI. But Dalit women are neglected in the decision making in PRI. Therefore, in this research analysis, I mark why they are neglected? Which is the most crucial factor related to harassment? This is the focus of the present study.

Findings of the Study

The findings of the present study are considered through gender and subaltern approaches.

In this district, a total of 206 SC women represent PRI. The researcher has tried to cover 100 per cent sample for the study but some respondents were inaccessible because of their personal problems. Sometimes their family members were ill, and sometimes, they met but they could not give their response. As a result, the researcher has taken only 171 (83%) respondents for this study and among these 153 are from reserved posts and 18 respondents are from on open posts.

Generally, we have seen that, the quota reservation in educational admissions and service is not filled properly because the system is totally against backward castes. And here SC women are elected on open posts; therefore, this situation is wonderful but notable point is that the relation between political power and political party is very closely associated. In the 73rd Amendment, 33 per cent reservation goes to the SC women. Therefore, various political parties give tickets to SC women. At that time they do not think of humanity and philosophy of equality, but they think about means to gain political power. The upper caste male members used SC women as a rubber stamp. Basically when reservation has gone to the post of *Sarpanch,* then upper caste people placed many SC women to contest for open post as well. At this level, they think only the political power of PRI.

Table 1

Post of Respondents and Names of the Scheduled Caste of the Respondents

Post of Respondent	*Name of the Scheduled Caste of the Respondent*				*Total*
	Buddhist	*Chambhar*	*Mahar*	*Mang*	
Gram panchayat	12	22	73	30	137
	8.8%	16.1%	53.3%	21.9%	100%
Sarpanch	3	4	15	8	30
	10%	13.3%	50.0%	26.7%	100%
Deputy Sarpanch	1	–	1	2	4
	25%	–	25%	50%	100%
Total	16	26	89	40	171
	9.4%	15.2%	52%	23.4%	100%

Table 1 shows the number of caste-wise respondents from Sangli district. The majority, 89 (52.0%) of members, come from Mahar caste, then Mang 40 (23.4%) and 26 (15.2%) of Chambhar Caste and remaining 16 (9.4%) are Buddhists. The survey has been done by an institution from Kolkata. They have found that in Maharashtra the population of Mahars is numerically large;

therefore, it is reflected in this study. But one thing is to be noted regarding those who are Buddhists is that the religious conversion of Dr B.R. Ambedkar and his followers have not been noted by government. Hence, they are treated as same as they were treated in their earlier caste. But, those who practiced Buddhism in day-to-day life enthusiastically say that 'we are Buddhists therefore, you should not include us in the old caste category, which is related to Hindu religion'. On this basis, the Buddhist category has been considered separately. Mostly, the Buddhist community is identified in the urban area but, in this study, researcher has found the Buddhist community is prevalent in the rural areas also.

Table 1 also shows that out of 171, only 137 respondents are members of PRI and 30 respondents are Sarpanchs and only 4 respondents are Deputy Sarpanchs. It means that 34 SC women enjoy higher position of decision-making process.

Table 2

Education and Post of Respondent

Education of the Respondent	*Post of Respondent*			*Total*
	Member	*Sarpanch*	*Deputy Sarpanch*	
Illiterate	25	7	–	32
	18.2%	23.3%	–	18.7%
Primary	57	13	1	71
	41.6%	43.3%	25.0%	41.5%
Secondary	49	6	3	58
	35.8%	20.0%	75.0%	33.9%
Higher Secondary	2	1	–	3
	1.5%	3.3%	–	1.8%
Graduate	2	2	–	4
	1.5%	6.7%	–	2.3%
PG	2	1	–	3
	1.5%	3.3%	–	1.8%
Total	137	30	4	171
	100%	100%	100%	100%

Table 2 shows that out of 171 respondents, 32 (18.7%) respondents are illiterate and majority 71 (41.5) of respondents have completed primary education and 58 (33.9%) respondents have completed secondary education and 3 (1.8%), 4 (2.3%) and 3 (1.8%) respondents have done higher secondary and graduate and post-graduate-level education respectively. In general highly educated people are not involved in the politics and the result of the present study also concludes the same. But 32 (18.7%) respondents are illiterate and the majority 71 (41.5%) respondents have taken primary education; therefore, we can say that SC women are less educated. Also the majority of respondents who have taken the post of Sarpanch are illiterate or educated up to primary level. So they are not aware of their administrative power. Therefore, their power is misused by upper caste people.

When we think of gender perspective, then we understand that the male have not allowed educated women to empowerment because men generally do not like to work under educated women. Sometimes women take credit for work done by them and this hurts the ego of male members. Even in the rural areas, male members do not give chance to the educated women for the fear of taking the credit of all the works. This happens in the illiterate society. But, in the well-organized society, the educated women have been given opportunities to manage a particular ward.

Table 3

Occupation of the Respondents

Occupation of the Respondents	*Frequency*	*Per cent*
Housewives	102	59.6
Housewives and service in semi-government	1	0.6
Housewives and business	1	0.6
Housewives and service in private sector	4	2.3
Housewives and social worker	2	1.2
Housewives and agriculture labour	52	30.4
Housewives and other work	7	4.1
Devdasi	2	1.2
Total	171	100

Table 3 shows that out of 171, majority 102 (59.6%) of respondents are housewives, and 52 (30.4%) respondents are engaged in agricultural work. When we think of women empowerment we have to take care of SC women as they are not economically sound and are dependent on other castes (mostly dominant castes). In such cases, it is futile to think that these women are capable of taking decisions.

Table 4

Occupation of the Husband and Total Agricultural Land of Respondent

Occupation of the Husband of Respondent	*Area of Agricultural Land (1 Guntha = 1089 sq. ft. approx.)*								*Total*
	(in Gunthas)					*(in Hectare)*			
	Landless	*20*	*40*	*60*	*80*	*One*	*One and Half*	*More than 2*	
NA	11	4	3	–	9	3	2	1	33
Government Sector	–	1	–	–	–	1	–	1	3
Semi-government sector	5	2	2	–	–	4	1	1	15
Private sector	4	9	1	–	4	–	2	–	20
Unorganized sector	25	26	6	–	12	6	1	–	76
Social worker	–	1	1	–	1	–	–	–	3
Business	1	2	1	–	–	–	–	–	4
Farming	–	3	1	1	3	1	3	1	13
Pensioner	1	–	–	–	–	–	–	3	4
Total	47	48	15	1	29	15	9	7	171

Table 4 shows that 47 respondents' families are landless, 48 having only 20 Gunthas land, 15 have 40 Gunthas, 1 has 60 Gunthas, 29 have 80 Gunthas, 15 have 1 hectare, 9 have one and half hectare and just a few respondent families have more than two hectares land.

Table 5

Type of Land of Respondent's Family

	Non-irrigated	*Irrigated*	*Wasteland*
Landless	84	152	146
20 Gunthas	33	5	12
40 Gunthas	13	2	2
60 Gunthas	2	0	0
80 Gunthas	23	6	4
1Hectaras	11	1	2
One and half Hectare	1	2	5
More than 2 Hectares	4	3	0
Total	171	171	171

Table 5 indicates that 84, 152 and 146 respondent families have no land neither non-irrigated, nor irrigated or nor wasteland. This table also shows that, from among the landholders, majority hold non-irrigated land and very few have irrigated land. So their economic position is very clear from the data in Tables 4 and 5. This is also concerned with income of the family which is dependent on the occupation of the husband of respondent. Table 4 shows that majority (76) of respondents' spouse work in the unorganized sector. Therefore, their economic position is very poor. Very few respondents' spouses are serving in government or semi-government service.

Generally upper caste women face only gender problem but they do not face class as well as caste discrimination but SC women definitely face caste problem. The majority of the rural areas connected with religious activity or these people project orthodox practices as Hindu culture and Dalits are victims. When we think SC women and their position, Gail Omvedt said Dalit women are 'downtrodden among downtrodden'. Her observation is right because 'culture' is more protective towards the male.

Table 6

Meeting and Decision in PRI

Participate in the Meeting	*Decision Maker in the Meeting*					*Total*
	Self (Respondent)	*Male Member of the Family*	*Upper Caste Male Member*	*Backward Male Member*	*Upper and Lower Caste Leader*	
Yes	31	12	90	6	6	145
	21.4%	8.3%	62.1%	4.1%	4.1%	100%
No	2	1	23	–	–	26
	7.7%	3.8%	88.5%	–	–	100%
Total	33	13	113	6	6	171
	19.3%	7.6%	66.1%	3.5%	3.5%	100%

Various thinkers have said that Dalit women face gender, class and caste discrimination. In the present study, Table 6 shows that out of 171 respondents, 145 respondents are participating in the PRI meeting and remaining are not. Also out of 171, 113 respondents say that the upper caste male members have taken decision in the meeting. It means that the SC women have not been involved in the PRI meeting. The reason for this is quite clear that SC women are being pressurized by the upper caste members for not opening their mouths in the meeting and sometimes they threaten and warn these women by saying 'you are lower caste therefore you have no right to say anything in the meeting, you just take care of your physical presence in the meeting'.

Table 7

Type of Harassment and Total Agricultural Land of the Respondents

Type of Harassment	*Area of Agricultural Land*								*Total*
	Gunthas				*Hectare*				
	NA	*20*	*40*	*60*	*80*	*One*	*One and Half*	*More than 2*	
None	12	18	6	–	16	1	2	2	57
Can't say	10	7	2	–	4	2	–	2	27
Lack of confidence vote	–	1	–	–	–	–	–	–	1
Casteism by Political members	11	18	4	1	4	7	5	1	51
Casteism by Administrative person	2	1	–	–	1	–	1	–	5
House burnt	–	–	–	–	–	–	1	–	1
Locked me at Office	1	–	–	–	–	–	–	–	1
Blame on character and torch ring	–	1	–	–	–	1	–	1	3
Pressure for Tanta Mukti gaon (Atrocity case)	1	–	–	–	1	–	–	–	2
Pressure for keep mum	6	1	2	–	1	1	–	1	12
Pressure to 'remain absent at the meeting'	–	–	1	–	2	–	–	–	3
Neglected for meeting	2	1	–	–	–	2	–	–	5
At the first meeting given the broken Chair	2	–	–	–	–	–	–	–	2
Name not included in Konsheela (Cornerstone)	–	–	–	–	–	1	–	–	1
	47	48	15	1	29	15	9	7	171

Table 7 shows that 57 (33%) respondents said that they have no harassment due to casteism and gender. But 27 respondents have not given an answer to problem concerned with harassment as gender and casteism. But researcher observes that they have a problem but they wouldn't say so, due to the pressure of upper caste male members. Table 7 gives the type of harassment faced by the respondent. Among these majority of respondents 51 (29.8%) face the problem of casteism by upper caste members and 5 by administrative person. These data also prove that those respondents who have agricultural land more than 1 hectare face these problems of harassment. These figures are not concerned with gender as well as economic condition but connected more with caste. Therefore, notable point is that the SC women's problem of casteism is caused by upper caste male members. This is the mindset of the upper caste people even today.

Conclusion

Various studies have been done by the many researchers concerning women's political empowerment. But very few studies have focused on Dalit and especially scheduled caste women. Therefore, this research area is neglected by researchers. In the present study, we find that SC women are facing various types of the problems. In general SC women face caste, class and gender discrimination. But the study concludes that SC women face gender problem in their home and in their community. But when they represent it in the PRI, majority of respondents do not face gender and class problem but they face caste problem created by the upper caste political male and female members.

Suggested Readings

Bandyopadhyay, Debabrata and Mukherjee, Amitava, 2006, *Empowering Women Panchayat Members*, Concept Publishing Company, New Delhi.

Bhagwat, Vidyut, 1998, *Locating Early Feminist Thought: A Review of Women's Situation from the 17th to the 20th century*, Monograph Published by Women's Studies Centre, Department of Sociology, University of Pune.

Government of India, 1955, Backward Class Commission Report, pp. 16–18.

Guru, Gopal, 1995, 'Dalit Women Talk Differently', *EPW*, 14–21 October , pp. 2548–2549.

Jha, Ashok Kumar, 2004, *Women in Panchayati Raj Institutions*, Anmol Publications Pvt. Ltd., New Delhi.

Kamble, N.D., 1932, *The Scheduled Castes*, Ashish Publishing House, New Delhi.

Kothari, R., 1994, 'Rise of Dalits and the Renewed Debate on Caste', *Economic and Political Weekly*, 25 June, pp. 1589–1594.

Meenakshi, J., 2007, *Women and Panchayati Raj*, Omega Publications, New Delhi.

Parvthamma, C., 1989, *Scheduled Castes and Tribes: A Socio-economic Survey*, Ashish Publishing House, New Delhi.

Patwardhan, Sunanda, 1973, *Change Among India's Harijans*, Orient Longman Limited, New Delhi.

Rege, Sharmila, 1998, *Dalit Women Talk Differently*, Women's Studies Center, University of Pune.

Report of Scheduled Caste's Commission, 1968–1969, p. 186.

Salve, R.N., 1998, *Impact of Government Welfare Measures on Scheduled Castes of India*, Mulnivasi Publishing, Aurangabad.

Singla, Pamela, 2007, *Women's Participation in Panchayati Raj: Nature and Effectiveness*, Rawat Publications, Jaipur.

Wankhede, G.G., 1999, *Social Mobility and Scheduled Castes*, Rawat Publications, Jaipur.

6

Labour Market Discrimination

Prakash Kamble

Labour is an important factor in the process of production and it plays a vital role in speeding up the socio-economic development of the economy. It is a human factor in the absence of which no single economic activity can be initiated. Hence, labour has a special significance in the development of economic activities, and rapid and all round economic development of the economy. But the importance of labour has not been recognized by the society. Due status, importance and treatment are not being given to labour as a factor of production in general and as a human being in particular. The discriminatory treatment is meted out to labour. Labour discrimination is practiced all over the world. And the bases of labour discrimination are caste, race, class, gender, ethnicity, colour, religion and so on. India is also a country in which there is a domination of bases of labour discrimination such as caste, class, gender, religion, etc. Hence, labour discrimination is practiced significantly in India. Labour discrimination has several evil consequences, and it can put greater social cost on the society as a whole. But it is neglected, and labour discrimination is practiced. This demands a study of the problem of labour market discrimination in the context of Indian economy. It is against this overall background that the present research study endeavours to assess the nature, extent, causes of the problem of labour discrimination, and policy guidelines to tackle the same.

Objectives of the Study

The major and important objectives of the present study are as follows:

1. To understand the concept of labour market discrimination;
2. To study the problem of labour market discrimination in the context of India;
3. To draw implications of labour discrimination in India;
4. To reveal policy guidelines for the problem of labour discrimination in India.

Hypothesis of the Study

The hypotheses of the present research study are as follows:

1. Labour market discrimination is practiced on the basis of gender and caste in India.
2. Wage discrimination is a mechanism of labour discrimination in India.

Data Base and Research Methodology

The present research relies exclusively on the secondary data. It covers the period from 1987 to 2005. The secondary data have been collected relating to employment generation and its structure, rural and urban components of employment, categories of labour, male–female participation in labour market, wage discrimination, agriculture and non-agriculture employment, unemployment and its categories from the sources such as National Sample Survey Organization Publications (NSSO), National Council for Applied Economics Research (NCAER) and others. This study makes use of quantitative techniques such as ratio analysis, simple growth rate (SGR), percentage difference, variance and other techniques in order to process the data by taking help of computer software packages such as Excel and SPSS. The important parameters used in the present study consist of volume of employment, nature of employment, nature and extent of unemployment, male–female participation in employment, scheduled castes (here after SCs) and non-scheduled castes participation in employment, wage discrimination between males and females, SCs and Non-SCs, agricultural labourers and non-agricultural labourers, etc.

The state-wise scenario of labour discrimination in India has also been examined.

Nature and Extent of Labour Market Discrimination in India

Labour market discrimination is a crucial problem especially in developing countries like India. This has a domination of religion, caste and gender-related ideas. This does not mean it is not a problem in developed countries like United States, United Kingdom and other countries. It is basically the problem of discrimination in the labour market. It is the unequal treatment given to labour especially on the bases of social, religious and economic criteria, such as caste, religion, gender, ethnicity and so on. If the same quality labour is given different treatment in one or the same employment or establishment, this is known as labour discrimination. It is the prejudices, wrong notions, traditions, biases, faulty ideas and ideology, incorrect line or direction of thinking that contribute to labour market discrimination. This can happen more frequently in those countries, which have domination of religion, caste and class ideology, traditions and blind beliefs, illiteracy, domination of males, biases and so on. We find the majority of such peculiarities in a country like India. Hence, we find labour market discrimination practiced to a great extent in India.

Labour market discrimination refers to the situation of unequal treatment of the workers, possessing the same education, training and employment experience or productivity level in hiring or in wage payment, but differing in some non-economic personal characteristics associated with race, sex or caste.[1] The free market solution is, however, not a final and practical remedy, as far a number of reasons market discrimination, particularly the labour market discrimination, might persist over long periods with or without prevalence of free market situation.[2]

Labour market discrimination is a broader concept having various issues and aspects. So far as labour discrimination in India is concerned, we find labour discrimination based on the criteria such as religion, caste, gender and class. Even though labour is qualified in all respects for a particular job or work, he is either deprived of that job opportunity or underpaid even after being absorbed in that employment. Likewise, suitable duties and responsibilities are not being given.

The assignment or division of occupations and property rights across castes is unequal and hierarchal with some occupations considered to be socially inferior.[3] Caste-based

Table 1

Organized/Unorganized Employment in India (15–59 years)

Category	*Rural*		*Urban*		*Total*		*Variance Rural*	*Variance Urban*	*Variance Total*
	1999–2000	*2004–2005*	*1999–2000*	*2004–2005*	*1999–2000*	*2004–2005*			
Organized	19.2%	14.3%	26.8%	23.6%	23.3%	18.7%	–12%	–5%	–11%
Unorganized	80.8%	85.7%	73.2%	76.4%	76.7%	81.3%	12%	5%	11%
Total	100%	100%	100%	100%	100%	100%	–	–	–
Growth Rate									
Organized	–	3.2%	–	1.1%	–	1.9%	–	–	–
Unorganized	–	10.7%	–	4.6%	–	7.7%	–	–	–
Total		9.4%		3.7%		6.5%			

Source: NSSO Rounds.

discrimination may involve limited access to markets such as land, inputs, consumer goods and social services, differences between prices charged or received and market prices.[4]

In the following part of this chapter, an attempt has been made to discuss the nature and extent of labour market discrimination in India.

The type of employment being generated in the economy can also be a basis of labour discrimination. Organized employment is preferred to unorganized employment on the grounds of salary, status, security, powers, etc. But organized employment is not available, especially to the people of backward classes. This can also have a gender bias.[5] Hence, the state of employment generation in organized and unorganized sectors with rural–urban dimensions is presented in Table 1.

It is revealed that total employment generation in India is dominated by the employment in unorganized sector than in the organized sector. Likewise, relatively it is dominated in the urban areas than rural areas. Only satisfactory thing is that employment growth is higher in rural areas than in urban areas. But it is dominated by employment in unorganized sector, which is conducive for labour discrimination. The technique of variance indicates that variations in employment in organized sector are negative and vice versa.

It is also important to study employment structure in India based on different categories or types of labour. It can also highlight some issues relating to labour discrimination in India.

It is observed from Table 2 that rural employment is dominated by self-employment that can have the problem of disguised unemployment, which is followed by other types of labour employment. Again, rural employment is dominated by agricultural labour, which has shown a negative growth during the period under study. Urban employment in India is dominated by regular wage/salaried employment, which is followed by self-employment. But regular wage/salaried employment has shown a significant negative growth. This reveals that self-employment does not allow labour discrimination, but regular wage/salaried employment has the feature of labour discrimination (Table 2).

Table 2
Employment Structure in Rural and Urban India

Population Type	*1993–1994*	*1999–2000*	*2004–2005*	*SGR*
		Rural		
1. Self-employed	555 (55%)	510 (51%)	565 (56%)	2%
2. Agricultural labour	275 (27%)	301 (30%)	241 (24%)	–12%
3. Other labour	75 (7%)	76 (8%)	106 (11%)	41%
4. Rural labour	350 (35%)	376 (38%)	346 (35%)	–1%
5. Others	95 (9%)	114 (11%)	88 (9%)	–7%
6. All	1000	1000	1000	
		Urban		
1. Self-employed	388 (39%)	393 (39%)	433 (43%)	12%
2. Regular wage/salaried	428 (43%)	402 (40%)	396 (40%)	–7%
3. Casual labour	129 (13%)	141 (14%)	118 (12%)	–9%
4. Others	55 (5%)	64 (7%)	53 (5%)	–4%
5. All	1000	1000	1000	

Note: Figures in brackets indicate percentages of all.

Source: NSSO Rounds.

Gender is the basis of labour discrimination in India; hence, male labourers are preferred to female labourers. But it is found that, this picture is changing slowly and gradually when we study unemployment rate and its structure in India. Table 3 presents necessary information regarding that.

From the Table 3, it is observed that unemployment based on CDS is increasing in both rural as well as urban areas in India. But it is considerably lower for females than males in rural areas. In urban area, unemployment based on CDS has been reduced, but more decrease is found among females than males. This is an indicator of falling gender bias in providing employment in India. The unemployment based on US status has reduced more for females than males in rural areas, but it has increased significantly for females in urban areas.

Table 3

Unemployment Rate in Rural and Urban Areas in India

Round Year	*Male*			*Female*		
	US	*CWS*	*CDS*	*US*	*CWS*	*CDS*
			Rural			
1987–1988 (43rd)	28	42	46	35	44	67
1993–1994 (50th)	20	31	56	13	29	56
1999–2000 (55th)	21	39	72	15	37	70
2004–2005 (61st)	21	38	80	31	42	87
Variance	–14%	–22%	236%	–124%	–45%	165%
			Urban			
1987–1988 (43rd)	61	66	88	85	92	120
1993–1994 (50th)	54	52	67	83	79	104
1999–2000 (55th)	48	56	73	71	73	94
2004–2005 (61st)	44	52	75	91	90	116
Variance	–55%	–44%	–78%	70%	82%	–140%

Source: NSSO Rounds.

Note: US = Usual Status, CWS = Current Weekly Status, CDS = Current Daily Status.

When we study female to male participation in agricultural and non-agricultural employment, women and managers, we found a significant labour discrimination based on gender bias.

The data in Table 4 adequately prove that gender-based labour discrimination is significant in India. Females are absorbed greatly in agricultural than non-agricultural employment. Likewise, female participation as managers is very insignificant. It is satisfactory only in Orissa. In non-agricultural employment, Andhra Pradesh, Karnataka, Madhya Pradesh and Gujarat are in better position than in all other states. Thus, it is a clear indicator of labour market discrimination on the basis of gender.[6]

Table 4
Gender-based Labour Market Discrimination

State	Female to Male Participation Ratios				
	Agricultural Casual	*Non-agricultural Casual*	*Variance*	*Workers*	*Managers*
Andhra Pradesh	63.9	57.1	–23.12%	21.1	8.2
Assam	27.3	6.3	–220%	27.5	3
Bihar	100	27.8	–2606%	8.8	3
Gujarat	92.9	45.5	–1123%	12.6	2.3
Haryana	25	20	–12%	7.1	1.4
Karnataka	78.6	50	–409%	21.9	5.3
Kerala	66.7	36.4	–459%	23.9	3.4
Maharashtra	133.3	25	–5864%	14.3	4.6
Madhya Pradesh	96	50	–1058%	12.2	4.4
Orissa	38.5	25	–91%	18.8	6.9
Punjab	42.9	10	–541%	7	1.6
Rajasthan	100	26.1	–2730%	10.9	3.3
Tamil Nadu	82.1	37.5	–995%	19.3	3.6
Uttar Pradesh	42.9	11.1	506%	7.3	2.7
West Bengal	61.9	33.3	409%	11.8	2.2

Source: NCAER 1999 REDS Survey and Esteve-Volart (2004).

Gender-based labour discrimination in India is not only practiced while providing employment, but also in the payment of wages/salaries. Thus, wages are a mechanism of labour discrimination in India. Table 5 represents the data regarding labour discrimination through wage discrimination.

Gender equality refers to women's enjoyment of equal rights in a number of dimensions. These include economic opportunities, access to public goods, participation in public decision making and employment. Although linked to some of these factors, wage discrimination is generally understood as referring to women being paid lower wages accounting for observable attributes.[7] It has long been noted that if women are discriminated against in the wage labour market, it would be rational for them to shift towards self-employment.[8]

It is revealed that labour market discrimination on the basis of wage differentiation is practiced in agricultural as well as non-agricultural employment. But it is higher in non-agricultural employment than in the agricultural employment. It is also different across the states in India. So far as agricultural employment is concerned, wage discrimination is absent in Assam and Rajasthan only. It is higher in Tamil Nadu, Kerala and Maharashtra. But it is lower in Uttar Pradesh, Gujarat, Punjab and Bihar. We found greater wage discrimination in Tamil Nadu, Orissa and Kerala, but lower wage discrimination in Assam, Uttar Pradesh and Haryana.

Labour discrimination in India also has a caste or caste-based group basis. It is practiced in providing employment as well as through wage discrimination. Though the occupational placement of caste groups varies across India, a common feature is the sharp contrast in status and income between scheduled caste (SCs) and scheduled tribes (STs) on the other hand and the so-called forward castes on the other hand.[9]

Table 5

Wage Rate Discrimination in India (in ₹ Per Day)

State	*Agricultural Labour*			*Non-agricultural Labour*		
	Male	*Female*	*Difference (%)*	*Male*	*Female*	*Difference (%)*
Andhra Pradesh	45.36	33.94	25%	46.34	33.64	27%
Assam	48.14	49.06	–2%	49.71	47.27	5%
Bihar	40.05	33.42	17%	45.82	35.28	23%
Gujarat	44.46	40.32	9%	54.98	38.57	30%
Haryana	74.14	59.00	20%	86.95	76.82	12%
Karnataka	43.22	31.92	26%	51.22	35.17	31%
Kerala	101.36	60.93	40%	107.14	60.81	43%
Maharashtra	43.26	28.37	34%	50.50	33.60	33%
Madhya Pradesh	32.30	27.42	15%	40.07	31.25	22%
Orissa	41.00	30.79	25%	61.92	35.00	43%
Punjab	68.53	59.13	14%	83.44	66.67	20%
Rajasthan	54.50	55.51	-2%	68.75	44.58	35%
Tamil Nadu	53.24	29.33	46%	67.80	33.18	51%
Uttar Pradesh	47.51	44.57	6%	61.74	57.86	6%
West Bengal	41.75	32.02	23%	50.47	37.90	25%
All India	46.35	33.70	27%	62.77	42.75	32%

Source: NCAER 1999 REDS Survey.

Table 6

Occupational Distribution among Wage Workers by Social Group, 2004–05 (in %)

Occupation	*Regular Workers*			*Casual Workers*			*Variance*		*Variance*	
	SC	*OBC*	*General*	*SC*	*OBC*	*General*	*I*	*II*	*I*	*II*
Professional/ technical	12	17	25	–	–	–	–12%	32	–	–
Administrative	1	2	6	–	–	–	–0.5%	8	–	–
Clerical	15	17	21	–	–	1	–2%	8	–	–
Sales workers	4	8	9	–	1	1	–8%	0.5	–	–
Service workers	26	13	10	2	2	3	+84%	–4	–	–0.5%
Farmers, fishermen, etc.	6	5	2	69	65	58	+0.5%	+ 4	+ 8%	+ 24%
Production workers	36	37	28	28	32	37	–0.5%	–40	–8%	–12%
Total	100	100	100	100	100	100				

Source: NSSO 61st Round, 2004–2005.

Note: I variance between SCs and OBCs; II variance between OBCs and Generals.

It is revealed from Table 6 that there is a very insignificant participation of SCs in socially prestigious and highly paid employment, especially in regular employment than OBCs and general category people. The OBCs are better than SCs, but worse as compared to the general. Surprisingly, participation of SCs and OBCs in casual employment is better than general category, but it is in socially inferior and lowly paid employment. Labour discrimination is also practiced through wage discrimination concerning caste or class basis. Necessary data are given in Table 7.

The data in Table 7 reveal that wage discrimination is higher in regular employment than in casual employment. It is lower between SCs and OBCs, but higher between SCs and general category. Likewise, it is also significant between OBCs and general category people. The overall wage discrimination is significant between SCs and general category as well as OBCs and general category especially in regular employment. Likewise, it is also of greater degree in socially prestigious and highly paid employment such as sales women, administrative, professional/technical employment than others in regular employment.

Table 7

Average Weekly Wage among Wage Workers by Social Group (in ₹)

Occupation	*Regular Workers*			*Casual Workers*			*I Wage difference between SC & OBC*	*II Wage difference between OBC & General*	*III Wage difference between SC & General*	*I*	*II*	*III*
	SC	*OBC*	*General*	*SC*	*OBC*	*General*						
Professional/technical	1536	1551	2096	–	–	–	–0.97	–35%	–36%	–	–	–
Administrative	2422	2719	4223	–	–	–	–12	–55%	–74%	–	–	–
Clerical	1330	1419	1679	–	–	–	–7	–18%	–26%	–	–	–
Sales workers	510	544	898	470	453	402	–7	–65%	–76%	4%	113%	14%
Service workers	677	664	911	294	367	388	2	–37%	–35%	–25%	–6%	–32%
Farmers, fishermen, etc.	493	478	603	233	232	242	3	–26%	–22%	0.42%	–4%	–4%
Production workers	791	821	978	384	417	413	–4	–19%	–24%	–9%	0.95%	–8%
Total	920	1028	1558	278	295	314	–12	–52%	–69%	–6%	–6%	–13%

Source: NSSO 61st Round, 2004–2005.

Note: I – variance between SCs and OBCs II – variance between OBCs and Generals III – variance between SCs and Generals.

Discrimination causes 15 per cent lower wages for SCs/STs as compared to equally qualified others.[10] The bad news is that in the absence of a control of grades, SC/ST candidates get wages that are between a fifth and a third lower than those in the general category.[11]

Implications and Policy Guidelines

The thorough study of the problem of labour market discrimination in the context of India clearly and adequately reveals some implications for India. On the basis of that it is also possible to draw some policy guidelines. Hence, the present section of the chapter endeavours to reveal implications for Indian economy, as well as policy guidelines in order to deal with the problem of labour market discrimination in India.

The important implications for an Indian economy relating to labour discrimination are the increasing employment in unorganized sector of the Indian economy creating a conductive environment for labour discrimination in India. It is more possible in agricultural labour, regular wage/salaried employment than casual and self-employment in rural as well as urban areas of India. It is revealed that unemployment based on US status has declined significantly among the females in rural areas than urban areas – which are a good thing. But increase of labour discrimination in urban areas to a significant extent indicates higher gender-based labour discrimination. We also found greater gender-based discrimination in non-agricultural employment and in the post for managers and they are mostly absorbed in agricultural employment. This is also different across the states in India. Labour market discrimination is practiced through wage discrimination with gender bias. It is greater in non-agricultural employment than the agricultural employment and also is different across the states in India. Labour market discrimination based on caste/class is greater in regular employment with socially prestigious and highly paid employment than socially inferior and lowly paid employment. Besides this, labour discrimination based on wage discrimination is also higher in regular and socially prestigious employment with highly paid employment. Labour discrimination is higher for SCs than OBCs, but it is greater for both of them when compared to general category people.

Hence, in order to deal with the problem of labour market discrimination in India the policy guidelines are described as follows:

> It is necessary to attempt for promoting employment in organized sector than in the unorganized sector. For this the government need to play an important role and should have control over the employment in the unorganized sector. The active role of the government through its interference – in the form of acts, laws and their rigorous implementation in agricultural employment and regular wage/salaried employment – is necessary. It is essential to control gender-based labour discrimination through appropriate labour policies especially in non-agriculture employment and in the employment such as the participation as managers, with due control of wage discrimination. Likewise, the intervention of government is essential. Laws, acts, policies and their honest implementation concerning labour discrimination and wage discrimination against SCs and other categories of backward classes should be undertaken. More importantly, gender, caste, class and religion-based discrimination of labours in India are a problem of the fixed mind set, prejudices, blind beliefs and faulty line of thinking. This can be tackled through education, training, awareness, research, participation of government, non-government organizations, social groups, organizations with greater emphasis on students and youth of India.

Concluding Remarks

Labour market discrimination is a major and crucial problem before the world in general and before India in particular. It has various issues and aspects with a broader scope. The present study is an attempt to explore various dimensions of the problems of labour market discrimination in India. But there is plenty of scope for further research on this topic. The micro level study especially based on the primary data will be more beneficial and fruitful in dealing with this problem. The necessary data are a vital problem in research on this topic. The present study is an honest attempt to analyse the problem of labour market discrimination in India. Both the hypotheses of the present study have been tested and proved with adequate empirical support. It is a fact that labour discrimination is practiced on the basis of gender bias as well as caste or class. And wage discrimination is a mechanism of labour discrimination. There can be other bases of labour discrimination as well as mechanism in India. But the present study is restricted to gender and caste/class-based labour discrimination with a prominent mechanism of wage discrimination coupled with priority in employment.

Notes

1. Sukhadeo Thorat, 2007, 'Remedies Against Market Discrimination', A Research Paper, Institute of Dalit Studies, New Delhi, p. 2.
2. Ibid., p. 3.
3. Sukhadeo Thorat, 2007, *Economic Exclusion and Poverty in Asia: The Example of Castes in India,* 2020 Focus Brief on the World's Poor and Hungry People, Washington, DC, IFPRI, p. 2.
4. Ibid., p. 3.
5. L.C. Mallaiah, 2006, 'Economic Discrimination of Women in Indian Labour Market', A Research Paper, Dr Babasaheb Ambedkar Central University, Lucknow (UP), India, p. 1.
6. Ibid., p. 2.
7. Deininger, Jin, Nagarajan, 2006, 'Gender Discrimination and Returns to Self Employment: Evidence from Rural India', A Research Paper, NCAER, New Delhi, p. 3.
8. Ibid., p. 5.
9. Atte Madheswaran, 2009, 'Caste Discrimination in the Indian Labour Market: Evidence from the National Sample Survey', *Economic and Political Weekly,* 44(34), 24–28 August, Mumbai, p. 1.
10. Ibid., p. 2.
11. Somanathan Chakravarty, 2008, 'Discrimination in an Elite Labour Market? Job Placements at IIM Ahmedabad', *Economic and Political Weekly,* 1 November, Mumbai, p. 50.

7

Caste Discrimination versus Democratic Equalization in India

Ravsaheb Janu Katti

Several groups from Asian and African countries, which suffer from discrimination due to reasons other than race or colour, have been negotiating with the UN Commission on Human Rights to bring them under its purview and treat them as discriminated groups for the purpose of Committee on the Elimination of Racial Discrimination (CERD).

Dalit communities from Nepal, the *Methor* community from Bangladesh (traditionally sweepers and manual scavengers) and the *Rodi/Rodiya* and *Pallar/Paraiyar* communities from Sri Lanka face discrimination in employment, practices of social distance and denial of resources, etc. Dalit communities from Pakistan (like Dalits in India except in Muslim society, they face the concept of ritual pollution, concepts of privilege and shame and *Buraku* community from Japan (at the bottom of the Japanese class System and they are viewed as filthy and or non-human beings) are some of the communities representing the matter to UN.

The scheduled castes who are the ex-untouchables constitute more than 17 per cent of the total population (about 170 million) in India, occupy the lowest rank in the caste hierarchy and live in subjugation. They are exploited by the upper castes and hence have been suffering from disabilities such as untouchability and stigmatized degraded status since times immemorial for no fault of theirs.

It was due to the radical, bold stand that Dr B.R. Ambedkar, a highly educated and active leader born among the untouchable community, made on the behalf of the untouchables in 1930–1931 at the Round Table Conference in London. As a result of his intervention at the Round Table Conference, the architect of the Indian Constitution provided them special provisions, namely Articles 14, 15, 16, 17, 25, 29, 44, 46, 49, 325, 330, 334 and 335 of the Indian Constitution, to safeguard the downtrodden.

Since independence, many laws have been introduced in India banning caste discrimination, untouchability and exploitation in all their manifestations. Special commissions have been set up to monitor the progress made in eradicating caste discrimination. But the existing national legislations to prevent caste-based discrimination in India have not been effective due to poor implementation, which itself is the result of lack of political will of the government. In spite of various legislations, the implementing agencies and monitoring bodies continue to show severe discrimination against the scheduled castes. In other words, the government has enacted laws, but the implementing authorities, police, courts and others are all against the asprishyas (Punalekar, 1988).

Why Such Typical Discrimination in India Only?

India is a country of villages with inequalities like any other countries. But, the Hindu social organization in India is traditionally divided into two substrata, known respectively as *Dwija* (twice-born clean castes) and *Ekaja* (once-born as hereditary polluted castes). The *Dwija* comprises three higher *varnas*: the *Brahman*, the *Kshatriya* and the *Vaishya* with their subdivision into castes. The *Ekaja* or the *Shudra* consists of lower castes that are meant to serve the *Dwija* and are, thus, placed lower in the social order of Hindu society. The whole system is known as *Chaturvarna Vyavastha* or fourfold division of Hindu society.

According to the ancient Hindu scriptures such as *Manusmriti* and some other *Shastras*, there are four *varnas*: the *Brahmins* (priests, teachers and scholars), the *Kshatriyas* (kings and warriors), the *Vaishyas* (agriculturists and traders) and

Shudras (artisans and service providers). The Bhagavad Gita says *varnas* are decided based on *Guna* and *Karma*.

The fourfold division of Hindu society which included *Ati-Shudras* or *Panchamas* is composed of many untouchable subgroups. As the *Shudras* stood at the bottom of fourfold hierarchical Hindu order, the *Ati-Shudras* also stood at the lowest bottom, and both were governed by *Brahmanical* laws and customs. With regard to the scheduled castes, the present ex-untouchables known as *Ati-Shudras*, *Antyajas* or *Shudra* of *Chaturvarna* system are right from the origin of caste system are dispossessed castes. Whatever their name, the stigma remains in one form or the other, since the stigma is attached to them by birth and cannot be ritually or socially eliminated.

It is said that untouchability was unknown to the *Vedic Aryans*. Hindus have no explanation regarding the origin of untouchability. They try to explain it in terms of fictitious belief in caste purity, taboo and inequality of castes. Hindus take strong support from caste system and religion to oppress the Mahars (ex-untouchables) and deprive them even of the basic minimum needs. The first explicit use of the word *Asprishya* (ex-untouchables) was made by Vishnu. V. From fifth to seventh century A.D. or possibly even later, there were approximately 104 of lower subcastes.

In order to trace the traditional social status of the ex-untouchables or dispossessed castes, one has to turn over the pages of Indian history. During the Vedic period, the last *varna*, that is *Shudra* was considered untouchable. They had no civil or religious rights in the society. This practice of untouchability and discrimination between the *Dwija* and *Ekaja* or *Shudra* was later passed on to the people below the rank of *Shudra* but with a higher degree of rigidity and intensity of untouchability as per the caste norms associated with purity and pollution.

During the post-Vedic period, the *Panchamas* or those who came into being from mixed unions between the *varnas* had to lead a life of sub-human conditions or even a life equal to animals. During that time a householder was exhorted to throw some food for them after all the members of the household had taken meals and the outcastes were to eat along with the crows and dogs outside the house. They were not permitted to use public wells or enter into the Hindu temples. They were treated as beasts; their shadows on streets during the day time were considered obscene. So they were not allowed to walk on the street during the day time. Thus, untouchables were denied all human rights.

Dr B.R. Ambedkar, in his work under the title *The Untouchables* (1948), says that there is no racial difference between untouchables and other castes. According to Dr Ambedkar, the divisions in our society began with a primitive society that consisted of many local communities or tribes. In the beginning, all these communities were nomadic in nature. But with time, and because of intratribal warfare, they scattered into three groups: a settled community, a *raider* community belonging to nomadic tribes and a broken men's community consisting of people of the defeated tribes. Here, according to Dr Ambedkar, the last group is important because it is these broken men who were forced to seek refuge in villages inhabited by other tribes or clans. They were given refuge, but made to reside on village boundaries. They were also assigned dirty occupations such as scavenging, monitoring (watchman) leather-working and so on. All the men, whether living within or outside village boundaries, had been Buddhists as they did not adhere to the sacrificing of animals to the Vedic gods/goddesses. When the people living within village boundaries reconverted to Hinduism, the descendants of the broken men continued to be Buddhists and eat beef, which the Hindus had given up to be one better than the Buddhists. This led to their being treated as untouchables.

In order to remove the age-old practice of untouchability and thereby improving the socio-economic status of the scheduled castes, over the periods many social movements have taken place in many parts of India by various social reformers. Among the earlier reformers, Chakradhar, Ramanuja, Kabir, Chaitanya, Eknath, Tukaram, Rohidas, Chokhamela and others of medieval period could be cited as notable men who fought against caste inequality.

During eighteenth century, the British government introduced certain legislations such as the Caste Disabilities Removal Act 1850. The British government also introduced legislation relating to education of all children without any caste distinction and some other administrative reforms, such as Morley–Minto Reforms of 1909, the Montagu–Chelmsford

Reforms of 1910 and the Government of India Act of 1935. In the nineteenth century, Brahmo Samaj under Raja Ram Mohan Roy, the Arya Samaj founded by Swami Dayanand Saraswati, Ramakrishna Mission founded by Shri Ramakrishna Paramahamsa and Swami Vivekananda actively campaigned against untouchability and casteism.

Dr Ambedkar was the first educated and active leader born among the scheduled caste people (ex-Mahar), who tried to unite the untouchables and created a semblance of unity. In 1924, he formed Bahishkrit Hitakarini Sabha, an educational and cultural organization which aimed at improving the social conditions of the untouchables. In 1929, he had made the first organized attempt to get rid of this casteism by publicly burning the *Manusmriti*. In 1942, Ambedkar founded the Scheduled Caste Federation and taught his caste men to fight for their rights. He organized a *Satyagraha* for the use of public lake at Mahad in Maharashtra in 1927. In the following years 1929–1930, the temple entry campaign at Kalaram Mandir, Nasik, and Parvati temple at Pune was launched.

Apart from Ambedkar's persistent and consistent efforts to improve the position of the scheduled castes in Maharashtra, in the nineteenth century, the most important social reformer was Jyotiba Phule. He openly came out against untouchability and propagated education of the untouchables, women and the downtrodden by starting a school for these people. He founded Satyashodhak Samaj (society in search of truth) in Maharashtra in 1873. Vitthal Ramji Shinde opened schools and hostels for the emancipation of the untouchables, founded the Depressed Class Mission and did substantial research work. Shahu Chhatrapati and Sayajirao Gaekwad, former rulers of the state of Kolhapur and Baroda respectively, supported the movement for the upliftment of the untouchables. Basaveshwar, the great social philosopher, religious leader and a social reformer of the twelfth century, not only preached equality among humankind but also boldly condemned the disparities based on caste system, gender and occupation. He arranged an intercaste marriage between the daughter of Madhuvayya a Brahmin and the son of Haralayya an untouchable. Basavanna allowed the women to take active part in religious discussion through *Anubhav Mantap*. He gave religious equality to women to undergo the process of *Linga Diksha* on par with men. He rejected discrimination made on the basis of *Kayaka* (Occupation). He struggled hard to establish an ideal welfare state by launching a crusade against casteism, superstitions, inequality, unsociability and exploitation which were going on in the name of religion. There were a few personalities who were involved directly in the struggle either for change or reform who deserve a mention here; they are Mahatma Jyotiba Phule, Dr B.R. Ambedkar and Basavanna from Karnataka.

The British government arranged three Round Table Conferences to discuss various issues. One of such issues was to discuss the problem relating to the scheduled castes. Dr Ambedkar was nominated as a representative of the scheduled castes for all these conferences. Dr B.R. Ambedkar had rightly remarked in London in 1930 at the First Round Table Conference that 'even 150 years of British Rule did not alter a little the position of the untouchables'. So, in the Second Round Table Conference (August, 1932), Dr Ambedkar demanded a separate electorate for scheduled castes. Finally, British government announced their decision, what is known today as Communal Award. According to this, the scheduled castes were granted separate seats in the provisional assemblies and they were given the right to double vote in which they could elect their own representative and were also entitled to vote for general constituencies too.

It was due to the radical, bold stand that Dr B.R. Ambedkar took on behalf of the scheduled castes at the Round Table Conference in London that the Indian Constitution guaranteed fundamental rights, established universal suffrage, abolished untouchability and guaranteed reservation in legislature and government services for scheduled castes. There is no doubt that none of these would have been possible without the interventions made by Dr Ambedkar, to ensure that Independent India would be based on a democratic constitution that guaranteed equality, fundamental rights and dignity to all – regardless of caste for gaining self-respect. After a long struggle by Dr Ambedkar, the legal disabilities of the scheduled castes were removed and equality of all before law was assured to scheduled castes on par with the caste Hindus.

On the other hand without giving a crushing treatment to caste-rule as part of Hinduism, Mahatma Gandhiji started a movement to bring attitudinal changes among the Hindus and retaining caste identity given to *Shudras* with another name *Harijan*. In 1933, Gandhiji started the Harijan Sevak Sangh (HSS) for the upliftment of the *Harijans* and their families. The HSS opened schools and hostels for the children of the untouchables. But the movement led by earlier reformers and the legislations introduced by British government could not succeed in reducing discrepancies that persisted in Indian caste system.

Since independence, the government has greatly intensified its efforts to improve as rapidly as possible the social and economic condition of the scheduled castes. The Constitution of India, as is clear from its preamble, aims at securing all the citizens of India 'Justice' social, economic and political, 'Liberty' of thought, expression, belief, faith and worship, 'Equality' of status and of opportunity; and promoting among them all fraternity assuring the dignity of the individual and the unity of the nation.

In order to achieve these objectives, a number of provisions have been made in the Constitution to remove the social disabilities from which the scheduled castes suffer. To fulfil the constitutional provisions, the Indian Government has passed various legislations to enforce the abolishment of 'untouchability' and remove the barriers of caste discrimination, making the socio-economic progress of the scheduled castes imminent. This included the following:

1. The Protection of Civil Rights (Untouchability Offence) Act 1955.
2. The Bonded Labour (Abolition) Act 1976.
3. The Employment of Manual Scavengers and Construction of Dry Latrines (Prohibition) Act 1993.
4. Jogini Act No. 10.
5. The Scheduled Castes/Scheduled Tribes (Prevention of Atrocities) Act 1989 and Rules 1995.

The changing concept of 'caste' in India has found that there is still pernicious manifestation of untouchability in the day-to-day life of scheduled castes and any deviation from the traditional set practices is not tolerated by the caste Hindus. In 2006, a survey of practice of untouchability in 565 villages in 11 major states of India was undertaken; the survey concluded that out of 565 villages in 35.8 per cent of the villages Dalits were denied entry into village shops. In 48.4 per cent of the villages, Dalits were denied access to water sources, in 25 per cent of villages Dalits were paid lower wages than non-Dalits, in 37 per cent of villages Dalit workers were paid wages from a distance to avoid physical contacts, in 64 per cent of villages Dalits were restricted from entering the Hindu temples, in 73 per cent of villages Dalits were not permitted to enter non-Dalit homes and 70 per cent of villages Dalits and non-Dalits could not eat together.

Béteille (1966) who studied the *Brahmans, non-Brahmans* and the scheduled castes of the Village Sripuram in Thanjavur District of Tamil Nadu found that the centre of power has shifted from the *Brahmans* to the *non-Brahmans* but the position of scheduled caste people remained the same. The policies of the government bring the Dalits on par with the upper castes in political and economic fields, but they will not end their exclusion. The process of inclusion has to operate at formal and informal and public and private spheres of life. The struggle for a dignified human life and human living must continue and, more so, at the grassroots. In fact, Dr B.R. Ambedkar considered the heart of the problem of untouchability to be the caste system, and that its destruction alone can lead to the emancipation of the untouchable.

Various studies relating to scheduled castes have been reviewed extensively. A large number of studies have dealt with the structural position and condition of scheduled castes. They have also highlighted the disabilities of the scheduled castes. Thus, the historical burden of laws, mainly the punishment laws, is reflected in the life of scheduled castes of both modern and contemporary period. Hence, in this study, an attempt has been made to understand socio-economic and political aspects of discrimination as well as agricultural labour exploitation and the perception regarding who are responsible for caste-based discrimination and by whom that can be tackled.

Status of Scheduled Castes in Karnataka

In Karnataka, the scheduled castes form a sizeable part of the state's population. Scheduled castes are known by different names in different parts of the state and comprise many subcastes and communities. The majority were formerly classified as untouchables and they generally lived in a segregated area or separate colony on the outskirts of villages. The predominant castes among the scheduled castes are *Adi Karnataka, Holeya, Chalavadi, Mahar, Mala, Madiga, Mang, Mochi, Adi Dravida, Samagar, Dhor, Banjara* and *Bhovi.* The spread of the scheduled caste population by caste/subcaste is not uniform throughout the state. At present, there are about 101 subcastes that have been recognized as scheduled castes in Karnataka. The population of scheduled castes in Karnataka has increased from 3.12 million in 1961 to 8.56 million in 2001. The share of the Scheduled caste population in the total population which was 13.22 per cent in 1961 increased to 16.21 per cent in 2001. The share of the scheduled castes population of India in 2001 is about 16.26 per cent, which is almost equal to that of Karnataka. The sex ratio of the scheduled castes has shown a marked improvement increasing from 962 in 1991 to 973 in 2001, higher than the sex ratio of scheduled castes at the all India level (936). In Karnataka, as in other parts of the country, the scheduled castes are largely concentrated in the rural parts of the state. Almost 75 per cent live in villages and depend upon agricultural labour or agriculture-related activities for subsistence. The majority of scheduled caste cultivators own marginal and small holdings, which are not viable and drive them towards indebtedness and poverty. In 2001 about 20.54 per cent and 43.41 per cent of scheduled caste workers are reported to be cultivators and agricultural labourers respectively.

At the all India level, about 72 per cent of scheduled caste households have an annual income of less than ₹ 20,000. In Karnataka scheduled caste households which fall into the income group of ₹ 20,000 to 40,000 per annum constitute 21.30 per cent and 19.50 per cent respectively.

The literacy rate among scheduled castes was 27.62 per cent in 1981. It increased to 52.87 per cent in 2001. The female literacy rate among scheduled caste in 1981 was 15.48 per cent which increased to 41.72 per cent in 2001, which is higher than the all India scheduled caste literacy level.

Generally, the housing conditions of scheduled castes have improved considerably, primarily because of the massive efforts of the government in providing houses through various housing programmes such as Ashraya, Ambedkar Housing Programme, Indira Awaas Yojana, Nirmal Bhagya Yojana, etc.

The scheduled castes suffer from a lack of social resources; they have also been denied access to both material and cultural resources. In addition to material deprivation, they have experienced social exclusion, which is manifested in their poor access to human development.

Objectives

With this broad background, an attempt has been made to understand the discrimination dimension at the micro-level in Shedbal village of Athani Taluk of Karnataka state. The major objectives are as follows:

1. To understand the socio-economic and political discrimination.
2. To understand agricultural labour exploitation.
3. To understand the perception of the respondents.

Four ex-untouchable castes *Holer, Samagar, Madigar* and *Dhor* located in Shedbal village were purposefully selected for the present study. For evaluating the discrimination and exploitation, selected indicators such as entry into shop, hotel, house and temple sharing of food with upper castes, freedom for caste, voting in Gram Panchayat Election were taken.

Social Discrimination

Social discrimination is observed in public and private domains. First of all, the social interaction largely occurs between scheduled castes and upper castes in the context of economic exchange. We have identified three important spheres of social interactions first, shop, second hotel and the third temple. The first two are private areas wherein interaction takes place daily because the basic needs are derived from shop which is owned by a private individual but it initiates intersection with the public in which all are involved. According to Government Act, while giving licenses to run a shop or a hotel, certain rules are accepted to be followed strictly. On the basis of caste and religion or language, the owner is not permitted to observe discrimination against the lower castes while conducting the business activities. As in the eyes of the law, all are equal. So is the case with private cum public space. There are number of studies that have pointed out the practice of discrimination against the lower castes in shopping activities and hotel activities. The practice of untouchability is found to be the part of caste system, and the issue of social discrimination is probed into. So the objective of study was to understand the nature of and practice of social discrimination. Therefore, the question relating to entry and exchange activities that take place in shop and hotels was dealt with.

An empirical study of social discrimination is undertaken. The study begins with the entry point either into shop or hotel or temple.

Table 1

Respondents Entry into Shop

Response	*Sub–castes*				*Total*
	Madigar	*Samagar*	*Holer*	*Dhor*	
Yes	4	3	2	1	10
	25%	37.5%	25%	12.5%	100%
No	11.4%	5.4%	1.3%	50%	4.1%
	31	53	150	1	235
	13.2%	22.6%	63.8%	.4%	100%
	88.6%	94.6%	98.7%	50.0%	95.9%
Total	35	56	152	2	245
	14.3%	22.9%	62.0%	.8%	100%
	100%	100%	100%	100%	100%

Source: Primary data (Collected during 2005–2006).

The data in Table 1 show that there are no 100 per cent free entries into the shop. Out of 245, 235 (95.9%) respondents stated that they have not made entry into shop due to prohibition by the owner of the shop, only 10 (4.1%) respondents stated that on rare occasions they have made entry into shop. It speaks about the continuity of practice of discrimination on the basis of untouchability (caste basis).

As far as entry into a hotel is concerned, all the respondents stated that from 1970 onwards the entry into hotel has been open and it has widened. The level of social discrimination in allowing free movement to take eatables from the pot like upper caste in rare situations was probed into.

The data in Table 2 show that only 10 (4.08%) respondents have access to the pot. Remaining 235 (95.9%) scheduled castes respondents said there is no free movement to take eatables from pot like upper castes. In the context of free movement to take water from water tank, this table also indicates that 221 (90.2%) of respondents do not have free movement to take water from water tank, like upper castes. The data indicate the dominating social discrimination in the hotels.

Table 2

Social Discrimination Based on Sharing Eatables and Taking Water in Hotel

Context	*Response*	*Sub-castes*				*Total*
		Madigar	*Samagar*	*Holer*	*Dhor*	
Freedom to take eatables from the pot like upper caste	Yes	2	3	5	–	10
		20%	30%	50%	–	100%
		5.71%	5.36%	3.29%	–	4.08%
	No	33	53	147	2	235
		14.0%	22.6%	62.6%	0.9%	100%
		94.3%	94.6%	96.7%	100%	95.9%
	Total	35	56	152	2	245
		14.3%	22.9%	62.0%	.8%	100%
		100%	100%	100%	100%	100%
Freedom to take water from water tank like upper castes	Yes	3	6	14	1	24
		12.50%	25%	58.33%	4.17%	100%
		8.57%	10.71%	9.21%	50%	9.80%
	No	32	50	138	1	221
		14.5%	22.6%	62.4%	0.5%	100%
		91.4%	89.3%	90.8%	50.0%	90.2%
	Total	35	56	152	2	245
		14.3%	22.9%	62.0%	0.8%	100%
		100%	100%	100%	100%	100%

Source: Primary data (Collected during 2005–2006).

The sharing of the items while eating with upper caste friends was probed into (Table 3) and it reveals that out of 245, 36 (14.7%) respondents stated that they have shared food items. Further to know the feeling of purity and pollution, another question was asked to the respondents that when owner/waiter supply the item who takes first, yourself or upper caste friend? Here most of the respondents have said that first the upper caste friends took the item, afterwards they take it but when they start eating item upper caste friend should not take it. The upper caste friends try to avoid and also say that they just had a meal so they can take or finished the item. Remaining 209 (85.31%) respondents stated that they shared the food items distributed by upper caste friend.

Table 3

Social Discrimination Based on Sharing Items with the Upper Castes in Hotel

Context	*Response*	*Sub-castes*				*Total*
		Madigar	*Samagar*	*Holer*	*Dhor*	
Sharing of items with upper castes	Commonly shared	2	9	25	–	36
		5.6%	25.0%	69.4%	–	100%
		5.7%	16.1%	16.4%	–	14.7%
	Distributed by upper caste friend	33	47	127	2	209
		15.79%	22.49%	60.77%	0.96%	100%
		94.29%	83.93%	83.55%	100%	85.31%
	Total	35	56	152	2	245
		14.3%	22.9%	62.0%	0.8%	100%
		100%	100%	100%	100%	100%

Source: Primary data (Collected during, 2005–2006).

The data from the Table 3 indicate that among friends the social discrimination is not observed but internally it shows the existence of hidden social discrimination.

Changing Food Pattern and Degree of Social Discrimination

Change in food pattern also contributes to bring about change in the social discrimination. As it was generally believed that those who are non-vegetarian, the degree of discrimination goes down. In this context, sharing of food into non-vegetarian hotel is probed.

As far as sharing of non-vegetarian food with upper caste is concerned, out of 245, 39 (15.9%) respondents shared the non-vegetarian food with upper caste friends (Table 4).

This indicates that the non-vegetarian hotels have less degree of social discrimination. The data indicate a dominating bias in allowing entry into non-vegetarian hotels by the lower castes. However, preparation of food and cleaning of the utensils by the lower castes is not open. The practice of social discrimination still prevails as it was noticed earlier. The cleaning of utensils is largely undertaken by Backward Castes followed by upper caste and Muslims.

Though a temple is public space and owned by none but by the village, it is found that the temple do not allow the entry of the scheduled castes.

Table 4

Social Discrimination Experienced by the Respondents in Non-Vegetarian Hotel

Context	*Response*	*Subcastes*				*Total*
		Madigar	*Samagar*	*Holer*	*Dhor*	
Sharing of non-vegetarian food with upper caste	No response	25	40	103	2	170
		14.7%	23.5%	60.6%	1.2%	100%
		71.4%	71.4%	67.8%	100%	69.4%
	Commonly shared	2	7	30	–	39
		5.1%	17.9%	76.9%	–	100%
		5.7%	12.5%	19.7%	–	15.9%
	Distributed by upper caste	8	9	19	–	36
		22.2%	25.0%	52.8%	–	100%
		22.9%	16.1%	12.5%	–	14.7%
	Total	35	56	152	2	245
		14.3%	22.9%	62.0%	0.8%	100%
		100%	100%	100%	100%	100%
Preparation of non-vegetarian food	No response	2	6	4	1	13
		15.4%	46.2%	30.8%	7.7%	100%
		5.7%	10.7%	2.6%	50.0%	5.3%
	Non-SC	33	50	148	1	232
		14.22%	21.55%	63.79%	0.43%	100%
		94.29%	89.29%	97.37%	50%	94.69%
	Total	35	56	152	2	245
		14.3%	22.9%	62.0%	0.8%	100%
		100%	100%	100%	100%	100%
Clean the utensils	No response	1	1	2	1	5
		20.0%	20.0%	40.0%	20.0%	100%
		2.9%	1.8%	1.3%	50.0%	2.0%

Cont'd...

...Cont'd

	Muslim	1	3	–	–	4
		25.0%	75.0%	–	–	100%
		2.9%	5.4%	–	–	1.6%
	Backward caste	33	52	145	1	230
		14.3%	22.6%	62.6%	0.4%	100%
		94.3%	92.9%	95.4%	50.0%	93.9%
	Upper caste	–	–	5	–	5
		–	–	100%	–	100%
		–	–	3.29	–	2.04
	Total	35	56	152	2	245
		14.3%	22.9%	62.0%	0.8%	100%
		100%	100%	100%	100%	100%

Source: Primary data (Collected during, 2005–2006).

Table 5

Social Discrimination Experience by the Respondents in Entry into Temple

Context	*Response*	*Subcastes*				*Total*
		Madigar	*Samagar*	*Holer*	*Dhor*	
Entry into the temple	Yes	27	36	137	1	201
		13.4%	17.9%	68.2%	0.5%	100%
		77.1%	64.3%	90.1%	50.0%	82.0%
	No	8	20	15	1	44
		18.2%	45.5%	34.1%	2.3%	100%
		22.9%	35.7%	9.9%	50.0%	18.0%
	Total	35	56	152	2	245
		14.3%	22.9%	62.0%	0.8%	100%
		100%	100%	100%	100%	100%

Source: Primary data (Collected during, 2005–2006).

To understand the social discrimination of scheduled castes for the entry into the inner parts of the temple, the data in Table 5 show that out of 245 respondents 201 (82.0%) of them said that there is entry into the temple but not in the inner part (*Garbha Gudi*) of the temple while 44 (18.0%) did not enter the temple. The subtle untouchability fear was found to be the cause of not entering the temple.

Among the 245 respondents, 44 (18%) of them have stated that there is no entry into the inner side of the temple. This table shows that 20 *Samagar* respondents and 15 *Holer* respondents were denied entry inside temple. Some were allowed entry into inner side of the temple: Holer 137 (68.2%) followed by *Samagars* 36 (17.95%), *Madigar* 27 (13.4%) and *Dhor* 1 (0.5%). The data in the table indicate that social discrimination in the entry of temple varies from person to person and from caste to caste. There is no total ban on entry into temple. The data indicate a healthy sign in the religious life of the village.

Table 6

Entry into the Inner Part of the Upper Caste House as Shown by the Respondents

Context	*Response*	*Subcastes*				*Total*
		Madigar	*Samagar*	*Holer*	*Dhor*	
Entry into the inner part of the house	No response	1	1	3	1	6
		16.7%	16.7%	50.0%	16.7%	100%
		2.9%	1.8%	2.0%	50.0%	2.4%
	Yes	1	5	9	–	15
		6.7%	33.3%	60.0%	–	100%
		2.9%	8.9%	5.9%	–	6.1%
	No	33	50	140	1	224
		14.7%	22.3%	62.5%	0.4%	100%
		94.3%	89.3%	92.1%	50.0%	91.4%
	Total	35	56	152	2	245
		14.3%	22.9%	62.0%	0.8%	100%
		100%	100%	100%	100%	100%

Source: Primary data (Collected during, 2005–2006).

Table 6 shows that out of 245, only 15 (6.1%) respondents state that the upper caste are allowed to enter inside their house, but they do not allow them to share the common cots. Remaining 224 (91.4%) respondents responded that they were not allowed to enter inside the house. The data in the table clearly show that there is existence of caste norms, that is purity and pollution.

In the village life, water has been found to be the cause of tension. But the tension is attributed to the practice of discriminatory use of water. The roots of discrimination are found in the practice of caste system. These are reflected in sharing of water. To what extent the legacy of practice of untouchability is retained is studied.

Shedbal village gets drinking water through overhead tank. The tap connections are distributed to the village people on personal and public basis. There are some public taps for water supply. All people belonging to different castes and religion residing near the tap collect water from these taps. In Shedbal village, public taps are installed in every street. On both the sides of the street, the residents of different castes are found. The existence of the tap created two situations. In the initial period when the tap began operating, upper caste members did show opposition the use of this tap by the lower caste members because of caste consciousness and practice of untouchability. When there were complaints against such responses regarding the use of tap, the gram panchayat, which controls the water supply system in the village, shifted the spot of the tap and installed it in another place.

In the second period, the use of tap did not find rivalry. However, the use of the tap by the lower caste members was not liked. At the time of field visits, the researcher himself observed the users' behaviour, which was not totally free from caste discrimination.

Table 7

Social Discrimination Experienced by the Respondents (Water Tap)

Context	*Response*	*Subcastes*				*Total*
		Madigar	*Samagar*	*Holer*	*Dhor*	
Allow to keep pots with upper caste pots	No response	7	3	4	–	14
		50.0%	21.4%	28.6%	–	100%
		20.0%	5.4%	2.6%	–	5.7%
	Yes	8	11	24	–	43
		18.6%	25.6%	55.8%	–	100%
		22.9%	19.6%	15.8%	–	17.6%
	No	20	42	124	2	188
		10.7%	22.5%	65.8%	1.1%	100%
		57.1%	75.0%	81.6%	100%	76.7%
	Total	35	56	152	2	245
		14.3%	22.9%	62.0%	0.8%	100%
		100%	100%	100%	100%	100%
Time allotment followed regularly	Not applicable	2	2	3	–	7
		28.6%	28.6%	42.9%	–	100%

Cont'd...

...Cont'd

		5.7%	3.6%	2.0%	–	2.9%
	Yes	6	16	65	–	87
		6.9%	18.4%	74.7%	–	100%
		17.1%	28.6%	42.8%	–	35.5%
	No	27	38	84	2	151
		17.88%	25.17%	55.63%	1.32	100%
		77.14%	67.86%	55.26%	100%	61.63%
	Total	35	56	152	2	245
		14.3%	22.9%	62.0%	0.8%	100%
		100%	100%	100%	100%	100%

Source: Primary data (Collected during, 2005–2006).

Table 7 shows that when the lower caste members do not get the supply of water, they go to collect water from the tap used by upper castes, which was not allowed by the upper castes. Out of 245, 188 (76.7%) respondents stated that they were not allowed to keep the pots with pots of the upper castes. There was the allotment of time for supplying water between SCs and non-SCs. As far as time allotment for supply of water is concerned, 151 (61.63%) respondents said that the time allotted for supply of water to the street of the upper castes is longer than for the SCs. Thus, the social discrimination, although diminishing – the discriminatory element in terms of touching of pots – is still dominant among the upper castes. The shows how hard it is to insist/get rid of the feeling of superiority and purity. The idea of pollution is also proved by the facts.

During rare occasions such as when SC members felt thirsty and request the upper castes to provide water, upper castes provide water directly pour the water or ask them to take a separate glass, which is kept outside the house.

The data in Table 8 reveal that out of 245, 139 (56.7%) respondents stated that when they are thirsty, they should not request the upper castes to provide water because they ask the scheduled castes to take separate glass, which is kept outside the house, or pour water from above. A total of 42 (17.14%) responded that the water is poured from above. Remaining 36 (14.7%) respondents stated that they got water directly from the upper castes.

Table 8
Social Discrimination Regarding Giving Water

Context	*Response*	*Subcastes*				*Total*
		Madigar	*Samagar*	*Holer*	*Dhor*	
To ease the thirst, the water is given directly or poured	No response	1	10	17	–	28
		3.6%	35.7%	60.7%	–	100%
		2.9%	17.9%	11.2%	–	11.4%
	Supplied directly	2	9	25	–	36
		5.6%	25.0%	69.4%	–	100%
		5.7%	16.1%	16.4%	–	14.7%
	Do not request	30	26	83	2	139
		21.6%	17.3%	59.7%	1.4%	100%
		85.7%	42.9%	54.6%	100%	56.7%
	Poured the water	2	13	27	–	42
		4.76%	30.95%	64.29%	–	100%
		5.71%	23.21%	17.76%	–	17.14%
	Total	35	56	152	2	245
		14.3%	22.9%	62.0%	0.8%	100%
		100%	100%	100%	100%	100%

Source: Primary data (Collected during, 2005–2006).

In some situations especially during agricultural operation, drinking water is shared commonly or separate pot is provided by the farmer is probed. The data in the table also show that out of 245, 232 (94.7%) respondents stated that separate pot is provided to them. Only 5 (2.0%) respondents said that they drink from the common pot. The data indicate that caste norms operate in such behavioural situations.

Economic Discrimination

Social discrimination impacts the economic activities of scheduled castes. Although all are free to undertake any economic activity in free India, the Indian villages are not yet free from the clutches of caste system, which imposes prohibition to pursue non-caste occupations or to disobey the rules of caste system by the upper castes.

Table 9

Economic Activity Not Undertaken Due to Opposition as Experienced by the Respondents

Sr. No.	*Response*	*Subcastes*				*Total*
		Madigar	*Samagar*	*Holer*	*Dhor*	
1.	Freedom to undertake any economic activity	4	16	18	–	38
		10.53%	42.11%	47.37%	–	100%
		11.43%	28.57%	11.84%	–	15.5%
2.	Opposition by upper caste represented	31	40	134	2	207
		14.98%	19.32%	64.73%	0.97%	100%
		88.57%	71.43%	88.16%	100%	84.5%
	Total	35	56	152	2	245
		14.3%	22.9%	62.0%	8%	100%
		100%	100%	100%	100%	100%

Source: Primary data (Collected during, 2005–2006).

Out of 245, 38 (15.5%) respondents felt that there was freedom to undertake any economic activity. However, 18 (11.84%) respondents belonging to *Holer* 16 (28.57%) *Samagar* and 4 (11.43%) *Madigar* responded that economic activity in terms of hotel and *Kirana* (grocery) shop was not undertaken due to their feeling of opposition by upper caste to these activities.

A respondent belonging to *Holer* caste opened a pan shop in the bus stand of Shedbal. It ran for few days but it was closed down because the business did not run due to his caste identity. Those who went to his shop belonged to his community but they were very few. As a result of adverse situation and loss he had to close down.

The discriminatory treatment is noticed in the field of economic activities. This is mainly because of the existence of caste system. The caste system does not give freedom to undertake any economic activity. This can be noticed from Table 9. Out of 245, 207 (84.5%) respondents said that they don't have freedom to undertake economic activity. Some economic activities such as running a hotel or a *Kirana* (grocery) shop are not allowed by the upper castes. Respondents further stated that the upper castes oppose such economic activities.

Political Discrimination

Since the implementation of Constitution of India, as a Democratic Republic form of government – with one man, one value, one vote (adult franchise), and equality, all entirely new political situation is found for scheduled castes. For centuries, political participation was denied to them. They were treated as servants. The question of participation in decision-making, implementation process did not arise. The *Shudras* were subjugated persons/group. After independence, these subjugated scheduled castes had to enter into democratic institutions. Traditionally, the upper castes exercised authority over the *Shudras*, the question of participating in democratic institutions was a challenge before the scheduled castes. For the upper castes, it was a question or challenge to treat them as equals.

Theoretically, democracy came into being but the upper castes who were conservative or liberal had to make space for scheduled castes who up to 26 January 1950 never challenged the power structure either formally under British regime or informally under *Varnashrama Dharma* the *Chaturvarna* system of sharing rights to rule and duties as part of *Dharma* – as a way of life for surviving caste. For upper castes, it was a challenge of not allowing the scheduled castes to show the behaviour based on the principle of equality. Even today, we find traditionally shaped personalities with such situation of domination of *Dharma* as duty to follow caste occupation. The challenge by the scheduled castes does not arise. Thus, from the traditional upper caste point of view, it was a challenge to retain 'master–slave subjugated' 'patron–client relations'. In such a situation of subjugation and discrimination, the Constitution of India stands on the side of the subjugated castes.

The political opportunity as such did not emerge spontaneously or naturally in the context of scheduled castes but due to the struggles launched by Dr B.R. Ambedkar, the political consciousness is developed. As a result of this, the people of India who accepted the democratic form of government had to consider seriously the democratic principles. Thus, the Constitution of India operates as a social source of creating political opportunities for the scheduled castes.

At the theoretical level, the scheduled castes are politically equal to others. According to Dr B.R. Ambedkar, in India, there is political equality. In this context, a situation arises that the exercise of one's own political right has a great political value. For others, it becomes an issue of sharing the political power given by the political institutions, which were monopolized before independence, but now, are being put forth as for sharing by all people under democracy.

In the political history of scheduled castes, we do not find their dominance over political institutions. Therefore, in the changed political set-up, the scheduled castes have a double challenge, namely, to face the challenges of scarcity of resources to obtain political power and to face the challenge of upper castes. In such a complex, odd and adverse situation, the political opportunities become very expensive in all senses.

The political opportunities are provided constitutionally and they are on paper, but in practical life, these political opportunities necessitate invocation to the upper caste on the one hand and initiate the process of empowerment of scheduled castes by themselves on the other hand.

In Shedbal village, as far as formal power structure is concerned on individual basis, one or two scheduled castes might have shown the source of political dominance. There is no sustainability of scheduled castes in the formal political power relations. The formal power structure provides opportunities to scheduled castes but the ground realities are not conducive to make a realization of the same. The detailed analysis of how the upper castes treat the scheduled castes and are denied political rights of scheduled castes during election is furnished later. During Gram Panchayat Elections for selecting a contesting candidate from scheduled castes, freedom given by the upper castes is analysed in Table 10.

During the election period, as far as the political right is concerned, especially the right to contest elections and right to be elected, the data in Table 10 show that out of 245, 233 (95.1%) respondents stated that the upper caste did not allow them to take decisions. The table indicates that the exposure to the upper caste treatment is larger among the *Holer* 146 (96.1%), followed by *Samagars* 52 (92.9%) and *Madigars* 33 (94.3%). The data indicate that during selection of a contesting candidate and the right to be elected, the scheduled castes in general and *Holer* in particular are kept out. The right to contest election and the right to be elected have been denied by the upper caste community members.

Table 10

Freedom Given by the Upper Caste as Shown by the Respondents during Gram Panchayat Election

Context	*Responses*	*Subcastes*				*Total*
		Madigar	*Samagar*	*Holer*	*Dhor*	
Allow to talk, express opinion and take decision	Yes	2	4	6	–	12
		16.7%	33.3%	50.0%	–	100%
		5.7%	7.1%	3.9%	–	4.9%
	No	33	52	146	2	233
		14.2%	22.3%	62.7%	0.9%	100%
		94.3%	92.9%	96.1%	100%	95.1%
	Total	35	56	152	2	245
		14.3%	22.9%	62.0%	0.8%	100%
		100%	100%	100%	100%	100%

Source: Primary data (Collected during, 2005–2006).

During the panchayat elections, the treatment pattern shown by the upper castes is analysed. To know the pattern of visits by the upper castes during election, out of 245, 156 (63%) respondents stated that the upper castes made frequent visits. About 28 (11.4%) respondents stated that they have never been visited.

Another important aspect of relations – the physical nearness – is concerned, 204 (83.3%) respondents said that they are not allowed to sit with upper castes. However, among them *Holer* 129 (63.2%), *Samagar* 42 (75.0%) and *Madigar* 31 (88.6%) said that they are allowed to sit.

The data in Table 11 show that, among the subcastes, the respondents have shown the treatments given by the upper castes, in the case of *Dhor* 2 (100%) respondents said that people are not allowed to sit together. This shows that segregation is still practiced. The physical segregation and valueless identity of scheduled caste, which existed during pre-independence period, have found to be eroded during post-independence period. It is reflected in the empirical data.

Table 11

During Election Period the Treatments Given by the Upper Castes as Shown by the Respondents

Context	*Responses*	*Subcastes*				*Total*
		Madigar	*Samagar*	*Holer*	*Dhor*	
Upper castes visit	Frequently	29	38	88	1	156
		18.6%	24.4%	56.4%	6%	100%
		82.9%	67.9%	57.9%	40.0%	63.7%
	Rarely	2	14	44	1	61
		3.28%	22.95%	72.13%	1.64%	100%
		5.71%	25%	28.95%	50%	24.90%
	Never	4	4	20	–	28
		14.3%	14.3%	71.4%	–	100%
		11.4%	7.1%	13.2%	–	11.4%
	Total	35	56	152	2	245
		14.3%	22.9%	62.0%	8%	100%
		100%	100%	100%	100%	100%
Allowed to sit together	Allowed	4	14	23	–	41
		9.8%	34.1%	56.1%	–	100%
		11.4%	25.0%	15.1%	–	16.7%
	Not allowed	31	42	129	2	204
		15.2%	20.6%	63.2%	1.0%	100%
		88.6%	75.0%	84.9%	100%	83.3%
	Total	35	56	152	2	245
		14.3%	22.9%	62.0%	8%	100%
		100%	100%	100%	100%	100%

Source: Primary data (Collected during, 2005–2006).

The prevailing impact of election on sharing of food was asked in order to know the closeness among the upper caste and lower caste. The data in the Table 12 indicate that, 202 (82.4%) respondents stated that during election period, food was shared separately. Only 25 (10.2%) respondents said that they had common food, 18 (7.37%) respondents opined that they don't go for food.

Table 12

Upper Castes Treatments during Election for Sharing of Food as Shown by the Respondents

Context	*Response*	*Subcastes*				*Total*
		Madigar	*Samagar*	*Holer*	*Dhor*	
During election period sharing of food	Common	1	6	18	–	25
		4.0%	24.0%	72.0%	–	100%
		2.9%	10.7%	11.8%	–	10.2%
	Separate	32	44	124	2	202
		15.9%	21.9%	61.2%	1.0%	100%
		91.4%	78.6%	81.6%	100%	82.4%
	We don't take it	2	6	10	–	18
		11.11%	33.33%	55.56%	–	100%
		5.71%	10.71%	6.58%	–	7.35%
	Total	35	56	152	2	245
		14.3%	22.9%	62.0%	0.8%	100%
		100%	100%	100%	100%	100%

Source: Primary data (Collected during, 2005–2006).

Table 12 indicates that they may be good friends or good party supporters but 82.4 per cent respondents' responses indicate the practice of segregation due to caste influence. The table indicates the rigidity of caste as diminishing marginally.

Besides knowing the sharing of food item during election for gram panchayat, the political participation, in terms of processions, was observed. It is found that the *Holers* have an upper hand in the participation during processions, followed by *Samagars* and *Madigars.*

'The voting was guided by whom?' was inquired by providing three responses, namely leader, parents and on their own. The responses of the respondents in Table 13 show that, among three, leaders are found to be guiding, followed by on their own decision and then by parents. Among the respondents, 146 (59.6%) were advised by leaders, followed by their own decision 93 (37.96%) and parents 6 (2.45%).

The data indicate that the parents do not influence on voting behaviours, but leaders do. It also shows that the right to vote freely has been denied by upper castes.

Table 13

Advice Taken for Casting Vote During Election as Shown by the Respondents

Context	*Response*	*Subcastes*				*Total*
		Madigar	*Samagar*	*Holer*	*Dhor*	
Whose advice taken for casting vote	Leader	30	33	81	2	146
		20.7%	22.8%	55.2%	1.4%	100%
		85.7%	58.9%	53.1%	100%	59.6%
	Parents	2	1	3	–	6
		33.33%	16.67%	50%	–	100%
		5.71%	1.79%	1.97%	–	2.45%
	On their own	3	22	68	–	93
		3.23%	23.66%	73.12%	–	100%
		8.57%	39.29%	44.74%	–	37.96%
	Total	35	56	152	2	245
		14.3%	22.9%	62.0%	0.8%	100%
		100%	100%	100%	100%	100%

Source: Primary data (Collected during, 2005–2006).

It was always commented that after elections the behaviour of the elected candidates changes compared to that during the elections. The figures in Table 14 indicate that this holds true. A total of 219 (89.4%) respondents said that they did not get equal treatment as against 26 (10.6%) respondents who said that they get equal treatment. Among the subcastes, more than 82 per cent respondents have said that they have changed so is the case of visits by upper caste members to scheduled castes. A few visits given by elected leaders is reported by 14 candidates (5.7%) as against 231 (94.3%) respondents said no visits were made.

With regard to assurances given by leaders, 232 (94.7%) respondents have said that the assurances given by them are not realized; among the subcastes the same trend is noticed. After election equal treatment, visits by the upper caste members and assurances given by the leaders are not realized and 95 per cent respondents responded negatively. As far as responses among the subcaste respondents, more or less the same percentage of respondents is observed in Table 14.

Table 14

Upper Caste Treatments after Election as Shown by the Respondents

Context	*Responses*	*Subcastes*				*Total*
		Madigar	*Samagar*	*Holer*	*Dhor*	
Equal treatment	Yes	6	8	12		26
		23.1%	30.8%	46.2%		100%
		17.1%	14.3%	7.9%		10.6%
	No	29	48	140	2	219
		13.2%	21.9%	63.9%	0.9%	100%
		82.9%	85.7%	92.1%	100%	89.4%
	Total	35	56	152	2	245
		14.3%	22.9%	62.0%	0.8%	100%
		100%	100%	100%	100%	100%
Upper caste members visit	Yes	5	3	6		14
		35.7%	21.4%	42.9%		100%
		14.3%	5.4%	3.9%		5.7%
	No	30	53	146	2	231
		13.0%	22.9%	63.2%	0.9%	100%
		85.7%	94.6%	96.1%	100%	94.3%
	Total	35	56	152	2	245
		14.3%	22.9%	62.0%	0.8%	100%
		100%	100%	100%	100%	100%
Assurances given by leaders are realized	Realized	1	1	11	–	13
		7.7%	7.7%	84.6%	–	100%
		2.9%	1.8%	7.2%	–	5.3%
	Not realized	34	55	141	2	232
		14.8%	23.5%	60.9%	0.9%	100%
		97.1%	98.2%	99.3%	100%	94.7%
	Total	35	56	152	2	245
		14.3%	22.9%	62.0%	0.8%	100%
		100%	100%	100%	100%	100%

Source: Primary data (Collected during, 2005–2006).

Labour Exploitation

In Marxism, exploitation is central and is defined in terms of the labour theory of value, to denote the extraction of surplus value or the difference between the value of what a worker receives in wages and that which is produced and appropriated by the capitalist.

As per the principles of justice/equality, the distributive system of (economic) agricultural production has to be applied. If this does not happen, it amounts to exploitation. As exploitation process is a given phenomenon, the exploited class and the exploiting classes continue to exist. Therefore, the questions relating to landless labourers as exploited class poor peasants or semi-exploited class are seen in the village. Hence, the questions are asked only to identify the nature of exploitation.

Exploitation in economic organizational sphere, in general, is carried out as per the laws of the capitalist economy or feudal economy. As far as laws of caste system are concerned, they are to be seen in terms of more extraction of work or historical status of labour (as readily available manpower) or ascribed role performed as woodcutter or gravedigger and so on (i.e. *Balutedar*).

Table 15

Availability of Work during the Year as Shown by the Respondents

Sr. No.	*Availability of Work*	*Subcaste*				*Total*
		Madigar	*Samagar*	*Holer*	*Dhor*	
1	Not applicable	4	16	43	1	64
		6.3%	25.0%	67.2%	1.6%	100%
		11.4%	28.6%	28.3%	50.0%	26.1%
2	3 months	26	25	68	1	120
		21.8%	21.0%	56.3%	0.8%	100%
		74.3%	44.6%	44.8%	50.0%	49%
3	6 months	–	–	7	–	7
		–	–	100%	–	100%
		–	–	4.6%	–	2.9%
4	8 months	–	1	3	–	4
		–	25.0%	75.0%	–	100%
		–	1.8%	2.0%	–	1.6%
5	10 months	–	–	1	–	1
		–	–	100%	–	100%
		–	–	.7%	–	0.4%
6	12 months	5	14	30	–	49
		10.2%	28.6%	61.2%	–	100%
		14.3%	25.0%	19.7%	–	20.0%
	Total	35	56	152	2	245
		14.3%	22.9%	62.0%	0.8%	100%
		100%	100%	100%	100%	100%

Source: Primary data (Collected during, 2005–2006).

To understand the nature of exploitation, the first requirement is that of availability of work for labourers. So we need to observe the data regarding the issue.

Table 15 shows that about 120 (49%) of the respondents got employment for 3 months in a year. The remaining respondents 49 (20%), 7 (2.9%) and 4 (1.6%) stated 12 months, 6 months and 8 months availability of employment in the village. Only one respondent stated that 10 months employment was available. Thus, the data indicate that an overwhelming number of respondents are involved in daily wage work throughout the year.

The subcaste-wise composition of labour force is studied. The wages paid to them are taken into account to know the extent of exploitation in the Shedbal village. The data relating to wages are obtained from village labourers and upper caste farmers while conducting the field survey.

Table 16

Additional Work Done by the Respondents

Sr. No.	*Hours of Work*	*Subcastes*				*Total*
		Madigar	*Samagar*	*Holer*	*Dhor*	
1	Not applicable	4	15	40	1	60
		6.7%	25.0%	66.7%	1.7%	100%
		11.4%	26.8%	26.3%	50.0%	24.5%
2	One hour	28	39	96	1	164
		17.1%	23.8%	58.5%	0.6%	100%
		80.0%	69.6%	63.2%	50.0%	66.9%
3	Two hours	3	2	15	–	20
		15.0%	10.0%	75.0%	–	100%
		8.6%	3.6%	10.6%	–	8.6%
	Total	35	56	152	2	245
		14.3%	22.9%	62.0%	0.8%	100%
		100%	100%	100%	100%	100%

Source: Primary data (Collected during, 2005–2006).

Among the labourers belonging to scheduled caste, 164 (66.9%) respondents stated that they generally work one hour more. Among these subcaste *Madigar* represented 28 (80%), followed by *Samagar* 39 (69.6%) and *Holer* 96 (63.2%). Again, the scheduled caste labourers who work more than two hours were 20 (8.6%) among the subcastes, *Holer* respondents represented 15 (10.6%), followed by *Madigar* 3 (8.6%) and *Samagar* 2 (3.6%). An additional hour of work for 'more than two hours' was observed in responses as well as the discussions with villagers held by the researcher.

The working hours of the labourers in the village are found in two patterns. First pattern is that the labourers work from 7 a.m. to 1 p.m. Within this duration of labour, half an hour is given for lunch. Thus, about 5 and half hours of labour are put in operation of agricultural activities. The second pattern is that the labourers work from 8 a.m. to 5 p.m. During this period of work, one hour is given for lunch. Thus, 8 hours are utilized for work.

During the discussion with employers and respondent labourers, it was found that 7 a.m. to 1 p.m. – five and half hour duration of work – was preferred by the labourers as against 8 a.m. to 5 p.m. hour duration preferred by employers. It was understood that in the village morning work hours were liked and prevailed mainly due to the preference of labourers who wanted to look after other activities such as collecting fodder for their domestic animals. While they complete their work, two or three hours are devoted to collect grass and fuel as well as to take care of animals and family members (children and old people).

However, as per the requirement of labour during seasons, the labourers adopt 8 a.m. to 5 p.m. working hours. Thus, in general, there is coordination and cooperation in arranging the working hours by the employers and agricultural labourers in the village. For each daily work, the daily wages for male and female are ₹ 60 and 30, respectively. This wage pattern was prevalent during the interview period (2006). Before the arrival of lift irrigation water (1980s) to the village, the wages were ₹ 5 and 2 for male and female, respectively. These wages went on increasing to ₹ 10 and 5 to ₹ 15 and 5, to ₹ 20 and 10, to ₹ 30 and 10, ₹ 40 and 15, to ₹ 50 and 20 and to ₹ 60 and 30. These changes in the wage pattern occurred during the last 30 years without following the minimum wage laws enacted by the Government of India.

However, this wage pattern was kept aside and increased wage pattern was adopted. For example, it was found that for harvesting short duration black gram (*Udida*, etc.), the labourers are badly needed because as soon as this crop is harvested the land is used for another crop without any gap. For intensive use of land, the farmers require labour force urgently. Therefore, such agricultural production needs labourers. The employers increase the wage from ₹ 60 to ₹ 70 or ₹ 80 for male and ₹ 30 to ₹ 40 for female labourers. This increase is caused by scarcity of labour and competition among the farmers.

What the data indicate is that still a large proportion of scheduled caste households continue to depend on the traditional occupation of waged labour. The wage pattern as indicated above shows that exploitation and discrimination prevails in the village. In the village economy, Minimum Wage Act is neither followed by employers nor asked for its implementation by the labour respondents. The traditional norms continue to operate in the agricultural production organization. The traditional wage pattern has changed but does not adhere to Minimum Wage Act.

Table 17

Wages Paid for Extra Work as Shared by the Respondents

Sr. No.	*Particulars*	*Subcastes*				*Total*
		Madigar	*Samagar*	*Holer*	*Dhor*	
1	No response	30	45	123	2	200
		15.00	22.50	61.50	1.00	100
		85.71	80.36	80.92	100.00	81.63
2	Give extra ₹ 10 or alcohol	–	4	9	–	13
		–	30.8%	69.2%	–	100%
		–	7.1%	5.9%	–	5.3%
3	Allow to collect grass from the field	5	7	20	–	32
		15.63	21.88	62.50	0.00	100
		14.29	12.50	13.16	0.00	13.06
	Total	35	56	152	2	245
		14.3%	22.9%	62.0%	0.8%	100%
		100%	100%	100%	100%	100%

Source: Primary data (Collected during, 2005–2006).

For additional work, the data in Table 17 show that few persons 13 (5.3%) get extra ₹ 10 or sometimes alcohol. Other labourer respondents 32 (13.06%) are allowed to collect grass from the owner's fields. Remaining 200 (81.63%) responded that these employers do not give extra payment for extra work. Daily wage labour is the characteristic of Shedbal's capitalist agricultural production. The labourer respondents during discussion stated that they are not attached to any farmer for their wages. They said that they are free to go to any farmer for work. But 50 years ago, the families of respondents were attached to a particular farmer's family. They were not allowed to deviate from the traditional contract.

Because of the object situation of not getting employment throughout the year, and because the farmers had to depend upon available monsoon water resource and avail more cheap assured labour from the labouring sections of the society, the payments were also not paid regularly. The labourers had to starve. They were docile and submissive, like semi-slaves who did not utter a word against their masters. This situation has changed. The worst exploitative system of feudal type has changed into capitalist system of exploitation with cheap daily wages. Hence, the hand-to-mouth condition is still prevalent among the scheduled castes of Shedbal village.

As an insider, I know the advantages and disadvantages. But I strongly say that some things cannot be brought in to the interview schedule such as economic and sexual exploitation. It is observed and also asserted that upper castes always try to exploit the scheduled castes in various ways. They try to buy fertile land, well-fed cattle and oxen and bulls from scheduled castes. Upper castes also had illegal sexual relations with one of the women labourers; they maintain the illegal sexual relation to extract more work from the labourers and also to get labourers to complete their agricultural works on time.

An attempt was made to understand the perception of respondents about the causes that lead to the continued existence of the caste-based discrimination such as untouchability and exploitation. Accordingly the causes for such phenomena were considered. The question posed to respondents was aimed at knowing the causes of discrimination among the scheduled castes. The question was open-ended. Their responses reflect their understanding. Therefore, the causes responsible for discrimination of scheduled caste are presented in their perception.

Table 18 shows a very interesting notion by the respondents that none of them attributed a single cause that led for their discrimination. A total of 216 (88.2%) respondents identified social, economic and political disabilities that existed in social system as the responsible causes of discrimination. Remaining 29 (11.8%) responded that a lack of political will of the government in implementing agencies and lack of unity among the scheduled castes as the causes of discrimination. It was also probed as to why such lack of will prevails among the officials. It was the upper caste feeling of superiority among the officials, which acted as obstacle in implementing the schemes. The lower caste officials were hesitant to help their own people because they were always under the constant fear of criticisms by the upper caste officials.

Table 18

Causes of Caste Discrimination as Felt by the Respondents

Response	*Subcastes*				*Total*
	Madigar	*Samagar*	*Holer*	*Dhor*	
Social structure	32	52	130	2	216
(Caste system)	14.9%	24.2%	60.0%	9%	100%
	91.4%	92.9%	85.6%	100%	88.2%
Lack of unity	3	4	22	–	29
	10.3%	13.8%	75.9%	–	100%
	8.6%	7.1%	14.5%	–	11.8%
Total	35	56	152	2	245
	14.3%	22.9%	62.0%	8%	100%
	100%	100%	100%	100%	100%

Source: Primary data (Collected during, 2005–2006).

Table 18 indicates that caste-based discrimination is considered to be the effect of multiple causes. Among them, the most important are continued existence of social, economic and political disabilities in the social system.

Many laws, as well as the Constitution itself, have been introduced in India banning caste discrimination, untouchability and their manifestations. Special commissions have been set up to monitor the progress made in eradicating caste discrimination. But to this day, the caste disabilities and discrimination continue to exist. Therefore, 'by whom this can be tackled' was probed by providing two alternations, namely, (i) Insider, including district, state and national authority, and (ii) outsider, including international authority.

Table 19
Who Can Tackle Caste Discrimination Effectively?
(As Shared by Respondents)

Response	*Particulars*	*Subcastes*				*Total*
		Madigar	*Samagar*	*Holer*	*Dhor*	
Insider	District authority	–	1	3	–	4
		–	25.0%	75.0%	–	100.0%
		–	1.8%	2.0%	–	1.6%
	State authority	2	3	7	–	12
		16.7%	25.0%	58.3%	–	100%
		5.7%	5.4%	4.6%	–	4.9%
	National authority	22	40	127	2	191
		11.6%	21.1%	66.3%	1.1%	100%
		62.9%	71.4%	83.6%	100%	78%
Outsider	International authority	11	12	15	–	38
		28.9%	31.6%	39.5%	–	100%
		31.4%	21.4%	9.9%	–	15.5%
	Total	35	56	152	2	245
		14.3%	22.9%	62.0%	8%	100%
		100%	100%	100%	100%	100%

Source: Primary data (Collected during, 2005–2006).

The data in Table 19 show that out of 245, 191 (78%) respondents stated national authority, 12 (4.9%) state authority and 4 (1.6%) district authority, remaining 38 (15.5%) responded that this can be only tackled by way of intervention of international authority.

Summary and Conclusion

Many Asian and African countries are found to suffer from discrimination. In India, discrimination is based on hereditary basis through the *varna* and caste system. The scheduled castes constitute more than 17 per cent of the total population; there are about 170 million in India who occupy the lowest rank in the caste hierarchy. However, the radical and bold stand of Dr B.R. Ambedkar and his intervention at the Round Table conference in London provided a breakthrough in tackling the caste discrimination.

Since independence, many laws banning caste discrimination, untouchability and exploitation have been introduced, but as rightly pointed out by Punalekar (1988), the real problem and obstacle in removing discrimination lies with the implementation of laws by authorities, police and other people.

Based on the empirical study conducted at Shedbal village covering four scheduled castes of *Holer, Samagar, Madigar* and *Dhor*, we can observe the followings things.

Social Discrimination

It was found that there was social discrimination even in small shops and hotels on the basis of untouchability practices. Though there is change in the nature of social relationship between the high caste and low caste, yet data show the existence of subtle social discrimination. There was subtle fear of untouchability among the scheduled castes and, therefore, they did not enter into the temple. But it varies from person to person and subcaste to subcaste. Overall, there was healthy sign in the religious life of the village, especially in village community festivals.

Economic Discrimination

There has been discriminatory treatment in the field of business and economic activity. The respondents opined that they did not have total freedom to undertake economic activity such as running pan shop, *kirana* (grocery) shop or (restaurant) hotel. The upper castes were not comfortable with such economic activities undertaken by the scheduled castes.

Political Discrimination

It was found that the scheduled caste communities have more exposure to higher castes. However, many respondents indicated the practice of political segregation due to caste. Voting was mainly guided by the leaders, followed by their own and parents' decision. The higher castes played an important role in influencing the voting behaviour of the scheduled castes. At the time of elections, the caste norms are undermined, but after election, they are reinitiated to retain the high caste image.

The data also indicate that still a large proportion of scheduled caste households continue to depend on the traditional occupation of wage labour. Wage pattern shows clear signs of exploitation and discrimination in the village. The Minimum Wage Act is not followed by the employers. The worst exploitative system of the feudal type has changed into capitalistic system of exploitation with cheap daily wages. Hence, hand-to-mouth condition is prevalent among the scheduled castes of Shedbal village.

The respondents felt that caste-based social structure with norms of purity and pollution ideas was responsible for caste discrimination, and they felt that it can be tackled mainly by the national authority and the international authority. Regarding the question of the effective way of irradiating caste discrimination and feelings of hatred between the scheduled castes and upper castes in Indian village, we recommend that the central and state governments should take productive steps to root out caste system and undertake developing economic enterprises or cottage industries involving all the village people irrespective of their caste background.

Suggested Readings

Ambedkar, B.R., 1948, *The Untouchables: Who Were They and Why They Became Untouchables*, Amrit Book Company, New Delhi.

Benjamin, N. and Mohanty, B.B., 2001, 'Ambedkar's Quest for the Right of Social Equality: An Interpretation', *Social Action,* 51, April/June.

Béteille, André, 1966, *Caste: Old and New – Essays in Social Structure and Social Stratification*, Asia Publishing House, Bombay.

Chakravarti, N.K. and Subedi, Shubhashree, 1995, 'Origin of Untouchability in Hinduism', *Man in India*, a *quarterly Journal of Anthropology*, 75(2).

Gill, M.S. and Singh, A.M., 1989, 'Reactionary Dissent by Caste Hindu Employee', *Social Change*, 19(3), p. 16.

Judge, Paramjit S., 2005, 'Caste Conflicts in Punjab: An Examination of Recent Jat-Dalit Clash in a Village', *Man and Development,* 27(3), p. 166.

Kamble, N.D., 1982, *The Scheduled Castes*, Ashish Publications, New Delhi.

Karnataka at a Glance (2003–04), Government of Karnataka.

Karnataka Human Development Report (2005).

Kshirsagar, R.K., 1986, *Untouchability in India: Implementation of the Law and Abolition*, Deep and Deep Publications, New Delhi.

Mohanty, R.P. *Dalit Development and Change: An Empirical Study*. 2003, Discovery Publication House, New Delhi.

National Campaign on Dalit Human Rights Report (2008).

Parvathamma, G., 1984, *Scheduled Castes and Scheduled Tribes: A Socio-Economic Survey*, Ashish Publications, New Delhi.

Punalekar, S.P. (1988), 'Identities and Consciousness: An Overview of Dalit Literature in Maharashtra', *Man and Development*, 10C4) (December).

Rangari, A.D., 1984, *Indian Caste System and Education*, Deep and Deep Publications, New Delhi.

Shah, Ghanshyam (ed.), 2001, *Dalit Identity and Politics*, Sage Publication, New Delhi.

Singh, Hoshiar and Malik, A.S., 2001, *Socio-Economic Development of Scheduled Castes in India: A Study of Haryana*, Aalekh Publishers, Jaipur.

Srinivas, M.N., 1972, *Social Change in Modern India*, Orient Longman, New Delhi.

Survey on Prevalence of Untouchability Practice and Discrimination in India (2006).

Thorat, Sukhadeo and Umakant, 2004, *Caste, Race and Discrimination Discourses in International Context*, Rawat Publications, Jaipur.

Wankhede, G.G., 1999, *Social Mobility and Scheduled Castes*, Rawat Publications, Jaipur.

8

Socio-economic Discrimination and Transformation of Dalits – Some Evidences

An Analysis Based on Dalit Autobiography

Praveen K. Jadhav

The discrimination against 'Dalits' in various social intercourses is being practiced since hundreds of years, which is based on the caste hierarchy. The social discrimination as 'untouchability' has been most critical and inhuman. Although the Constitution of India (Art. 14) has abolished the discrimination on the bases of race, religion, caste and gender, it is being practiced in many parts of India. Action Aid Report (2002) has given many evidences of practice of untouchability in the recent period. The scholars have explained several forms of social discrimination against Dalits. Some of them also have explained the need for protective discrimination (Thorat and Umakant, 2004). However, the economic discrimination against Dalits in a strict sense has not been the focus so far. Social discrimination is closely connected with the economic discrimination and it is hard to separate them from each other. In this effort very few scholars have explained the economic discrimination against Dalits. Sukhadeo Thorat and

This chapter is based on the 'Major Research Project' sanctioned by University Grants Commission (UGC), New Delhi. The author is grateful to UGC, New Delhi, for extending the financial support for the project.

Newman Katherine (2010) have identified various forms of economic discrimination against the Dalits. The authors have covered the discrimination in the field of wage, job, labour, rural market, health, school, food distribution scheme, etc. The practice of economic discrimination against Dalits is based on the social practices guided by the caste hierarchy. The stereotypical mindset of the non-dalits is creating the discrimination. Such discrimination can be found even in the contemporary period.

This chapter has also focused on economic discrimination against Dalits and the transformation of Dalits in the post-Ambedkar period. Severe discrimination has brought the Dalits to inhuman level, however, Ambedkarism or the movement led by Dr Ambedkar has brought the transformation among the Dalits. The present chapter gives some evidences of economic discrimination and transformation. It is true that the economic discrimination cannot be separated from social discrimination, since one determines the other. However, the objective of the author is to highlight only economic discrimination. The whole analysis has been presented on the basis of Dalit autobiography. The Dalit autobiographies can portray the real reasons of the discrimination over the years. These autobiographies can explore the realistic picture of Dalits. Although the Dalit autobiography is the story of an individual, this is equally the story of untouchables. For the present analysis, one famous Dalit autobiography titled, *Taral Antaral* (Kharat Shankar, 1988) has been selected. This Dalit autobiography represents the Dalit community as a whole. Hence, the study of this autobiography could be stated as the study of Dalit community. The main objective of this chapter is to give important evidences of economic discrimination and transformation of Dalits.

'Dalit' Autobiography and Autobiographer

The Dalit autobiographies explore the social life and transformation process of the Dalit as an individual and also as a group. These narrate the past and present social and economic position of the society. Arti Kusare-Kulkarni (1991: 31) writes, 'In the "Dalit" autobiographies, the autobiographer does not describe himself as the hero, but remains as "anti-hero". The surrounding social and cultural situation of the community, of the writer, is described as the hero. Various social references of the past and of the present are given. The "Dalit" autobiographers also narrate the magnitude of social awareness among the "Dalit" community, as well as, the psychological understanding of the Dalits and non-Dalits over various social and cultural issues. Therefore, the "Dalit" autobiographies are said to be "socio-literal" and hence, considered a social document'.

The life of the Dalit is painful and sorrowful. The social stratification treats the Dalits with cruelty and contempt. The pain and sorrow of the Dalits is reflected and narrated through the autobiographies. Many Dalit intellectuals have accepted this method of exploring reality of their 'self' and the 'society'. They can narrate the oppression, agony and anger of the Dalit masses. These social documents are the best source to analyse the social, economic and cultural reality of the Dalits over the years. These documents can help explain the position and the transformation of the Dalits in Maharashtra. Since the researcher's objective is to draw the social evidences, in general and not to draw the 'subjective' evidences, the Dalit autobiographies can be considered the base of analysis.

The selected Dalit autobiographer Mr Kharat Shankarrao (1921–2001) was born in a 'Mahar' (a caste in scheduled castes or in Dalit community) family, who represent the whole Dalit community. He was born in a village named Atpadi in Sangli district of Maharashtra state. The autobiographer has explained his life story in detail. He has narrated the various forms of discrimination based on caste system and the various stages of transformation. He also writes in the preface, 'This autobiography is not only a story of my life but also a story of all untouchables'. He was born in Mahar caste; he faced severe discrimination, despite that he brought the transformation in his life. He became an advocate and later a Vice Chancellor of a statutory university in Maharashtra. This chapter aims at giving the evidences of discrimination and transformation of the Dalits with the help of the selected autobiography.

Meaning of 'Dalit' and 'Discrimination'

The term Dalit has been defined differently by different scholars. Some scholars and activists have considered this term as relating to a more confined and defined group, whereas others have explored its usage in a wider and broader way. 'The word "Dalit" is a common usage in “Marathi”, “Hindi”, “Gujarati” and many other Indian languages. The word “Dalit” was first used in the new context in “Marathi” language by “Neo-Buddhist” activists, the followers of Babasaheb Ambedkar in the early 1970s. It refers to those who have been broken, ground down by those above them in social hierarchy in a deliberate way. There is, in the word, an inherent denial of pollution, karma and justified caste hierarchy' (Zelliot, 1978: 77). The word Dalit includes whom? This question is most important. There are different meanings in the different context. Ghanshyam Shah (2001: 17–18) writes that, ‘Dalits are the poor and downtrodden. Generally, “Dalit” includes those termed in administrative parlance as scheduled castes (SCs), scheduled tribes (STs) and other backward castes (OBCs). However, in day-to-day usage, in political discourse, the term is so far mainly confined to scheduled castes’. In more simple words, it can be stated that the Dalits are nothing but the ex-untouchables. This meaning seems to be more historical, practical and realistic. The researcher has also confined to this meaning or group in the analysis. The Dalits are scheduled castes and scheduled castes are the Dalits, for the study, Dalits and SCs are synonymous terms.

Economic discrimination is the form of discrimination based on economic factors. The discrimination in price, labour, wage and occupation is classified under economic discrimination. The economic discrimination has been recognized as a major cause of income inequality and poverty. Gary Becker (1971) argues that the discrimination is determined by the taste of the discriminator. In the context of India, social and economic discrimination has been more common. Dalits are discriminated against on social grounds. The social discrimination further determines the economic discrimination against the Dalits. The economic discrimination against Dalits can be found in the case of labour, wage, occupation, distribution of resources, services, etc. This economic discrimination is guided by the caste system. The higher castes dislike the lower castes, since the concept of pollution is attached to the Dalits. The existed form of discrimination against the Dalits has been more serious and hence is against humanity. In the social history of Dalits, the discrimination could be found in all segments, even in the ‘justice’. N.D. Kamble (1986) has explained the differences in the justice in the history, which brought the Dalits to severe exploitation. The discrimination against the Dalits continued even in the post-independence period. Even in Indian companies, discrimination could be found. Thorat and Newman (2007) have explained the existence of caste-based discrimination in Indian companies. Since, the present chapter deals with analysing the discrimination against the Dalits on the basis of selected autobiography, the other forms of discrimination based on caste have not been discussed in detail.

Socio-economic Discrimination Against 'Dalits'

The economic discrimination against Dalits has been an important reason for sustaining the poverty among the Dalits. The caste system forced discrimination and blocked Dalits from all rights and services. Kharat Shankarrao, the autobiographer, has explained the various forms of discrimination experienced by him and the Dalit community. Some of the evidences of economic discrimination against the Dalits have been given here.

Water and Discrimination

Water is a natural resource. All the people have equal right on this natural resource. But the distribution of this natural resource is not 'natural'. At a general level under defined circumstances, water and water facilities must be accessible to all, including the most vulnerable or marginalized sections of the population without any discrimination. But in rural areas, Dalits are discriminated in case of water accessibility. The method of distribution of water is based on caste hierarchy. The autobiographer has experienced this discrimination in his village. He writes, 'In the rural area, drinking water facilities were made available near the well or natural canal or at one established place. However, the sources of drinking water facilities were divided as per the caste hierarchy. The direction of flow of water (in the natural canal) was deciding the right of caste on the water. At the beginning of the flow, the "Brahmins" had the right of fetching the water, followed by "Sonars" (the gold smiths' caste) and the "Marathas" (economically dominant caste). After these places, "Kumbhar" (the potters' caste), "Sutar" (the carpenters) and "Lohar" (the blacksmiths' caste). At the end of the flow of water, there were places, where the "Mahars", "Matangs" and "Chambhars" had a right to fetch the water. The practice of fetching the water was perfectly based on the caste system or caste hierarchy'. This shows that 'water', which is a natural resource, was also divided on the basis of caste system. The water available to the 'Dalits' was not clean.

The autobiographer further gives the evidences of discrimination. He writes, 'Dominant castes had their own wells for drinking water. The "Dalits" did not have wells. They were dependent on the dominant castes. The "Dalits" had no right to fetch water from the wells of the "Marathas" and "Brahmins". The "Dalits" could get water from a distance, i.e. the member of dominant caste used to give a water place at a distance from the main source. The "Dalits" should not touch either the pot or the person of dominant caste. That was treated as "sin" or against the social rules'. Thus, the most essential natural resource 'water' was controlled by the upper castes. Dalits had no right over the water. This situation could be seen in most of the villages in Maharashtra.

Public Places and Discrimination

The autobiographer has explained the discrimination of Dalits at various public places. This discrimination was serious since this was blocking the most essential services to the Dalits. The autobiographer has faced discrimination at various places. Some of them have been given here.

Discrimination at School

Dalits were discriminated at the schools. Dalits were not allowed to sit in the school building or in the class room, but were allowed to sit outside the school, in open space. Teachers used to keep a distance from the Dalit students. The practice of 'untouchability' was followed by the teachers. Not only this but the other students from upper castes were also practicing the 'untouchability'. Dalit students were not allowed to drink water from the pot kept in the school. The segmentation process began from the school. The autobiographer has faced this situation. The education is available in the school. But school (upper caste teachers) discriminates the students on the basis of caste. Education is a process, which has formative effects on the mind, character and physical ability of an individual. This process transmits the knowledge, skill and values from one generation to another. Thus, education is most important and crucial factor in the development. But this most important factor was not properly offered to the Dalits.

Discrimination at the Hair Cutting Saloon

The hair cutting saloon is also a public place where service of hair cutting is made available to all. The barber belongs to *Nhavi* caste, which is assumed to be higher caste to Mahars. The autobiographer has experienced the discrimination at the hair cutting saloon too. The barber (the *Nhavi* caste person) was refusing to cut the hair of Dalits. The practice of untouchability was being followed by the barber. This resulted into two possibilities, as a solution, the hair of the 'Dalits' was being cut by family members or 'Dalit' children had to keep long hair.

Occupation and Discrimination

Employment is a contract between two parties: one is an employer and another is employee. The employer offers a wage for work or employment. There were certain occupations, which were being practiced by the Dalits. These occupations were based on caste hierarchy. The lower status and dirty occupations were offered to Dalits. The autobiographer's father was doing all such jobs, decided by the caste system, sometimes, wood-cutting and road repairing was also done by the Dalits. The autobiographer has given some of the forms of occupations of the Dalits, which are as follows:

(a) Occupation of messenger: Dalits were given the occupation of carrying the message from one place to another or from one village to another. Especially, the message about the death of a person had to be carried by the Dalits. The method of delivering the message was done considering the untouchability.

(b) Occupation of watchman: most of the Dalits were working as the watchmen in the villages. Their work was to protect the village. The nature of work was guided by the caste system. Against this work, they were offered handful of grains.

(c) Occupation of woodcutter: some of the 'Dalits' were working as woodcutters in the villages. They were offered less wage in terms of kinds.

(d) Occupation of carrying the dead animals: Dalits were given an occupation of carrying the dead animals from the village. They had to remove the dead animals from the village. This work was given by the caste system. Over hundreds of years, the Dalits were doing this work.

These occupations were given to the Dalits in the rural area. There was no change in these occupational structures. Some of the Dalits tried to break this structure, but the upper castes refused to accept this. The psychological understanding of the upper caste was based on caste hierarchy. Some of the Dalits had migrated to the city. They started to work as unskilled workers in the factories. They were living in the slums in the city.

Discrimination and Exploitation

Discrimination and exploitation are two sides of the same coin. Discrimination always leads to exploitation. In the case of the Dalits, the discrimination was based on the caste hierarchy. The intensity of discrimination was higher in the history. Over the years, there has been a decrease in the discrimination. However, discrimination still persists. The social, economic and cultural discrimination against the Dalits is nothing but exploitation. Such exploitation is beyond the measurable scale. In fact, there is no proper scale that can measure such discrimination and exploitation. The Dalits have united to fight against this discrimination. 'Deprived sections of the society in different parts of the world have organized themselves into protest movements to fight discrimination of various kinds based on colour, religion, caste and tribe. Their problem has been creating a new identity – the kind of image that they want to protect in order to gain self-respect, honour and status' (Rao, 1984: 191). Dr Ambedkar has fought discrimination against the Dalits. He organized a number of agitations, because of which the Dalits have obtained number of rights. In the real sense, Dr Ambedkar promoted the social reform movement.

Socio-economic Transformation of Dalits

Social and economic transformation is a process in which an individual or the society alters the socially ascribed status of their parents into a socially and economically achieved status for themselves. The process of transformation brings development in the society. The socio-economic transformation could be stressed among the elite Dalits. In general, a large section of the Dalit community is far from the process of transformation, but there is one elite group, existing especially in the urban area, which has gone through the process of socio-economic transformation. Noor

Mohammad (2006) has analysed the socio-economic transformation of the scheduled castes (similar word to Dalits) in Uttar Pradesh. For the analysis, the author has used selected parameters such as education, marriage, occupation, food, housing, clothing, standard of living and political awareness.

In case of elite Dalits in Maharashtra, the socio-economic transformation could be stressed. The selected autobiographer is a best example of a witness to the process of transformation. In spite of severe discrimination and exploitation, 'Dalits' had achieved the highest occupational mobility. The socio-economic transformation of 'Dalits' could take place due to the following circumstances.

Motivational Factor

In the process of overall transformation, 'motivation' is the most important factor. The motivational factor determines the socio-economic transformation of an individual. In case of the Dalits, this factor has valid significance. The motivation was given by Dr Ambedkar, the leader of the Dalits. Dr Ambedkar's thoughts and speeches inspired the entire Dalit community. The autobiographer (Mr Kharat) also was inspired and motivated by the thoughts of Dr Ambedkar. The autobiographer and the other Dalits were getting inspired through the newspaper named *Janata*. The autobiographer quotes; 'the speech of Dr B.R. Ambedkar brought the change in understanding of the "Dalits"'. The autobiographer quotes Dr B.R. Ambedkar as,

> we are human beings, but we have been treated like animals. The Hindu touchable castes kept us away from the mainstream. They made us slaves. They made us untouchables. Now onwards, we have to act as free human beings. We have to get our rights of humanity. We have to break the system of slavery and untouchability. For this freedom, we have to get united … . (Kharat, 201)

This message of Dr Ambedkar was given to the Dalits. The untouchables' movement led by Dr Ambedkar was spreading throughout Maharashtra. A new consciousness was being created. The speeches and thoughts of Dr Ambedkar were being published in the newspaper *Janata*. Some of the relatives of Mr Kharat had brought this newspaper in Mumbai. This paper brought drastic change in the mind of the 'Dalits'. Since then, the paper started reaching the village frequently. The Dalits wanted to free themselves from slavery and untouchability. All Dalit communities accepted Dr Ambedkar as their leader. The leadership and the movement of Dr Ambedkar brought confidence among Dalits. They really wanted a transformation.

Migration and Education

Migration and education have been the most important factors in the social and economic transformation of the Dalits. Dr Ambedkar had realized the importance of these two factors long back, hence he appealed the Dalit community to migrate to cities and get the work or education. Mr Kharat had also received inspiration about getting higher education. Mr Kharat quotes Dr Ambedkar's speech as,

> you (Dalits) have to send your children to school. Give them good education. You should leave the dirty work given by the Hindu touchable castes ... (Kharat, 201)

The autobiographer (Mr Kharat) and the Dalit youth realized the need of migration and education as told by Dr Ambedkar. He migrated to the city to get higher education. Many Dalit families migrated to cities in search of new employment. After the migration, Dalits started to work as unskilled worker in the factories and they sent their children to the school. They were living in the slums. This life was far better than earlier life. The Dalit elites have gone through social and economic transformation. The migration brought them various facilities, especially education. Hence, the second generation of the Dalits was able to get education. Many Dalit youth could get higher education. Dr Ambedkar gave a message of 'Educate, Agitate and Organise'. Due to this message, Mr Kharat completed his bachelor's degree in arts followed by degree in law. The educational progress of Mr Kharat was an output of Dr Ambedkar's thoughts. Similarly, the number of 'Dalits' (scheduled castes) who migrated to urban area and received higher education is increasing. The literacy rate among them is increasing.

Occupational Mobility

The educational progress of the higher educated Dalits in Maharashtra has promoted the occupational mobility. Many of the Dalits have obtained government jobs. The reservation factor played an important role in this regard. 'Education' and 'Reservation' have been the best combination for the transformation of the Dalits. The second and third generation of the Dalits have reached a satisfactory level. It is true that a large number of Dalits, especially, rural Dalits are away from the socio-economic transformation, but there exists a strong elite group in the urban area, that is representing the transformation.

In case of Mr Kharat (the autobiographer), after completing his bachelor's degree in arts, he became an advocate. He started his practice in urban area (Pune). After some years, he became the director of an established government bank. In the later years, he also became a Vice Chancellor of a statutory university in Maharashtra. The occupational mobility of Mr Kharat has been remarkable. In the context of caste hierarchy and its practice in society, the intergenerational and intragenerational occupational mobility of Mr Kharat was beyond imagination. Mr Kharat's father was illiterate. Mr Kharat, himself, went through a number of obstacles during his education. The caste barriers were hurdles in his development. However, he could reach to the highest post in educational system. One person from Mahar caste, which was being treated as 'untouchable' caste and who was blocked from educational facilities, now became the head of the educational system. The achievement of Mr Kharat was also an output of Dr Ambedkar's thoughts. Mr Kharat also writes that due to Dr Ambedkar's thoughts and agitations, he could move to a higher level. This generational occupational mobility – inter and intra – is a result of *Ambedkarism*. In a similar way, many Dalits (scheduled castes) have received the higher level jobs in the government sector. The representation of them in the higher posts in the central government sector is increasing over the years.

Conclusion

Dalits have gone through serious inhuman treatment and exploitation for hundreds of years. They have been facing high-degree social and economic discrimination based on the caste system. The caste hierarchy was blocking the 'Dalits' from the development. They had no free access to school or educational system. The public places were closed for them. The autobiographer, Mr Kharat, represents the Dalit community. He has faced all types of caste barriers. However, Dr Ambedkar's famous statement 'Educate, Agitate and Organise' brought a change in the mindset of the Dalits. Dr Ambedkar created an inspiration and motivation to Dalits, especially the youth. As a result of this, Dalits started to get education, in spite of all inhuman treatment. Mr Kharat completed his higher education and reached to the highest post in the educational system. This was the highest intrageneration occupational mobility. The achieved status of Mr Kharat was remarkable and he acknowledges his gratitude towards Dr Ambedkar. In general, the Dalits migrated to urban; they and their next generation received higher education. On the basis of education and reservation, they also got the employment. Thus, a social and economic transformation took place in case of the Dalits. The intensity of caste hierarchy, especially in urban area, has been declining. (At least, it is not visible. It might have taken an invisible form.) The rights of the Dalits are protected. The Dalits are organized to fight against the discrimination and exploitation. These changes among the Dalits took place because of Dr Ambedkar's thoughts and agitations. Even today, that is, 54 years after the sad demise of Dr Ambedkar, his followers or the Dalits remember him on all important occasions. The most powerful elite group among the Dalits, that is, 'Neo-Buddhists' are strong in their social, economical, political and cultural angle. They have established their separate social identity. The formation of identity is the biggest achievement. As a whole, despite severe discrimination and exploitation, many of the higher educated 'Dalits' could bring the social and economic transformation in their lives. This has been the result of the application of the thoughts of Dr Ambedkar.

References

ActionAid, 2002, Peoples Report on the Status of Untouchability in Maharashtra, Mumbai, Quoted in Thorat, Sukhadeo and Negi, Prashant (2006) '*Exclusion and Discrimination-Civil Rights Violation and Atrocities in Maharashtra*, Indian Institute of Dalit Studies, New Delhi.

Becker, Gary, 1971, *The Economics of Discrimination*, The University of Chicago Press, Chicago.

Kamble, N.D., 1986, *The Scheduled Castes*, Ashish Publishing House, New Delhi.

Kharat, Shankar, 1988, *Taral Antaral*, Continental Prakashan, Pune.

Kusare-Kulkarni, Arti, 1991, *Dalit Swakathane: Sahitya Roop*, Vijay Prakashan, Nagpur.

Mohammad, Noor, 2006, *Socio-Economic Transformation of Scheduled Castes in Uttar Pradesh*, Concept Publishing Company, New Delhi.

Rao, M.S.A., 1984, 'Social Movements Among Backward Classes and the Clocks: Homology in the Sources of Identity', in Rao M.S.A. (ed.), *Social Movements in India*, Manohar Publication, New Delhi.

Shah, Ghanshyam, 2001, 'Introduction: Dalit Politics', in Ghanshyam Shah (ed.), *Dalit Identity and Politics*, Sage Publications, New Delhi.

Thorat, Sukhadeo and Katherine Newman, 2007, 'Caste and Economic Discrimination: Causes, Consequences and Remedies', *Economic and Political Weekly*, 13 October.

Thorat, Sukhadeo and Katherine Newman (ed.), 2010, *Blocked by Caste: Economic Discrimination in Modern India*, Oxford University Press, New York.

Thorat, Sukhadeo and Umakant (ed.), 2004, *Caste, Race and Discrimination: Discourses in International Context*, Rawat Publications, Jaipur

Zelliot, Eleanor, 1978, 'Dalit New Cultural Context for an Old Marathi World', Contribution to Asian Studies, Quoted in Ghanshyam Shah (2001), *Dalit Identity and Politics*. 11: 77–78.

9

Geographical Discrepancy among Scheduled Caste Students in Academic Achievement

Vikas Sudam Kamble

The great social reformers Jyotiba Phule, Ch. Shahu Maharaj and Dr Babasaheb Ambedkar clearly recognized the universal truth, why *Bahujan* or Dalit – depressed people are so much deprived in all things? The answer is in the historical quotation of Jyotiba Phule

> Vidya vina mati geli | Mati vina niti geli |
> Niti vina gati geli | gati vina vitta gele |
> Vitta vina shudra Khachale |
> Ewadhe anarth eka avidyene kele ||

Dr Babasaheb Ambedkar wrote the Indian Constitution and provided equal educational opportunity for all. Since that day, deprived people, especially scheduled caste people, have started to learn and get education. After 50 years, they have achieved unprecedented success in every sector of life. It is an incredible ideal for those who were deprived, exploited and suppressed by social, political or any other system. Education is an important instrument for such kind of progress.

Scheduled caste people from Maharashtra are a great example of this development than any other state or territory in

India. Maharashtra state is geographically divided into five regions. Among them Vidarbha, Marathwada and Western Maharashtra have developed very well. However, a significant disparity is observed among caste to caste and region to region. Konkan and Khandesh or Northern Maharashtra has remained much deprived in the field of higher education. Hence, the present chapter is designed to study the regional disparity among the scheduled caste students.

Academic Stress

Stress is one of the popular fields for researcher. There is no field, in which stress does not exist. It is undivided part of modern life. Hans Selye is the father of stress study. He wrote several books and papers on it. Selye[1] defines stress as 'The non-specific response of the body to any demand after conducting extensive animal and human research'. He identified a predictable pattern of response to stress that he termed the 'General Adaptation Syndrome' (GAS). He identified three stages in this syndrome. The first stage is the alarm stage that is the immediate stress responses. The individual perceives a stressor that causes the body to begin a physiological response. This response is automatic and unconscious. It is at this point that the individual initiates the flight or fight response to the stimuli. The second stage is the stage of resistance. This is the stage where adaptation and coping occur. After using a large amount of energy available to the individual, the body enters the last stage. This third and final stage is termed exhaustion.

Stress has become an important topic in educational setting. It can give positive and negative effects on academic performance, if stress is not managed well. Smith[2] and Stevenson and Harper[3] mentioned, 'academic stress is mental and emotional pressure, tensions that occur due to the demands of college life'. Academic stress includes the students' perception of the extensive knowledge base required and the perception of an inadequate time span to develop it. Carveth, Gesse, and Moss[4] and other researchers pointed out that stress is the perception of discrepancy between environmental demands and individual capacities to fulfil these demands. Vermunt and Steensman[5] and Smith[6] have observed that at higher education various academic demands placed on students are based on deadline, which creates a lot of academic stress among students.

There are varieties of stressors in the academic context that have been identified by the several researchers. Sinha[7] observed academic stressors such as academic burden, high expectations, unrealistic ambitions, limited opportunities and high competitiveness; Fairbrother and Warn[8] identified too many assignments, competition with other students and failure; Ongori[9] observed interpersonal difficulties with teachers and other subjects, family problems, college or university level stressors and overcrowded lecture halls; and Erkutlu and Chafra[10] observed semesters system and inadequate resources to perform academic work and also point outs the pressure to perform well at the examination. All these stressors cause inconvenience for students.

It has been estimated that 10 per cent to 30 per cent students experience academic-related stress that affects their academic performance. Some academic stress, such as stress that comes from being exposed to new educational concepts and adjusting to new setting and taking on the larger workload, is normal among all college students. Too much academic stress can cause depression and physical illness, which can in turn negatively affect academic performance mentioned by Macgeorge, Samter, and Gillihan.[11]

One of the major causes of academic stress is adaptation to a new life or transaction of junior to senior level that suddenly takes place. Towbes and Cohen[12] also explain such type of stress. At this stage, students are facing new challenges such as new curriculum, deep and vast syllabus, anxiety of career, new relationships, college-related issues and so on. The college-related issues also affect the students during these days. Difference between new and old students and peer versus other students can also create a stress.

Academic Self-concept

We have been observing our overt picture or physical appearance since childhood. But we start to see our internal picture from adolescence. Who am I? How am I? What abilities and qualities I have? These questions arise in our mind during adolescent period. Answer of such a question is called self-concept. The self-concept is nothing but our understanding, observations and thoughts of our self. It is self-evaluation of image, motivation, emotions, interest, attitude, ability and hobbies, etc. The self-concept is an organized collection of beliefs about the self. Self-concept is the value that an individual places on his or her own characteristics, qualities, abilities and actions as noted by Woolfolk.[13] According to Wolffe,[14] the term self-concept refers to the ordered set of attitudes and perceptions that an individual holds about him or herself.

The importance of self-concept in educational setting has been researched by plenty of researchers. Byrne[15] concluded that 'self concept is a multidimensional construct, having one general facet and several specific facets, one of which is academic self concept'. The term academic self-concept can be characterized by two elements consistent with the Shavelson Model made by Strein.[16] First, academic self-concept reflects descriptive (e.g. I like Maths) as well as evaluative (e.g. I am good at Maths) aspects of self-concept. Second, self-perception associated with academic self-concept tends to focus on scholastic competence, rather than attitudes. Some researchers are giving their stress on different aspects. Reyes[17] defined that academic self-concept referred to as a person's perception of self with respect to achievement in school. Skaalvik and Hagtvet[18] defined academic self-concept as an individual's perception of self-efficacy in academic subjects.

Marsh and Hau[19] has put forward the view that academic self-concept is determined by student's frame of references, such students with high attaining peer will be more likely to consider themselves 'below average' than students of the same prior ability who are surrounded by lower attaining peers.

Marsh raised a question, Do changes in academic self-concept lead to changes in subsequent academic achievement? This question has a big practical implication among educational world. He concludes that such type of research is critically important in that it has established that increase in academic self-concept leads to increase in subsequent academic achievement and other desirable educational outcomes. Hence, self-concept is not only an important outcome variable in itself, but also plays a central role in mediating the effects of other desirable educational outcomes.

Academic Achievement

Academic achievement is extremely important, particularly in the present situation. All the parents and teachers give more stress on academic achievement right from the beginning of the primary education. Today, a great kind of academic achievement at higher education level is very important to get job. Various companies and institutes follow selection and recruitment on the basis of academic achievement and other developments.

In general terms, academic achievement refers to the overall educational progress among school or college students. According to Good,[20] academic achievement means knowledge attained or skills developed in the school or college subject. Shaik[21] and his colleagues defined it as the specified level of attainment of proficiency in academic work designed by test score. Shapiro[22] defines academic achievement as academic assessment of performance. Subramanyam and Rao[23] said that, 'Academic achievement is related to the acquisition of principles and generalizations and the capacity to perform efficiently with certain manipulation, objectives, symbols and ideas'. Singh[24] says academic achievement of a student measures knowledge, understandings or skills in a specified subject. Moreover, academic achievement is an essential tool or device for measuring the quality and quantity of pupils learning outcomes in a subject of students or group of subjects.

Today, we do not find the considerable number of scheduled caste students from school going to college or higher education. It is very necessary that government should provide attention towards scheduled caste students especially among the Konkan region and make strong plans to increase the number of scheduled caste students in higher education.

Scheduled Castes

Scheduled castes means such castes, races or tribes or parts of groups which are deemed under Article 341 (The President of India specifies the castes, races and tribes, to be included in the list of scheduled caste in relation to a particular state or union territory, once such a list is notified with respect to any state or union territory) for the purpose of this constitutional provision. 'The Government of India Act 1935 used the term scheduled castes for the first time. Then the Government of India published a list of scheduled caste in 1936'. A total of 417 castes were listed but actually there were 450 castes, considering each of the caste/subcastes, etc. which are grouped together as a separate entity. In the present study, three castes are considered, namely Buddhist, Mahar and Charmkar. Buddhist means those students who have converted themselves from all the scheduled castes.

Western Maharashtra

Maharashtra state has six administrative divisions. But geographically, Maharashtra has five main regions, namely Vidarbha region (Nagpur and Amravati division), Marathwada region (Aurangabad division), Khandesh or Northern Maharashtra region (Nasik division), Konkan region (Konkan division) and Desh or Western Maharashtra region (Pune division).

Desh or Western Maharashtra has five districts, namely Pune, Sangli, Satara, Kolhapur and Solapur. In addition to Sangli, Satara and Kolhapur districts are considered for the present study. Moreover, on account of paucity of time and funds, this research is limited to three districts.

Konkan Region

Konkan region has seven districts, namely Sindhudurga, Ratnagiri, Raigad, Thane, Mumbai district, Mumbai suburb district and New Mumbai. But only three districts are considered for present research, namely Sindhudurga, Ratnagiri and Raigad. The living conditions of Konkan people are very miserable especially the people from Schedules Castes and tribes. There is a lack of social, economic, political and educational awareness among scheduled caste people. They still don't realize that education is the only base of all types of development. They have less ability to acquire higher education. All these factors are responsible for educational deprivation among them.

Statement of the Problem

Education is the only base of all kinds of progress of scheduled caste people. Ample research has been done on them. Some of the topics of research are its social and economic mobility of scheduled caste people, poverty of scheduled caste, the role and status of scheduled caste women, legal awareness, social and political mass movement of scheduled caste, etc. Such kinds of research have been carried out by several researchers. And there is no comparative study conducted on the regional disparity in higher education of scheduled caste students.

This chapter focuses its attention on the way the scheduled caste students face new challenges of higher education, the level of academic stress they experience and how they look towards higher education.

Purpose of the Study

The purpose of this study is to determine if there is a significant difference in the academic stress, academic self-concept and academic achievement among the scheduled caste students of Western Maharashtra and Konkan region, and also to provide suggestions to foster academic self-concept and academic achievement and reduce the level of academic stress of these students.

Objectives of the Study

Following objectives were considered to conduct this project:

- To measure the geographical region disparity on academic stress experienced by students due to its various sources.
- To find the geographical region discrepancy on academic self-concept and its various sources.
- To find the disparity of geographical region on academic achievement of students.
- To understand the impact of caste on academic achievement of students.

Hypotheses of the Study

Following hypotheses were formulated to perform the study:

1. Konkan students will experience significantly more academic stress than students from Western Maharashtra.
2. The level of academic self-concept and its various components will be significantly more among the students from Western Maharashtra than Konkan students.
3. Students from Western Maharashtra would have significantly high academic achievement than Konkan students.
4. academic achievement of students would be significantly affected by different castes.

Significance of the Study to Higher Education Administration

After independence, the Government of India has taken a number of steps to strengthen the educational base of the persons belonging to scheduled castes. Various plans and schemes are initiated and effectively run through opening a number of new departments and programmes. Crores of rupees have been utilized for the development of weaker sections of the society.

However, even today, various regions remain socially and educationally deprived. These sectors could not develop by providing only such kind of plans and schemes. Instead of such provisions, it is necessary to initiate different kinds of plans for the people who live in such deprived regions.

Such kind of projects should be conducted at the micro level to find out the basic academic problems of these students. The government also should motivate and economically support such projects with free hand. Present research project is carried out on such kind of deprived regions and it is observed that Konkan students are not only very poor on educational background but also very poor on cognitive abilities such as thinking, decision making and level of aspiration. They have a lot of inferiority complex, quite shy, less confident for leadership, less tolerant and so on. Moreover, these students have low academic self-concept and they suddenly became victims of academic stress and get frustrated.

Through this project, the researcher has suggested some ways to overcome these disparities for the great kind of future success for Konkan students. If government pays attention to these suggestions, it would be more beneficial to make future plans and schemes for the higher education of scheduled caste students, which will in turn help, to increase their social, economical status and living conditions.

Methodology

Sample

For this study, only senior college students enrolled in BA, BCom. and BSc. during the 2008–2009 were included. A total of 900 samples were collected from the Shivaji University, Kolhapur and University of Mumbai, Mumbai jurisdiction. But finally only 600 students were considered for analysis of data.

The present chapter is limited to Western Maharashtra and Konkan region; hence samples consisted of 300 students from Western Maharashtra and 300 students from Konkan for this project. There are six districts from Western Maharashtra but only three districts, namely Sangli, Kolhapur and Satara are considered for collecting the sample. Similarly, though six districts are included in the Konkan region, only Sindhudurga, Ratnagiri and Raigad are considered for this study. Hundred samples are collected from each district of Western Maharashtra and Konkan region.

Moreover, the sample is collected on the basis of several other criteria such as gender, residence and caste. There are so many castes within the scheduled caste, but for convenience and availability of specific caste only three castes, namely Buddhist, Mahar and Charmkar are included. One important fact is that Buddhism is a religion and not assumed to be a caste; however, it belongs to Scheduled caste in India. Two hundred students from each caste are selected. The age range of students is 18 to 22 years. Gender and residence criteria are also considered to match the subjects. Finally, sample is collected by the quota sampling method for convenience.

Tools

Three tools are used in this study.

(i) Academic Stress Scale (For College Students) (ASS)

This scale has been developed to identify the sources of academic stress among college students by Dr Rajendran and Dr Brinda (1991). The scale has 52 items on a five-point scale varying from the responses of 'no stress' to 'extreme stress'. The scale measures five sources of academic stress, namely personal inadequacy, facilities at the college and hostel, interpersonal difficulties with teachers and parents, attitude of teachers and attitude of management. A high score on the scale indicates high academic stress and low score denotes low academic stress. The scale depicts high reliability and validity with 81 per cent variance explained.

(ii) Academic Self-Concept Scale (ASCS)

This scale is standardized by Dr Anil Kumar (1998) and has been used to assess the level of academic self-concept. It measures the dimensions such as academic abilities and interest, academic interactions, self-confidence, study preparation, academic time, academic future, examination, mode of study, etc. High score on the scale indicates high academic self-concept, while low score denotes low academic self-concept. The scale has high reliability and validity.

(iii) Academic Achievement Score (AAS)

Academic achievement is usually defined in three ways: the grades earned in school or college, student's performance and score achieved on standardized test of academic achievement. In the present study, for the consideration of academic achievement of students, the percentage of their previous year final examination and percentage of current year examination were collected. The total of these two scores of each subject was converted into grade point of average (GPA).

Research Design

This study has used a descriptive and comparative approach between Western Maharashtra and Konkan region including an exploratory factorial research design was used. Academic achievement is one and the only dependent variable, while academic stress and academic self-concept are major independent variables. 3 × 3 factorial design was employed to see the comprehensive effect of these variables. Academic stress and academic self-concept was considered on three levels, namely high, average and low.

Moreover, there are other three independent variables such as geographical region, considered on two levels, namely, Western Maharashtra and Konkan, caste considered on three level, namely Buddhist, Mahar and Charmkar, gender and residence or area which was considered on two levels. The effect of these three variables on GPA was studied by using 3 × 2 × 2 factorial design.

Procedure for Data Collection

The detailed plan of work was discussed with the principals and permission was sought from them. The names and addresses of various colleges of Shivaji University, Kolhapur, and University of Mumbai, Mumbai jurisdictions, were collected. Then permission was sought from the principals of selected colleges from these jurisdictions to administer the psychological scales on their graduate students, through the letter. When researcher obtained permission from various principals in willing, orally and through telephonic communication, and finally the date of visit was fixed.

On the day of the visit to these colleges or in the concerned classroom, each participant was assured confidentiality and privacy about their responses. It was also explained that participation is voluntary and without compulsion. After rapport formation each subject was given an academic stress scale. They were asked to fill the demographic information in the front page of the scale. After giving instructions regarding the responses to the items, participants were asked to complete the whole scale without omitting any item. After finishing this task the second scale (academic self-concept) was administered and the study proceeded in the similar way.

At the end of the data collection, the annual percentage of marks of their previous year's examination was collected from the result ledger of the college. After six months, when annual examination of the participants was over and the result were announced researcher again visited these colleges and current year percentage of marks of the participants was collected from the result ledger.

Data Analysis

All the items of the academic stress scale were scored and summed up according to five different sources. The total score was obtained by summing all items. The high score on scale indicated high academic stress, while low score shows low academic score.

The results from the academic self-concept scale were also hand scored by the researcher. Row scores were determined for each component of the scale. Then all totals on each component were summed as academic self-concept index. A high score denotes high academic self-concept, while low score reveals low academic self-concept.

Row scores from ASS and ASCS were entered into SPSS programmes data sheet and statistical analysis was done. Descriptive and inferential statistics were performed to get the results. The *t*-tests and one-way analysis of variance (ANOVA) was used to calculate the difference between academic stress, academic self-concept and academic achievement score. Scheffe's post-hoc-multiple comparisons were also done to find out which pair shows the most significant difference. Two way and four way analysis of variance were done to see the main effect of independent variables as well as to see the interaction effect of several combinations. All statistical analysis has been made through SPSS programmes by the researcher.

Results and Discussion

The purpose of this study was to determine the significant difference between Western Maharashtra and Konkan students in academic stress, academic self-concept and academic achievement.

Table 1

Geographical Comparison on Academic Stress

Stressors	*Region*	*N*	*Mean*	*Standard Deviation*	*t*
Personal inadequacy	W Mah	300	14.25	12.75	30.88**
	Konkan	300	55.16	19.07	
Facilities	W Mah	300	12.02	8.86	36.92**
	Konkan	300	45.04	12.70	
Interpersonal difficulties	W Mah	300	8.21	4.64	28.42**
	Konkan	300	25.02	9.13	
Attitude of teachers	W Mah	300	10.60	9.16	29.51**
	Konkan	300	42.18	16.10	
Attitude of management	W Mah	300	4.87	4.37	31.33**
	Konkan	300	18.67	6.25	
Academic stress	W Mah	300	49.99	38.09	33.27**
	Konkan	300	186.07	59.73	

W. Mah = Western Maharashtra, * 0.05, ** 0.01.

1. Geographical Comparison on Academic Stress

Scheduled caste students are developing rapidly and steadily. However, there is no similarity among all of them. We can find regional imbalance and caste differences among them. Maharashtra is divided on certain geographical phenomena. Among them Konkan remains most deprived because of various aspects.

Table 1 shows how Western Maharashtra and Konkan regions differ on academic stress. Students from Western Maharashtra show a low level of academic stress but students from Konkan region show a greater level of academic stress. They have 49.99 and 186.07 mean as well as 38.09 and 59.73 SD, respectively. The *t*-value of mean difference is 33.27, which is significant on 0.01 level of alpha.

Table 1 shows that Konkan students suffer intensely due to personal inadequacy of facilities provided at the college and hostel, interpersonal difficulties with teachers and parents, attitude and teachers and attitude of management. They have a high level of stress on these sources than the students of Western Maharashtra. Western Maharashtra and Konkan students differ significantly on sources of academic stress.

2. Geographical Comparison on Academic Self-concept

Table 2 shows a clear picture of total academic self-concept and its various dimensions. Academic self-concept is nothing but an overall understanding of the educational process. In the present study, the researcher has found the students from Western Maharashtra show the highest level of academic self-concept. On the contrary, Konkan students show a low level of academic self-concept; hence, it reversely affects their academic achievement and results in low educational performance.

Table 2

Geographical Comparison on Academic Self-concept

Dimension ASCS	*Region*	*N*	*Mean*	*Std. Deviation*	*t*
Ability and interest	W Mah	300	35.35	4.05	26.21**
	Konkan	300	13.84	13.32	
Interactions	W Mah	300	14.19	1.47	41.14**
	Konkan	300	5.48	3.35	
Self-confidence	W Mah	300	23.49	2.86	31.25**
	Konkan	300	9.09	7.45	
Study preparation	W Mah	300	32.49	4.00	51.19**
	Konkan	300	11.76	5.75	
Academic time	W Mah	300	23.23	3.01	52.41**
	Konkan	300	10.04	3.14	
Academic future	W Mah	300	14.03	1.49	35.75**
	Konkan	300	6.37	3.39	
Examination	W Mah	300	18.44	2.62	45.79**
	Konkan	300	7.58	3.15	
Mode of study	W Mah	300	22.95	3.20	39.39**
	Konkan	300	8.97	5.24	
Academic self-concept	W Mah	300	183.78	20.74	28.15**
	Konkan	300	93.13	51.76	

W. Mah = Western Maharashtra * 0.05, ** 0.01.

Mean and SD of the students from Western Maharashtra on academic self-concept is 183.78 and 20.74, respectively, as well as mean and SD of Konkan students is 93.13 and 51.76, respectively. The *t*-value of mean difference is 28.15, which is significant on 0.01 level of confidence.

Academic self-concept has eight different dimensions. Western Maharashtra and Konkan students strongly and significantly differ on all these dimensions. Western Maharashtra and Konkan students have a mean score respectively 35.35 and 13.84 on academic abilities and interest, 14.19 and 5.48 on academic interactions, 23.49 and 9.09 on self-confidence, 32.49 and 11.76 on study preparation, 23.23 and 10.04 on academic time, 14.03 and 6.37 on academic future, 18.44 and 7.58 on examination dimension and 22.95 and 8.97 on mode of study. It could be also seen that all the mean scores of Western Maharashtra students show a greater level of academic self-concept, while all the mean scores of Konkan students show lowest level. Hence, all these mean differences significantly differ on 0.01 level of alpha.

Table 3

Geographical Region Comparison on Academic Achievement

Variable	*Region*	*N*	*Mean*	*Std. Deviation*	*t*
GPA	W Mah	300	59.69	8.15	18.22**
	Konkan	300	47.36	8.42	

W. Mah = Western Maharashtra, ** 0.01.

3. Geographical Region Comparison on Academic Achievement

Deprivation does come not only from social backwardness but also from geographical causes. Scheduled caste students of Western Maharashtra are aware of socially, politically and much more educationally. Education is the base for overall development of these students. But the key point is that Konkan students are not providing their concentration on education. Hence, they remain deprived on various aspects of life. The hidden truth of their miserable condition could be in their personal ability or social condition. Government should make new special plans and schemes for such deprived people.

Table 3 clearly shows that Konkan students have a lower academic achievement than Western Maharashtra students. There is a significant difference between students from Western Maharashtra who have a 60 per cent academic achievement and Konkan students who have 47 per cent academic achievement, which is very low.

4. Caste-wise Comparison of Academic Stress

Higher education is a stage of transition where students have just finished their school education and entered into college life. They are confused, anxious and tense about their future. Such stressful situation might create a lot of academic problems for them.

Students from three different castes are significantly different from each other. Table 4 shows that *F* value 4.05 is significant at 0.05 level of alpha. Table 5 revels that Buddhist students experience less academic stress than other caste students. Buddhist students may have more potential, more capabilities, bold and dashing with positive attitudes than other student's, that is Mahar and Charmkar students, hence, are less stressed.

Table 4

Summary of One-Way ANOVA for the Stressor 'Academic Stress'

Sources of Variance	*Sum of Squares*	*Df*	*Mean Square*	*F*	*Sig.*
Between Groups	57,272.17	2	28,636.08	4.050*	0.018
Within Groups	4,22,0747.29	597	7069.92		
Total	42,78,019.46	599			

* 0.05.

Table 5

Scheffe's Post-hoc Multiple Comparison on 'Academic Stress'

Caste	*N*	*Subset for alpha = 0.05*	
		1	*2*
Buddhist	200	104.27	
Charmkar	200	123.82	123.82
Mahar	200		125.99
Sig.		0.06	0.96

Means for groups in homogeneous subsets are displayed.

5. Caste-wise Comparison of Academic Self-concept

Academic self-concept is the overall understanding of academic life. It affects all types of development at school and college. Students who have a high level of academic self-concept could be higher in other tasks. Though Buddhist, Mahar and Charmkar students belong to the same category meaning they are scheduled castes, they are different in many areas such as economic background, social and educational awareness, values, ideals and so on. Variation in such things makes lots of difference in lots of matters among these students. It is seen from Table 6 that academic self-concept is a matter in which researcher finds a significant difference among three types of students [$F(2, 597)$, 9.57, $p < 0.01$]. Table 7 shows that difference between Buddhist and Mahar students about academic self-concept is 23.32, which is strongly significant, and difference between Buddhist and Charmkar students is 21.45, which is also significant at 0.05 level of confidence. Table 7 shows that Buddhist students have 153.38 mean score of academic self-concept while Mahar and Charmkar students respectively have 130.06 and 131.93 mean score. Buddhist students have high degree of self-concept than others.

Table 6

Summary of One-Way ANOVA on 'Academic Self-concept'

Source of Variance	*Sum of Squares*	*Df*	*Mean Square*	*F*	*Sig.*
Between groups	67,174.51	2	33,587.25	9.570**	0.000
Within groups	20,95,268.53	597	3509.66		
Total	21,62,443.04	599			

** 0.01.

Table 7

Scheffe's Post-hoc Multiple Comparison on 'Academic Self-concept'

Caste	*N*	*Subset for alpha = 0.05*	
		1	*2*
Mahar	200	130.06	
Charmkar	200	131.93	
Buddhist	200		153.38
Sig.		0.952	1.000

Means for groups in homogeneous subsets are displayed.

6. Caste-wise Comparison of Academic Achievement

Table 8 reveals that if three caste students are compared on GPA, significant difference is found among them. *F* value of 9.38 is significant on 0.01 level. If a comparison is made between Mahar and Charmkar students on GPA, we may not get a significant difference among them (Table 9). Though Charmkar students are high on economic background they were not high on GPA, and other variables than Mahar students. But Buddhist students are significantly different from these two castes. The reasons of differences could be because of social, educational or political awareness. Specifically, social movements could be responsible for such a kind of difference among Buddhist and Charmkar students.

Table 8

Summary of One-Way ANOVA on Academic Achievement

	Sum of Squares	*Df*	*Mean Square*	*F*	*Sig.*
Between groups	1,949.69	2	974.84	9.38**	.000
Within groups	62,000.26	597	103.85		
Total	63,949.96	599			

** 0.01.

Table 9

Scheffe's Post-hoc Multiple Comparison on Academic Achievement

Caste	*N*	*Subset for alpha = 0.05*	
		1	*2*
Charmkar	200	52.09	
Mahar	200	52.42	
Buddhist	200		56.07
Sig.		0.95	1.000

Means for groups in homogeneous subsets are displayed.

Conclusions

Following conclusions were drawn from this study regarding scheduled caste students of Western Maharashtra and Konkan region.

1. Scheduled caste students from Western Maharashtra and Konkan region are significantly different on academic stress and its various sources. Scheduled caste students of Konkan have been experiencing a high amount of academic stress while students from Western Maharashtra experienced low level of academic stress.
2. Scheduled caste students from Western Maharashtra and Konkan region are significantly different on academic self-concept and its various components. Scheduled caste students of Western Maharashtra possessed high level of academic self-concept, while Konkan students had a low level of the same.
3. The results of this study indicate that scheduled caste students of Western Maharashtra have a higher academic achievement than Konkan students.
4. Significant caste differences were found on academic stress experienced by scheduled caste students due to interpersonal difficulties, attitude of teachers and attitude of management. Buddhist students are significantly different from Mahar and Charmkar students; they have a low level of academic stress.
5. Significant caste difference was found regarding the academic self-concept. Buddhist students have a high level of academic self-concept, while Mahar and Charmkar students have average level.
6. The results of this study also indicate that Buddhist students have a high academic achievement than Mahar and Charmkar students.

Recommendations

The following recommendations are suggested on the basis of the findings of this research.

1. The Government of Maharashtra should start a comprehensive stress management programme for scheduled caste students, especially for scheduled caste students who live in educationally deprived region such as Konkan, at the initial stage of higher education and continuing until postgraduation. These programmes should emphasize study habits/skills, time management or future planning skills, healthy lifestyles and effective adjustments or coping skills.

2. University Grants Commission should take a commitment from the professors who belong to scheduled castes that each of them should keep personal contacts with at least 20 scheduled caste students to enhance their academic progress of such students. Moreover, such professors should provide their attention to develop the academic abilities and interest, self-confidence and positive attitude of students. They further should work making available a complete package of academic competence to their students.
3. The Government of Maharashtra should form a commission for educationally deprived sections to find out the causes of such deprivation and make suggestions for comprehensive remedies.

Notes

1. H. Selye, 1976, *Stress in Health and Disease,* Butterworths, Boston.
2. A. Smith, 2002, 'The Scale of Perceived Occupational Stress', *Occupational Media Journal,* 50, pp. 294–298.
3. A. Stevenson and S. Harper, 2006, 'Workshop Stress and the Student Learning Experience', *Quality Assurance Education,* 14(2), pp. 167–178.
4. J.A. Carveth, T. Gesse, and N. Moss, 1996, 'Survival Strategies for Nurse-midwifery Students', *Journal of Nurse–Midwifery,* 41(1), pp. 50–54.
5. R. Vermunt, and H. Steensman, 2005, 'How Can Justice be Used to Manage Stress in Organizations?', *Handbook of Organizational Justice,* 383410, pp. 383–410.
6. A. Smith, S. Johal, E. Wadsworth, G.D. Smith, and T. Peters, 2000, 'The Scale of Occupational Stress: The Bristol Stress and Health at Work Study', *HSE Book,* Sudbury.
7. U.K. Sinha, 2000, Academic Stress and its Management. *Proceedings of the Orientation Course in Clinical Psychology,* AIIMS, New Delhi.
8. K. Fairbrother and J. Warn, 2003, 'Work Place Dimensions: Stress and Job Satisfaction', *Journal of Managerial Psychology,* 18(1), pp. 8–21.
9. H. Ongori, 2007, 'A Review of the Literature on Employee Turnover', *African Journal of Business Management,* 1(3), pp. 49–54.
10. H.V. Erkutlu and J. Chafra, 2006, 'Relationship Between Leadership Power Bases and Job Stress of Subordinates: Example from Boutique Hotels', *Journal of Management Research News,* 29(5), pp. 285–297.
11. E.L. Macgeorge, W. Samter, and S.J. Gillihan, 2005, 'Academic Stress, Supportive Communication and Health', *Communication Education,* 54, pp. 365–372.

12. L.C. Towbes and L.H. Cohen, 1996, 'Chronic Stress in the Lives of College Students: Scale Development and Perspective Prediction of Distress', *Journal of Youth and Adolescence,* 25, pp. 199–217.
13. A. Woolfolk, 2001, *Educational Psychology*, 8th ed., Allyn and Bacon, Needham Heights, MA.
14. K. Wolffe, 2000, 'Growth and Development in Middle Childhood and Adolescence', in: A.J. Koening and M.C. Holbrook (eds.), *Foundation of Educations*, pp. 135–156.
15. B. Byrne, 1984, 'The Academic Self Concept Nomological Network: A Review of Construct Validation Research', *Review of Educational Research,* 54, pp. 427–456.
16. W. Strein, 1993, 'Advances in Research on Academic Self Concept: Implication for School Psychology', *School Psychology Review,* 22, pp. 273–284.
17. L.H. Reyes, 1984, 'Affective Variables and Mathematics Education', *Elementary School Journal,* 84, pp. 558–581.
18. E.M. Skaalvik and K.A. Hagtvet, 1990, 'Academic Achievement and Self Concept: An Analysis of Causal Predominance in a Development Perspective', *Journal of Personality and Social Psychology,* 58, pp. 292–307.
19. H.W. Marsh and K.T. Hau, 2003, 'Big-Fish-Little-Pound Effect on Academic Self Concept : A Cross Cultural (26 country) Test of the Negative Effects of Academically Selective Schools', *American Psychology,* 58(5), pp. 364–376.
20. Good, V., 1993, *Dictionary of Psychology*, 3rd ed., McGraw-Hill Book Company, New York.
21. S. Shaik, V.D. Reddy, and D.B. Rao, 2007, *Values and Academic Achievement*, Discovery Publishing House, New Delhi, pp. 26–27.
22. E.S. Shapiro, 2000, 'Academic Achievement of Performance', in Alan E. Kazdin (ed.), *Encyclopedia of Psychology,* Vol. 1, Oxford University Press, New York.
23. K. Subramanyam and S. Rao, 2008, 'Academic Achievement and Emotional Intelligence of Secondary School Children', *Journal of Community Guidance and Research,* 22(2), pp. 224–228.
24. K.S. Singh, 2009, 'Impact of Leadership Behavior on Teachers Job Satisfaction and Public Academic Achievement', *Indian Psychological Review,* 72(1), pp. 41–44.

10

Modern Casteism in Gujarat State

Socio-economic Effects and Remedies

M.H. Makwana and Pradip Prajapati

Gujarat state has always been considered as the most progressive and developed state. Before independence, many progressive states were there in Gujarat, such as Baroda, Gondal, Bhavnagar, which were ruled by some of the kings, where many developmental steps were taken and work was undertaken for enlistment and development of the untouchables. Even during the British Period, missionaries and administrators had worked for the enhancement of these groups. Thereafter, Mahatma Gandhi had also tried to abolish untouchability by reducing casteism. Ambedkar movement and ideology had also played a very significant role in creating unity and awareness among the untouchables. Taking the history into account, if an analysis of casteism and its effects is made with reference to different societies in Gujarat, the picture is not different from the other parts of the country, even after 66 years of independence. Of course, the nature and means of casteism are different in different societies, but ultimate aims and goals of the upper classes are the same as their counterparts elsewhere.

The construction of caste is based on socio-economic, political conditions, as well as pride and vanity of groups. The caste structure is ascribed and imposed and none wants to be known as belonging to lower strata of society and resent and oppose the caste stratification which has a derogatory nomenclature. By its very rigid nature, the caste structure has in-built characteristics for continuous alteration. From 855 castes in 1881 census, the number has grown up to 4635 castes, as recorded in 1931 census. The caste system is affected by domicile, language, diversity of occupation, dictation of rulers and proximity to kings. Though there were claims to higher *varna* and superior caste status, it was not accorded a formal recognition till 1901.

As casteism continues, it also furthers the fragmentation of Indian society. In fact, one could say that it has practically killed the Vedic society and has brought about numerous divisions and social conflicts that everyone finds in India today. Even among the Hindus, there has been fighting along the caste, ethnic and sectarian lines for hundreds of years. This is one of the main reasons why the country has been weakened to such a degree that they could not properly defend themselves in a unified way from the genocide under the Muslim invasions and modern fundamentalism. This sort of fragmentation was also a factor that helped Hindus to endure two centuries of British persecutions.

It is the premise of the Vedic Friends Association that it is not one's birth that is most important to divide on caste, but one's consciousness, intentions and spiritual awareness, which supersedes the rank of one's lineage. It is this consciousness that actually determines one's personality, character and abilities, not merely one's birth. And therefore, casteism today does not help the society to advance spiritually. In fact, it helps promote contempt and disapproval among the people of different castes and ethnic groups.

For this reason, even till today one still sees the socio-economic effects of the modern caste-based philosophy of the Indian societies given in the next section. And these are developed on the basis of capitalism waves that when the *Shudras* and Dalits felt that they are disliked by fellow Hindus, they become Muslims or Christians or Buddhists in the attempt to find greater acceptance elsewhere and avoid distinctions. Hence, there has been social disharmony. Otherwise, there would have been no need for parts of India to be divided in order to create Bangladesh and Pakistan, which have since become nothing more than moral enemies of India. Have any lessons been learnt? Apparently not. Ethnic intolerance is on the rise in many parts of India.

Socio-economic Effects of the Castes-based Philosophy of the Different Societies

More particularly, after the capitalist wave, casteism in upper castes has become stronger in the sense that they help each other in various activities such as agriculture, politics and education, which ultimately has adversely affected the deprived classes. A few examples are given as follows:

1. Poverty existed right from the independence among the downtrodden of the society, more particularly among scheduled castes (hereafter SC), scheduled tribes (hereafter ST) and other backward classes (hereafter OBC) and therefore constitutional provisions such as reservation policy in education, service and other sectors have been implemented to eradicate poverty and socio-economic inequalities so that social and economic development can be realized by these deprived classes.

   As a result, people of these groups entailed education and jobs marginally. This is a kind of sharing that was not digestible to the upper classes, for whom there is a strong hold on education and jobs even today. Therefore, they started harassing and victimizing SCs, STs and OBCs, for no reason. Hence, government has enforced the Atrocity Act to protect SCs and STs against such kind of harassment and victimization, but this act has become very ineffective due to the dominance of some of the upper class police authorities, politicians and judicial people, influencing each other the way they like.

   The influential police authorities do not arrest the accused immediately and judicial authorities have now started granting anticipatory and regular bails to the accused even though there is no such provision in the Atrocity Act. And therefore, the ultimate aim of the government to implement the Atrocity Act now remains only on paper.

   Besides, to make reservation policy ineffective, the upper caste people in politics and policy makers introduced 'new' ideas such as anti-reservation agitation of 1981 and 1985, in which Government of Gujarat had withdrawn and interchangeability of reserved seats of SCs and STs in education and services had been introduced to prevent SC, ST and OBC classes from the benefit of education and jobs.

After implementation of New Economic Policy in 1990, privatization in Government Undertakings and in education is seen as the anti-SC and ST product of their evil minds, which has adversely affected such deprived groups.

2. On the one hand, upper castes have started preventing SCs, STs and OBCs from their rights and benefits, by one or the other way (as explained above); on the other hand, they have started helping their own brethren through the social gathering and their NGOs by establishing educational institutions, by providing hostels and other facilities and financial arrangements to their children for the overall development of their castes. This is not there among lower classes.
3. In Gujarat, SCs are the agricultural labourers in rural areas and therefore it was their bread and butter but they did not get their wages even according to the Minimum Wages Act. Not only that, these people do not get work because of migration of the labour from the other parts of the country, and therefore they have to migrate from their native place to an urban location.

   On the other hand, more and more small and marginal farmers are becoming landless labourers and number of large farmers has gone up. What they wanted is large numbers of labourers for their farming activities. Therefore, all the labourers collectively started bargaining with large farmers to have work on the basis of contracts but not on daily wages. This, in fact, was a rational and economical transaction but here also the farmers have started making commitments for agricultural work on farms and outside with the families of other farmers internally instead of giving work to the farm labourers. The result, again, is increase in poverty and hence, most of these people have been moving towards urban places (i.e. urbanization) for their livelihood.
4. Because of such kind of urbanization, on one hand, villages are being destroyed and on the other, urban authorities have failed to provide them all the facilities and amenities and therefore, poverty in urban areas has gone up more than the rural poverty and obviously, the victims are from lower castes and tribals.
5. As far as unemployment is concerned, SCs and STs are mostly engaged in unorganized sectors and therefore, the same is the case of severity of unemployment among these castes.

Facts and Figures to Support their Presented Arguments

1. Gujarat shines in the world.
2. Large business houses, especially multinational corporations, started operating in Gujarat.
3. Gujarat is becoming now hub of IT sector and other service sectors along with phenomenal rise of business tycoons.
4. According to Forbes List 2008, India added 16 new billionaires making 53 billionaires living in India with a net worth of $335 billion equal to one-third of India's GDP, of which majority are Gujaratis.
5. There has been a huge growth in middle class with the income range of 2 to 10 lacks per annum. A study conducted by National Council for Applied Economic Research (NCAER) reveals that the number of middle class has reached to 28.4 million by 2008–2009.

All these development created an impression to the world that Gujarat is growing as super power and a leading state in India. But, on the other hand, if we move to the other side, this glimpse and rosy picture fades off.

Though the decade of 1990s experienced high growth, it could not improve the life and living standard of weaker sections of the society, that is SC, ST and OBC, which can be realized from the facts given as follows:

1. As many as 19 per cent of people living in rural areas belong to household that cannot afford more than ₹ 12 a day per person on consumption and in town and cities about 22 per cent belong to household whose daily per capita expenditure is less than ₹ 19.
2. Such abysmal level of the consumption is surely linked to very low wage rate. In rural areas, the average daily wage of casual labour in 2005–2006 was ₹ 59 for men and ₹ 38 for women, whereas in urban area, the wage rates were ₹ 81 and ₹ 45, respectively, that is in both the areas it was below the statutory minimum.
3. The pattern is unrelenting in all the aspects of quality of life:
   (a) In villages, 50 per cent of families live in *kuccha* or *semi-pucca* homes
   (b) 74 per cent of households still use firewood for cooking and kerosene for lighting their homes.

> This is unbelievable for life in a high performing economy, but unfortunately, it is true (Employment–Unemployment Survey, NSSO).

All these lead to the reality that there exists inequality not only at income level but also in consumption expenditure, human development, regions, social groups, etc. in Gujarat state as it is in entire India.

Socio-economic Inequalities among Different Social Groups

Looking at the modern change in casteism, the present study attempts with a limited objective to study the socio-economic inequalities in the light of income level, consumption expenditure and educational status among social groups in Gujarat state, particularly after the implementation of New Economic Policy in India.

(i) Poverty Incidence by Social Groups

The Eleventh Plan in India is characterized by achieving the faster and inclusive growth, where in common parlance the inclusive growth can be defined as irrespective of any social groups, all people residing in India should get equal chance for education, employment and get proper return from the same. But it is sad to note that even after 66 years of independence nationals still talk about and researchers study about disparity through social groups. Some groups are considered lower, have less social network, avail less opportunity, have less education and hence are poor.

Using NSS consumption data, the Sachar Committee Report (GoI 2006) provides poverty incidence by social categories as under for which the committee has divided total population into rural and urban categories.

Table 1 shows that SC/STs fall in the category of 'most poor' in both rural and urban area. SC/STs residing in urban area show 46 per cent of poverty ratio in 2004–2005 as against 41 per cent of those residing in rural area. Even reduction in poverty ratio is higher (9% point) in rural area and 6 per cent point in urban area in SC/ST category. Rural Muslims have 33 per cent poverty ratio in the year 2004–2005 and urban Muslims have 44 per cent poverty ratio in the same year. All Hindus and other Hindus have less poverty ratio. Other category also has less poverty ratio but poverty has declined by 4 per cent point in urban area and by 9 per cent point in rural area.

Table 1

Poverty Incidence by Social Category: 1987–1988 to 2004–2005

	Rural			*Urban*		
	1987–1988	*1993–1994*	*2004–2005*	*1987–1988*	*1993–1994*	*2004–2005*
All Hindus	40	36	28	36	31	27
SCs/STs	54	50	41	55	51	46
Other Hindus	33	29	21	32	26	22
Muslims	43	45	33	53	47	44
Others	25	27	18	27	23	16

(ii) Employment Pattern among Social Groups

One of the major reasons for high incidence of poverty among SC/ST, Muslims and other backward classes is that they are mostly engaged in unorganized sector. Unorganized workers are mostly unskilled workers and hence they are mostly working in unorganized enterprises or households and are excluded from social security benefits provided by employers. They face different kinds of vulnerabilities and risks. Most common of those is job insecurity and social insecurity. They generally fall in the category of 'Extremely Poor, Poor and Vulnerable'. The distribution of unorganized workers in different poverty status by social groups for the year 2004–2005 is given in Table 2.

Table 2 gives the distribution of unorganized workers by social groups in each poverty status category. It clearly reveals that in extremely poor and poor categories highest percentage of workers are unorganized workers (44.9%), followed by 33.6 per cent of unorganized workers from Muslim community. Together, 91.4 per cent (44.9 + 33.6 + 12.9) of unorganized workers belong to extremely poor and poor category and come from SC/ST, Muslim and OBC groups. And in the case of marginal and vulnerable group, 40.6 per cent of unorganized workers are from OBC category, followed by SC/STs 30.5 per cent and 10.8 per cent of unorganized workers belong to Muslim community. Together, their share totals to 84.4 per cent.

It can be therefore seen that majority of the people in these social groups are engaged in unorganized sector and hence they are poor.

(iii) Educational Status of Social Groups

The level of education is also an important determinant of poverty. Illiterate or less educated people are forced to work as manual labourers in unorganized sectors. Many times they are self-employed as tailors, vendors, greengrocers, plumbers, etc. The distribution of the population in different educational levels in different poverty status groups across the different social groups are summarized in Table 3.

Table 2

Percentage Distribution of Unorganized Workers in Different Poverty Status by Social Groups (2004–2005)

Poverty Status	*Total*	*SC/ST*	*OBC*	*Muslims*	*Others*
Extremely poor and poor	100	44.9	33.6	12.9	8.9
Marginal and vulnerable	100	30.5	40.6	10.8	18.1
Poor and vulnerable (1 + 2)	100	34.3	38.7	11.3	15.6
Middle and high income group	100	16.4	35.6	7.6	40.4
Total	100	30.5	30.5	10.5	20.9

Note: Row does not add up to 100 as the distribution by social status does not include non-reporting cases in 2004–2005.

Source: Computed from NSS 50th and 61st round survey on Employment-unemployment, 1993–1994, 2004–2005.

Table 3 reveals that social category is a major factor affecting poverty status. Illiterate people are poorer but it is found that illiteracy with certain social groups is more prone to poverty. Like among SC/STs, Muslims and OBCs have high percentage in poor and vulnerable group, whereas in the case of others (high caste Hindus, Sikhs, Christians), illiterate poor and vulnerable section's percentage is comparatively less.

People with primary education belong to SC/STs, Muslims and OBC have 89.7 per cent, 87.2 per cent and 83.6 per cent of population in poor and vulnerable group. And with same level of education in others category population in poor and vulnerable group is 66.9 per cent. Similarly, it is found that with middle education, secondary and graduates also, SC/STs, Muslims and OBCs have more percentage of people in poor and vulnerable group than 'Others'.

Table 3

Percentage Distribution of Population in Specific Educational Categories by Poverty Status and Social Groups

Social Category	*Poverty Status*	*Illiterate*	*Up to Primary*	*Middle and Above but Below*	*Secondary and Above Graduate*	*Graduate*	*Total*
SC/ST	Poor and vulnerable	91.2	89.7	80.7	65.4	47.8	85
	Middle and high	8.8	10.3	19.3	34.7	52.2	15
	All	100	100	100	100	100	100
Muslims	Poor and vulnerable	89.5	87.2	76.5	63.1	43.4	81.3
	Middle and high	10.6	12.8	23.6	36.9	56.6	18.7
	All	100	100	100	100	100	100
OBC	Poor and vulnerable	85.6	83.6	74.3	59.9	39.4	76.3
	Middle and high	14.5	16.4	25.7	40.1	60.6	23.2
	All	100	100	100	100	100	100
Others	Poor and vulnerable	70.6	66.9	57.7	39.5	21.6	50.9
	Middle and high	29.4	33.1	42.3	60.5	78.4	49.1
	All	100	100	100	100	100	1000
All	Poor and vulnerable	86.1	83.3	71.2	52.4	29.7	72.6
	Middle and high	13.9	16.7	28.8	47.6	70.3	27.4
	All	100	100	100	100	100	100

Source: Computed from NSS 50th and 61st round survey on Employment-unemployment, 1993–1994, 2004–2005.

Hence, it is noticeable that there is congruence between educational status and poverty status and social groups and poverty status. Low social status groups, with less education, are more prone to fall in category of poor and vulnerable.

(iv) Consumption Pattern of Social Groups

Along with disparity in employment and education status, it could also be realized that the consumption expenditures divided the people with same poverty status but different social groups is more important indicator in relation to the present study. Therefore, average monthly per capita expenditure (MPCE in ₹) and work participation rate (WPR) by social groups and poverty status are to be examined and accordingly it is given in Table 4.

Table 4

Average MPCE (₹) and WPR (%) by Social Groups and Poverty Status

Year	*Extremely Poor and Poor*		*Marginal and Vulnerable*		*Middle and High*		*All*		*Ratio of Cons*
	MPCE	*WPR*	*MPCE*	*WPR*	*MPCE*	*WPR*	*MPCE*	*WPR*	
1993–1994									
SC/ST	156	44.1	276	48.2	617	50.5	255	46.6	4
Muslim	174	30.2	294	33.7	662	37.6	295	32.9	3.9
OBCs	NA	NA	NA	NA	NA	NA	NA	NA	NA
Others	168	39.5	301	41.5	714	42.8	364	41.4	4.2
All	164	40	294	42.4	697	43.4	328	41.9	4.2
2004–2005									
SC/ST	303	40.9	516	46.5	1118	49	520	45	3.7
Muslim	174	30.4	556	34.7	1279	37.4	611	33.9	3.7
OBCs	324	37.7	541	44.2	1211	48.1	632	43.6	3.7
Others	349	35.6	608	39.9	1611	41.6	1039	40.6	4.6
All	321	37.7	550	42.7	1388	44.3	695	42	4.3

Note: Others include OBCs in 1993–1994, NA = not available, ratio = average MPCE of middle and high income group/average MPCE of extremely poor and poor.

Source: Computed from NSS 50th and 61st round survey on Employment-unemployment, 1993–1994, 2004–2005.

The foremost outcome that is shown in Table 4 is the increase in MPCE for all social groups from 1993–1994 to 2004–2005. During the years 2004–2005, MPCE in extremely poor and poor, varies from ₹ 303 to ₹ 349, where SCs/STs have lowest MPCE of ₹ 303 and others account for highest MPCE of ₹ 349. On the other hand, WPR of SC/ST is highest followed by OBCs. The Muslims have lowest WPR.

MPCE is highest in 'marginal' and 'vulnerable' category during 2004–2005 and lowest for SC/ST group, whereas WPR for SC/ST is highest. And middle and high income group enjoys very high MPCE for all the social groups. In that too, MPCE of others is highest and MPCE of SC/ST is the lowest. The WPR of SC/ST is the highest during the period.

Therefore, it can be interpreted from the above findings that:

(i) 'Others' in all poverty status have high MPCE and SC/STs have lowest MPCE.

(ii) WPR of SC/STs is highest in all poverty groups, whereas Muslims have lowest WPR irrespective of any poverty status.

(iii) The average MPCE of middle and high income groups were about four times that of the extremely poor and poor group for the year 1993–1994 as well as 2004–2005.

Conclusions

It can be concluded from the aforesaid analysis that because of the strong casteism in upper castes they help each other in various activities such as agriculture, politics and education. Deprived groups of the society are more deprived in terms of education, employment opportunities; and therefore, the disparity among those belonging to the social categories of Backward Class and non-Backward Class socially as well as economically has worsened with time.

Further, a much more powerful factor responsible for this is the household size and dependency ratio. Mostly in poor class and poor social group, the ratio of illiteracy is high, which increases the dependency ratio. More number of children is dependent on parents and makes economic condition worse.

Discussion and analysis so far brings us to the conclusion that there is segmentation based on social groups. 'Poor' are not the same in all social groups. SC/ST poor, Muslim poor, OBC poor and other poor have different depth of poverty. This can be more clarified from the Table 5, drawn from the above indicators discussed.

Table 5

Systematic and Hierarchical Segmentation of Social Groups across Economic Groups (Ranking)

Social Groups	*Share of Unorganized Workers in Total Workers*	*Incidence of Extremely Poor and Poor*	*Incidence of Poor and Vulnerable*	*Low Education among Poor and Vulnerable*	*Low Education among Unorganized Workers*	*Proportion of Middle and High Income Groups among Social Groups*
Others	1	1	1	1	1	1
OBCs	2	2	2	2	2	2
Muslim	3	3	3	3	3	3
SC/ST	4	4	4	4	4	4

Note: Ranking is in descending order, 1 indicates most favourable position and 4 indicates the least favourable position.

Table 5 shows that SC/ST population forms the bottom layer in all respects and others attain higher position followed by OBCs and Muslims. The inequality existing in many economic categories is a matter of great concern and has severe implications.

Casteism among the upper castes has become stronger by all means, which ultimately has adversely affected the deprived classes as discussed earlier. Therefore, considering these, it is more important to study the psychology and philosophy of the upper class people regarding their belief of daily life and standard of living.

Implications

The centre and the states together must deal with this problem on a priority basis. One cannot let large parts of the country be trapped in a prison of discontent, injustice and frustration that will only breed extremism. The spread of Naxalism in more than 100 districts in the country is a warning sign. Pockets of despair where communalism has left scars are also festering with anger. In all areas, despair is the result of visible failures of the state apparatus to ensure good governance and create an environment where the bulk of the people experience the benefit of development.

Special efforts must be made to remove discontent, dispense justice, instil a sense of fairness among the people and give them dignity and hope. Otherwise, not only will the growth momentum in the rest of the country be disrupted, but we also will not attain the dignity and pride of a good society. The Backward Regions Grant Fund provides a new instrument to deal with this problem.

Suggestions

It is clear from the above analysis that the social and economical inequalities exist even after 66 years of independence between different social groups and to our utmost surprise these inequalities are more in urban areas than in rural even within the same social group. This is because of the bitter truth of psychology of untouchables that still prevails in Indian societies. Actually, there is no word like untouchable in any of the Vedic scriptures. This has been a modern invention. As it stands today, it is a great curse to Hinduism. It attacks the core of its spiritual philosophy and has resulted in large numbers of Hindus converting to other religions. Therefore, it needs to be replaced by the genuine *varnashrama*. However, there are many groups of Vedic followers that are open for everyone and do not divide people or consider their status according to their birth.

Therefore, instead of dividing people/society on caste, religion and ability, more attention is to be given to the development of all the people, which can only be possible when the development of urban economy will co-exist with the development of rural economy. The authors, therefore, suggest following policy suggestions for the overall development of economy and accordingly socio-economic welfare of the people.

The pre-condition of the development of Indian economy is to develop rural sector through the development of agricultural sector. Therefore, following steps are needed to be taken to improve the standard of living of the people by providing them better job opportunities and reducing poverty and inequalities prevailing in certain social groups in India as seen above:

1. Agricultural sector should be treated not as a primary but as an industrial sector and developed accordingly, providing all the facilities given to the industrial sector.
2. To support this sector, agro-based industries and also ancillary to small and large industries should be established in rural areas.
3. Concentrated efforts should be made to implement new agricultural strategies through credit schemes and provide some incentives such as insure the farmers and landless labourers against uncertainties as well, so that there will be modernization in agricultural activities even on small and marginal farms.
4. Agro-based industries should be established in the rural areas according to the crops cultivated on the bases of agro-climatic zones, providing adequate incentives to these industries, managed and controlled either by private, public or co-operative sectors, which will increase the agricultural output and develop the rural sector. Also,
   (a) Exploitations of the small farmers and landless labourers by moneylenders, middlemen and large farmers would be reduced.

(b) Investment would be forthcoming in rural areas so that modernization in agricultural sector will be possible, which will help in reducing underemployment and disguised unemployment and hence poverty.
(c) Reduce inequalities between the regions and also interpersonal indifferent social groups.
(d) Problem of urbanization would be mitigated.
(e) Increase in income will create better awareness and demand for consumer goods, infrastructural facilities, education, health, higher rate of literacy, which will lower mortality rate, increase in life expectancy, etc.
(f) Consumption expenditure will increase which results in improvement in the living standard.

Thus, development of urban economy would co-exist with the development of rural economy because of increase in consumption expenditure and mitigation of urbanization with the ultimate result of development of economy as a whole.

Such policy changes certainly would achieve the predetermined goals under New Economic Policy (NEP). However, it must be remembered here that the implementation of such policy implications require a very strong 'Political Will'.

Suggested Readings

Arjun, Sengupta, Kannan, K.P. and Raveendran, G., 2008, Paper Presented on 'Revisiting the Poverty Issue: Measurement, Identification and Eradication' at the International Seminar organized jointly by the Institute for Human Development, New Delhi, A.N. Sinha Institute of Social Sciences, Patna, and the Asian Development Research Institute, Patna, during 20–22 July 2007.

Arun, Sengupta, 2001, *Reforms, Equity and the IMF*, Haranand Publications, New Delhi.

Balakrisnan, P. and Parameswaran, M., 2007, 'Understanding Economic Growth in India: A Prerequisite', *Economic and Political Weekly*, 42(27/28), 14 July.

Bhardwaj, V.P. and Prajapati, Pradeep, 2002, 'Economic Reforms in Indian Agriculture: Myths and Reality', *Anvesak*, 32(2), July–December.

Draft of Eleventh Five Year Plan in India.

Dutt, R. and Sundaram, K.P.M., 2008, *Indian Economy*, Himalaya Publications, New Delhi.

Government of India, 2006, 'Social, Economic and Educational Status of the Muslim Community in India: A Report', Prime Minister's High Level Committee, Cabinet Secretariat, New Delhi.

——, 2007, *Poverty Estimates for 2004–05*, Planning Commission, New Delhi.

Makwana, M.H., 2011, *Dalits in Western India*, Shanti Prakashan, New Delhi.

Rao, C.N. Shankar, 2004, *Sociology of Indian Sociology*, S. Chand, New Delhi.

Thorat, Sukhadeo, 2010, 'On Social Exclusion Addressing Inter-Social Group, Graded and Multiple-Group Inequalities Through Inclusive Policy', I.P. Desai Memorial Lecture at Centre for Social Studies, V.N. South Gujarat University, Surat (Gujarat), May 2010.

11

Pesticides and Health Discrimination

A Case of Dalit Agricultural Workers in India

Dhanraj A. Patil

The thoroughly reactionary *varna* and caste system has hounded Indian society for thousands of years. India is the only country in the world where such a system came into being and still exists. The *varna* and caste system was sanctified by the Hindu religion and by the *Vedic* scriptures. This was the main reason for its consolidation. The distinctiveness of the caste system was that it was hereditary, compulsory and endogamous. The worst affected by the caste system and its social oppression has been the Dalits, or *Ati-Shudras*, or scheduled castes. Albeit in a different way, the *adivasis* or scheduled tribes in India have also faced social oppression over the ages. Along with the curse of untouchability, the Dalits had no right to have any property. They had to eat the foulest food, including leftovers thrown away by the higher *varnas*; they were not allowed to draw water from the common well; they were prohibited from entering temples; they were barred from the right to education and knowledge; they had to perform menial jobs for the higher castes; they were not allowed to use the common burial ground; they were not allowed to live in the main village inhabited by the upper *varnas* and they were deprived of ownership of rights to land and property, leading to a lack of access to all sources of economic mobility. Thus, Dalits were subjected to both social exclusion and economic discrimination over the centuries. In one form or the other, this continues even today in most parts of the country. In this context, the present study tries to analyse one of the unexplored patterns of the health discrimination and exploitation of Dalit agriculture workers by the capitalist forces in a modern society full of risks.

Thus, considering the importance of the subject, an empirical investigation has been carried out purposively in Western Maharashtra, which is one of the high cash crop zones of Maharashtra state.[1]

Background and Rational of the Study

According to the 2001 Census, scheduled castes comprise 16.2 per cent of the total population of India, that is, they number more than 17 crore. Scheduled tribes comprise 8.2 per cent of the population, that is, they number more than 8 crore. Both together constitute 24.4 per cent of the Indian population, that is, together they number more than 25 crore. Almost every socio-economic indicator shows that the position of scheduled caste families is awful. In many cases, their plight is getting worse. Let us have a look at some of the major indicators.

Land

In 1991, 70 per cent of the total SC households were landless or nearly landless (owning less than one acre of land). This increased to 75 per cent in 2000. In 1991, 13 per cent of the rural SC households were landless. However, in 2000 this saw a decline and was 10 per cent. As per the Agricultural Census of 1995–1996, the bottom 61.6 per cent of operational holdings accounted for only 17.2 per cent of the total operated land area. As against this, the top 7.3 per cent of operational holdings accounted for 40.1 per cent of the total operated area. This gives an indication of land concentration in the hands of a few.

Agricultural Worker

In 2000, 49.06 per cent of the working SC population was agricultural labourers, as compared to 32.69 per cent for the STs and only 19.66 per cent for the others. This shows the preponderance of Dalits in agricultural labour. Between 1991 and 2001, the number of agricultural labourers in India increased from 7.46 crore to 10.74 crore, and a large proportion of them were Dalits. On the other hand, the average number of workdays available to an agricultural labourer slumped from 123 in 1981 to 70 in 2005.

Poverty

In 2000 35.4 per cent of the SC population was below the poverty line in rural areas as against 21 per cent among others ('Others' everywhere means non-SC/ST). In urban areas the gap was larger: 39 per cent of SC against only 15 per cent among others. The largest incidence of poverty in rural areas was among agricultural labour followed by non-agricultural labour, whereas in urban areas the largest incidence of poverty was among casual labour followed by self-employed households. The monthly per capita expenditure (MPCE) for all household types was lower for SCs than others.

Employment

In 2000, the unemployment rate based on current daily status was 5 per cent for SCs as compared to 3.5 per cent for others in rural and urban areas. The wage labour households accounted for 61.4 per cent of all SC households in rural areas and 26 per cent in urban areas, as compared to 25.5 per cent and 7.45 per cent for other households (Human Right Watch, 2007).

Pesticides in Indian Agriculture

Post-independence, population was growing at a much faster rate than food production. This called for drastic action to increase yield. The action came in the form of the Green Revolution involving expansion of farming areas, double cropping existing farmland using irrigation and using high-yielding variety (HYV) seeds. The Green Revolution of the 1960s was confined to the northern states of Punjab, Haryana and parts of Uttar Pradesh and to strategic crops, mainly wheat and rice. More than 70 per cent of the country's farmland remains rain fed, while a significant proportion of agricultural land (150 million hectares) is now classified as 'wasteland'. The liberalization of the Indian agricultural economy started in 1991. The major impact has been the shift from 'lower value' or subsistence food crops to higher value cash crops (such as cotton or oilseeds). This shift had created massive impact especially on the use of pesticides in Indian agriculture.

The promotion of HYV that marked the Green Revolution has led to the large scale use of chemical pesticides. Increase in the use of chemical pesticides can result in various health and environmental problems such as pesticide poisoning of farmers and farm workers, cardiopulmonary, neurological and skin disorders, foetal deformities, miscarriages, lowering the sperm count of applicators, etc (Bag, 2000). The Indian pesticide industry is the fourth largest in the world. Of the total market, around 75 per cent is accounted for by insecticides.

At present, India is the largest producer of pesticides in Asia and ranks twelfth in the world for the use of pesticides with an annual production of 90,000 tonnes (Government of India 2007).

According to Mr Pradeep Dave, President, PMFAI, and Chairman and Managing director, Aimco Pesticides Ltd., 'Pesticide consumption in India is low – less than 800gm per acre against 16 kg per acre in the US. We want the government machinery to educate farmers about the use of pesticides through scientific programmes. All over the world better crop protection is used and here the government discourages the use of pesticides' (Sabbu 2001). Over the past decade, the high prices of HYV cotton crops encouraged tens of thousands of small and marginal farmers in the region to shift from traditional food crops to cotton. By switching to the cotton meant costly investments in seeds, fertilizers and pesticides which were possible for the small peasants of Telangana only through loans typically secured with their land or the gold ornaments of their wives. Now, in the thousands of homes, dreams lie shattered amidst the ruins of thousands of families. A pall of despair and shocks lies over the region today, where at least 180 debt-ridden cotton farmers committed suicide in a short spell of just 3 months (Kanekar 1999). The food we eat today contains a concoction of banned and restricted chemicals such as DDT, benzene hexachloride (BHC), aldrin, dieldrin, lindane and many others. And the food is their route to the human body. This results in functional disorder and disease. It all began with the Green Revolution, which saw indiscriminate use of chemical fertilizers and pesticides. It left behind enormous toxic loads of contaminants in the environment, which eventually found their way into humans through the food chain (Rangrajan, 2001).

India had adopted the environment-friendly integrated pest management (IPM) approach for combating pests and diseases as a cardinal principle of its plant protection strategy way back in 1985. By adopting the IPM technology on rice, they have not only saved on pesticides but also improved conditions for restoring the ecological balance in this rich agricultural belt. However, in most cases, the farmers gave up this practice and reverted to pesticides use soon after the projects under which they took to it were over. Besides the lack of necessary follow-up action on the part of the promoters, there are other reasons as well for the failure of interest in this technology to endure without official patronage (*Business Standard*, 1999).

The Political Economy of Agricultural Modernization and Liberalization

Historically, modernization of agriculture was to lead to changes in relation of production from a feudal system to capitalist mode. In India, factors such as caste, colonial influence and uneven development led to complex relations and development. During the mode of production, debate in the 1960s and 1970s indicated these relations were characterized variously semi-feudal, semi-colonial, early capitalist, to semi colonial systems (see Habib, 1984; Patnaik, 1990). The new seed fertilizer technology especially those arising from the Green Revolution has resulted in the increase of land rents and lower labour wages (in real terms). Only the big farmers, mainly those who are producing for the market, could make use of government support. The marginal farmers have in fact been further marginalized under the new regime of modern agriculture and Green Revolution. In fact, most farmer suicides are connected to pauperization and indebtedness which the so-called government support in the form of part subsidies for seeds, credit and fertilizers have brought in.[2]

Methodology

This study deals to analyse the handling of agro-chemicals and health-related problems that arises among the Dalit agricultural workers and its linkage in one of the cash crop zones of Maharashtra state. Some of the specific objectives are as follows:

1. To study the socio-economic characteristics, awareness level and precautionary measures adapted by Dalit agricultural workers in the study area.
2. To suggest policy implications for reducing pesticide-induced health problems.

For the present study Shirol region of Kolhapur district was selected purposively as a unit of study for the following two reasons:

1. This region comes under one of the high cash crop zones of Maharashtra state.
2. The percentage of agricultural labour is also high in this region.

The operational meaning of Dalit agricultural workers for the present study refers to all the caste belonging to scheduled castes (SCs) in the study area. After necessary discussions with the concerned stakeholders and for the convenience of the study, a total of 100 Dalit agricultural workers have been selected by using accidental sampling procedure. Information has been collected through structured and pilot tested interview schedule during January to February 2010. It was decided that for the convenience of the workers, interviews would be taken in the field, in the forenoon hours. The interviews were conducted in the local language, namely *Marathi*; however, some of the interviews of migrant workers were also been conducted in *Kanada* language.

Dalit Agricultural Workers and Pesticides Exposure: An Analysis

This section discusses the major findings within following categories:

(a) Socio-economic characteristics of agricultural workers
(b) Pesticide use pattern by agricultural workers
(c) Information Sources of pesticides
(d) Precaution and handling of pesticides
(e) Pesticides and health impacts
(f) Caste and health discrimination

Socio-economic Characteristics of Agricultural Workers

A consideration of the history of agrestic hierarchical subordination of one class by another inevitably becomes a history of the evolution of the class of agricultural workers in India

(Patnaik, 1990). Agricultural worker is not the creation of the British economic policies alone as it has been in existence since the inception of the caste system (see Kosambi, 1965; Habib, 1971; Béteille, 1972). According to Suresh Tendulkar and K. Sundaram (2000), the social groups most vulnerable to poverty have been identified to be the scheduled caste households and the scheduled tribe households with both these groups having above average level of poverty indicators in the rural and the urban population. The primary exposure status to pesticides was ascertained based on whether or not the agricultural workers are involved with spraying pesticides. It was noted that majority of male respondents (73%) were closely linked with pesticide spraying than female respondents (5%). The average age of male respondents was 35–45 years.

The level of education and illiteracy has contributed to the poor awareness on the use of agro-chemicals especially pesticides. However, 50per cent of respondents received no formal schooling, while 36 per cent merely read and write *Marathi* and *Kanada* language. Shirol region is situated on Karnataka–Maharashtra border, majority of agricultural workers have migrated from Karnataka state. Due to the fertile soil and availability of water resources, most of the landless workers prefer to work in this region. However, ₹ 1,500–2,500 is the average monthly income of both male and female respondents (Table 1).

Among the economic groups, the most vulnerable groups are the agricultural labour households (rural) and the casual labour households (urban) each having the highest level of the poverty indicators in their respective population segments. The agricultural workers constitute the most important segment of Indian agrarian social structure; the number of rural agricultural workers have grown, which is about 258 million (Info Change, 2010). They are the worst exploited socially, economically and politically. A big chunk of them comes from the scheduled castes and scheduled tribes who still continue to be the victims of social oppression. However, they have been identified as chronically poor, which further creates multiple risks (Deshingkar, 2010). Hence, it would be unreal to talk about the agrarian hierarchy in India in isolation from the division into a caste which is an important feature of Indian Society (Béteille, 1972). According to, Warriner (1969: 141), 'the agrarian structure of India is neither a large estate nor a peasant system, but a system of caste'.

Table 1

Socio-economic Background of Respondents (N = 100)

Sr. No.	Socio-economic Characteristics	Male	Female	Total
1	*Marital Status*			
	Unmarried	21	9	30
	Married	58	12	70
2	*Age*			
	21–30	7	2	9
	31–40	22	6	28
	41–50	28	7	35
	51–60	13	6	19
	Above 60	9	0	9
3	*Education*			
	Illiterate	39	11	50
	Merely read and write	19	7	36
	Marathi/Kanada	16	3	19
	Fluently read and write	5	0	5
	Marathi/Kanada			
	Fluently read and write			
	Marathi/English			
4	*Monthly income:*			
	1500–2000	21	8	29
	2000–2500	25	3	28
	2500–3000	18	6	24
	3000–3500	15	4	19
5	*Involvement in pesticide spraying*			
	Yes	73	5	78
	No	6	16	22
	Total	79	21	100

Source: Primary data.

Pesticide Use Pattern by Agricultural Workers

Table 2 explores that most commonly used pesticides according to the workers were Dimethoate/Rogor (70.51%), endosulphan (62.82%) and Unalphos/Ekalux (52.56%). Likewise 6.41 per cent of the workers used pesticides that are extremely hazardous. Rogor, Unalphos/Ekalux and endosulfan are classified as

Table 2

Pesticide Use Pattern by Agricultural Workers

S. No.	*Pesticide: Common Name (WHO Classification)*	*Chemical Category*	*No. of Agricultural Workers*	*%*
1.	*a. Extremely hazardous*			
	1. Phorate	Organophosphate	5	6.41
	b. Highly hazardous*	Organophosphate		
	2. Monocrotophos	Combination	36	46.15
	3. Profenofos and	pesticide	17	21.79
	Cypermethrin	Carbamate	3	3.84
	4. Carbofuran			
2.	*Moderately hazardous**			
	5. Dimethoate/Rogor	Organophosphate	55	70.51
	6. Unalphos/Ekalux	Organophosphate	41	52.56
	7. Endosulphan			
	8. Carbaryal	Organochlorine	49	62.82
	9. Chlorpyrifos	Carbamate	11	14.1
	10. Cyhalothrin			
	11. Fenthion	Organophosphate	8	10.25
	12. DDT	Pyrethroid	4	5.12
		Organophosphate	9	11.53
		Organochlorine	6	7.69
3.	*Slightly hazardous**			
	13. Malathion	Organophosphate	4	5.12
	Unlikely to present acute hazard in normal use*			
	14. Carbendazim	Carbamate	6	7.60
	15. Atrazine	Triazine	2	2.56

* World Health Organization (WHO) classification of pesticides.

moderately hazardous by WHO. while Monocrotophos is classified as highly hazardous.[3] A very few workers, that is 5.12 per cent used the pesticides in the class III (slightly hazardous) and unlikely to present acute hazard in normal use. Due to the fertile soil and modern agricultural tools and techniques, farmers use maximum pesticides on crop and especially on vegetables in the study area.[4] However, apart from WHO classified pesticides, labourers were also using few other popular pesticides in their fields such as Methoxychlor, Lindane and Dicofol from organochlorine category. Organochlorine group pesticide was used widely in the United States in 1960s to 1970s, this impart acutely toxic and very persistent pollutants in the environment. In this category, many pesticides are proven to be carcinogenic, reproductive toxicants or both (CEPA 1998).

Few organophosphates group pesticides were also found in the study area, these are Malathion, Methylparathion, Chlorpyrifos and Diazinon. The pesticide contains the chemical formulations Aldicarb and Carbaryl along with this synthetic Pyrethroid is also being used popularly in the study area. The Pyrethroid includes Permethrin and Cypermethrin formulation. Herbicides used for the control of weeds have different chemicals such as Alachlor, Atrazine and Simazine. Herbicide is designed to kill the plants rather than animals and is less acutely toxic to humans than the insecticides. But many of them are classified as probable or possible carcinogens by United States and Environment Protection Agency (EPA-US 1999). Fumigants are also used as agrochemicals but their use is very rare in the study area and only to sterilize soil and in structural pest control. Fumigants have the ability to diffuse organic matters in the soil. Fumigants tend to be rapidly absorbed across the pulmonary membrane and through skin (Arora 2007). Fumigants are classified under 'deadly poisonous' category and they act as a carcinogen and are found to be in use in the study region especially in the green house agriculture commodities (Takagi et al. 1997).

Information Sources of Pesticides

It was observed that the retail shop owners/agricultural marketing agents were the key sources of information regarding proper usage of pesticides (55%). However, 43 per cent of workers consulted with fellow workers and only 21 per cent of workers considered government or any other agricultural authorities as their source of information.

It is interesting to note that Table 3 explores merely 9 per cent of agricultural workers know the proper usage of pesticide from their respective land owners; in fact they are educated and are well aware about the scientific and proper utilization of the pesticide. But they did not think that it is their moral responsibility. The agricultural workers are uneducated, poor, work hard in their land and take maximum risk during pesticide use, but they are not able to get proper information from the land owner.

Table 3

Information Sources about Proper Pesticide Usage (N = 100)

S. No.	*Sources of Information*	*Yes*	*No*	*Total*
1.	The retail shop owners/agricultural marketing agents	55 (55%)	45 (45%)	100 (100%)
2.	Fellow workers	43 (43%)	57 (57%)	100 (100%)
3.	Government/agricultural officials	21 (21%)	79 (79%)	100 (100%)
4.	Land owner	09 (9%)	81 (81%)	100 (100%)

Source: Primary data.

However, because of their illiteracy workers are very often unable to read the information written on the labels. They face problems, which are as follows:

- The labels may not be in the local language, as in the case of pesticides which are smuggled into the country illegally. In Cambodia, a study found that 95 per cent of the pesticide bottles sold was not labelled in Khmer, but in a foreign language – English, Chinese or Malay.
- The listing of contents may be in scientific jargon rather than in commonly understood language. Thus, the label may state the chemical composition of a pesticide rather than its popular name such as *lindane, parquet* and so on.
- In PAN AP's own research, plantation workers have noted that the labels are often removed from pesticide containers, thus making it very difficult to know whether they are made to be sprayed (Rengum 2006).

Precaution and Handling of Pesticides

Handling of pesticide concentrations and application of diluted formulation requires the use of appropriate personal protection equipment as a precaution against pesticide exposure. This would include the use of gloves, masks, protective clothes, personal hygiene, appropriate footwear, head gear and many others as indicated in the respective pesticide labels (FAO 1990).

Table 4

Protective Measures during Pesticides Use (N = 78)

S. No.	Protective Measures	Yes	No	Total
1	Did you take any personal protective precaution while using pesticides?	9 (12%)	69 (88%)	78 (100%)
2	Did you cocktail different kinds of pesticides?	45 (58%)	33 (42%)	78 (100%)
3	Did you use scarf/mask during pesticide spraying?	23 (30%)	55 (70%)	78 (100%)
4	Did you use bare hands to mix pesticides?	21 (27%)	57 (73%)	78 (100%)
5	Did you use gloves while using pesticides?	2 (0.3%)	76 (97%)	78 (100%)
6	Did you chew tobacco/gutkha or were smoking while spraying pesticides?	47 (60%)	31 (40%)	78 (100%)
7	Did you consume wine while spraying pesticides?	3 (0.4%)	75 (96%)	78 (100%)

Source: Primary data.

The workers in the study were not much keen to take necessary personal protective measures while handling pesticides. In all 88 per cent of agricultural workers reported that they took no precaution while handling and spraying pesticides. Furthermore, 58 per cent of workers prefer to make a cocktail of different kinds of pesticides before spraying (see Table 4). It was found that maximum amount of the pesticides was sprayed on the fruit and vegetables, leafy vegetables and vegetables grown in the green house. Workers used to mix the different pesticides in a plastic or metal drum with water or some time they used pesticides later. Around 27 per cent of workers mix the pesticides directly using bare hands and 70 per cent did not use scarf/mask during pesticide spraying. The situation is worse especially regarding the use of gloves while spraying and mixing pesticides. Only 0.3 per cent used gloves while using pesticides, while some of them use plastic carry bags as an alternative to gloves.

However, extended working hours and unsafe drinking water and lack of sanitation facilities create more health risks. Majority of agricultural workers toil 10 or more hours in the hot sun, for instance an average 8 to 12 hours daily, in the study area. It has been observed that many workers spray at high noon, despite the fact that pesticide use is not recommended between the peak sun hours of 10 a.m. to 4 p.m. Further, pesticide exposure through drift and water contamination creates greater risks to agricultural workers. Children of agricultural workers are particularly vulnerable to agro-chemical exposure as they play, live and help in the fields. Agricultural workers, and often their children, are regularly exposed to pesticides in many ways: mixing or applying pesticides; planting, weeding, thinning, irrigating, pruning, harvesting and processing crops; or living in or near treated fields. The study also found that pesticides carried from field to home on parents clothing and skin put workers' children at risk. As one of our respondents explained:

> I am the pesticide sprayer and I often get wet with the liquid that they use on the plants. My clothing does not protect me, it is too thin and my arms get wet. After spraying, I often used to go home and due to inadequate water I don't take bath or even don't change cloths. I have had headaches, dizziness, nausea, stomach pain and vomiting. (Personal interview)

According to Human Right Watch, only 9.84 per cent of households belonging to a scheduled caste have access to sanitation, and 20 per cent do not have a safe source for drinking water (Human Rights Watch, 2007).

It is also pertinent to note that due to the bad smell, majority of the workers (60%) suffer from eye irritation, throat infection, and they also suffer from other problems as they chew either tobacco/gutkha or smoke while spraying.[5,6] However, very few (4%) workers expressed the fact that they consume country liquor/wine during spraying to avoid the adverse effect of pesticides.[7] It is very serious, not only health-related problem but also a social problem that is gradually defusing among the other (non-sprayer) workers too. For physiological reasons, initially workers consume wine to avoid the adverse effects of pesticides but later they are not able to control their drinking and started drinking regularly and soon became acute daily drinkers. This process further leads to various social problems such as indebtedness, domestic violence, unemployment, acute poverty and so on.

Thus, the above empirical realities show that how poverty is responsible to make them more vulnerable and create multiple risks which are directly associated with pesticides. However, in a welfare democratic country it is the states prime social accountability to take necessary steps in this regard.

Figure 1

Poverty and exclusion

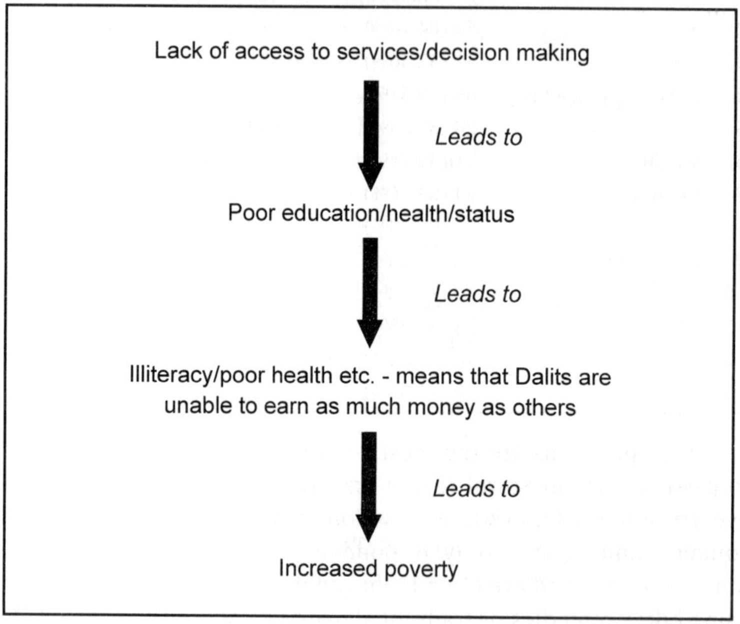

On this background, R.J. Das (2001: 112) critically comments, 'if the democracy could empower people irrespective of their class and caste background, one must wonder why the majority of Indians are below or very close to the line of absolute poverty'. Hence, the typically poor, undereducated, often undocumented Dalit agricultural workers are an especially vulnerable population that has been all too easy for large agribusinesses to exploit.

Pesticides and Health Impacts

The signs and symptoms related to pesticide exposure were included in the interview schedule. The workers who are actually involved in pesticide use were asked whether they experienced these signs and symptoms during or immediately after pesticide spraying days and non-spraying days. These symptoms and signs were reported by a large number of workers.

Table 5

Signs and Symptoms among the Population under Study (N = 78)

S. No.	*Signs and Symptoms*	*Pesticide during Applying Day*	*Pesticide during Non-applying Days*	*Total*
1	Eye irritation	64 (82.05%)	14(17.94%)	78 (100%)
2	Nausea	50 (64.10%)	28 (35.89%)	78 (100%)
3	Giddiness	41 (52.56%)	37 (47.43%)	78 (100%)
4	Breathing problems	55 (70.51%)	23 (29.48%)	78 (100%)
5	Fever	28 (35.89%)	55 (70.51%)	78 (100%)
6	Vomiting	31 (39.74%)	47 (60.25%)	78 (100%)
7	Cramps	24 (30.76%)	54 (69.24%)	78 (100%)
8	Itching	76 (97.43%)	24 (30.76%)	78 (100%)
9	Convulsions	12 (15.38%)	66 (84.61%)	78 (100%)
10	Burning sensation	10 (12.82%)	68 (87.17%)	78 (100%)
11	Hives	58 (74.35%)	20 (25.64%)	78 (100%)
12	Diarrhoea	10 (12.82%)	68 (87.17%)	78 (100%)
13	Tremor	09 (11.53%)	69 (88.46%)	78 (100%)

Skin problems are the most common health problem linked to pesticide use in Shirol region (see Table 5); itching (97.43%) eye irritation (82.05%), and vision problems were also very common among the study respondents. These are regarded as minor ailments and are often managed by the workers themselves using home remedies or traditional *ayurvedic/hakim* treatment. A number of more severe symptoms are also reported, for which agricultural workers either go to a doctor or hospital. These include breathing problems (70.51%), dehydration and vomiting (39.74%), cramps (30.76%) and diarrhoea (12.82%). There were 9 cases of hospitalization among the 62 cases of sickness reported in the survey. It was found that agricultural workers are relatively free from illness during non-pesticide applying days. However, among men there is a higher frequency of signs and symptoms, but some of the female workers (6%) felt stomach problems sometimes during or after spraying.

This is also important in the context that females are the major part of a family and when a woman gets sick or dies due to sickness, the family is left behind in crisis and chances of social disintegration are increased.[8]

Caste and Health Discrimination

On the basis of the study it has been found that Dalits have been facing acute health problems due to pesticide exposure. In a democratic country it is the prime social accountability of the responsible actor's, namely the state, pesticide industries and the land owners. In this context Chaudhari rightly pointed out that, 'Indian planning was meant to benefit the industrial capitalists and the rich farmers' (1995: 11). On this background as one of my respondents says:

> We have always been working in others' field. As *majdoor* (worker) my father worked here, we work in everybody's field. We knew we get fewer wages and work in an inhuman, risky environment. But the government and political leaders are silent on our plight. why? Because we are vice-less! (Personal interview)

Furthermore, the following paragons elucidate how far these actors are responsible and accountable for?

Land Owners: New Bourgeoisie Class

During the last four decades, the Indian capitalist class has vastly expanded. In addition to the national industrial large bourgeoisie, the capitalist class also includes the agricultural bourgeoisie, especially, the fact that large landowners are a part of the class base of the state (Das 1998).

The same fettles have been found in the study area, although maximum agricultural workers robustly expressed the fact that land owners never give proper information or any precautionary measure or protective equipments to prevent from various toxic pesticides, but the conditions are more severe as far as the capitalist exploitative mentality is concerned.

I have also come across instances where land owners have not revealed to the agricultural workers the particular pesticide that is being sprayed. Furthermore, land owners have a traditional belief that maximum pesticide gives quicker and safe produce, hence they keep silent about its toxicity and harmful effects and keep pressurizing the agricultural workers to use maximum pesticides. However, the capitalist relations of production also do not allow them to do anything in favour of the workers.

Thus, in such a predicament, they are simply treated like a product, just use and throw!

Are They Socially Responsible?

After knowing this, the data of the present study indicate negative impressions since majority of agriculture workers responded that they do not receive any kind of training regarding the use of pesticides as well as they are not happy for not properly informing them of the dangers of exposure to pesticides.

Reports from many parts of India indicate that farmers indiscriminately use mixtures of pesticides and follow the 'extension advice' given to them by dealers and local marketing agents (see Jeyaratnam 1987; Indira Devi 2007; Kuruganti 2010). There are no campaigns for them being taken up either by the government (agriculture department or health department) or the pesticide industry to educate the agricultural workers about the dangers of pesticides. The pesticide industry would have us believe that its products are safe and effective. The pesticide manufacturers adopt a variety of fictitious marketing strategies to promote their products.

Since majority of the workers are illiterate and untrained, they make them think that pesticides usage as recommended by the dealers would solve their pest management problems (CSA 2007).

Building Alliances Role of EJMs

The environmental justice movements' (EJMs) critical attention to the relationships between social inequalities and pollution resonates with much pesticide drift activists for whom poverty and political disenfranchisement are key variables in explaining and farming pesticide drift. Pesticide drift activists spotlight the ways in which social inequalities are experienced particularly by farm workers and their families by poverty, job insecurity and disregard by authorities and language barrier, and lack of access to health care and legal assistance prevent adequate regulatory response, medical treatment and analysis of pesticide drift:

> most of the worker communities, especially specifically in these accidents, is low-income communities of backward castes (Dalits), and that they have very little political clout. A lot of them are migrant farm working communities ... the exploitation of these communities have not been able to project themselves in the past. But we hope to empower them that are our aim, to educate and empower. (Drift activist, Personal interview)

Like developed countries, in India the environmental justice movement towards pesticide drift has not yet been matured and organized except in Kerala, Karnataka and few other regions. However, it could be a dawn of massive mass movement for the betterment of human and environment sustainability.

Conclusions and Policy Implications

The study shows the silent voices that talk about the harmful and unmanageable effects of pesticides on agricultural workers in general and Dalit agricultural workers in particular who are one of the most deprived and unorganized segments of Indian agrarian society. Agricultural workers particularly Dalits have emerged as the most risk prone sections of the modern agrarian society due to pesticides. Due to acute poverty,[9] they cannot afford visiting the doctors regularly, partially because earning a livelihood gets priority over health issues and partially because of ignorance. For medical practitioners treating pesticide poisoning cases, it is just another source of income and for the pesticide industry, it is business as usual. Meanwhile, the government chooses to turn blind eye to the issue, preferring to blame the victims for their ignorance and negligence in wrongly handling pesticides. The exact extent of occupational accidents due to pesticide is unclear; no efforts are forthcoming from the government to begin any surveys to assess the problem. In India, regulatory and support infrastructure to present agricultural workers from such a toxic environment, deal with victims of pesticide poisoning and promote ecological sustainable farming alternatives simply do not exist. And the pesticide industry denies that pesticide exposure and poisoning are issues to be connected with.

Finally, as it is observed the lack of scientific awareness, chronic poverty and collective pressure from agricultural workers and public actors such as environmental justice/pesticide drift activists and media have been considered to be a cause of this situation. In this context Dreze and Sen (1995: 87) comment that 'successive governments in India have had reason enough to rely on the unending patience of the neglected and deprived millions in India, who have not risen in fury about their socio-economic problems'.

Thus, there is an exigent need to provide a distinct and effective legal regime to the agricultural workers that not only support the mandates of welfare state but also fulfil the mandate of social security. The government should also conduct caste-wise survey of agricultural workers in the pesticide prone areas. And immediate bans on WHO classified acute hazardous type of pesticide such as endosulfan at least in the 'pesticide prone regions' in India.

Thus, there is ample scope for reducing pesticide exposure through training. An extension strategy focusing on this aspect alone would result in an improvement in the health of the workers who are involved in the handling of pesticides. Support could be provided by subsidizing the supply of protective gear and by setting up general awareness creation programmes.

Policy Implications

On the basis of the present study and discussion with agricultural scientists, doctors and comments of previous studies following suggestions have been made to reduce pesticide-induced health problems in agrarian social structure.

1. Land Reforms

The central and state governments must immediately set in motion the process of land reforms whereby land will be redistributed gratis to the landless agricultural labourers and poor peasant. All loopholes in the present laws must be plugged. And necessary training of organic agriculture should be given.

2. Strengthening the Existing Regulatory Mechanism

It includes the Insecticide Act 1964. To incorporate ADI (acceptable daily intake) in addition to MRL (maximum residue limit), the registering and re-registering procedures for agro-chemical manufacturers should be strengthen. Also the existing laws should be modified including deterrent punishment of violation as the exposure leads to death or damage to unsuspecting peoples. In this context, Dr M.S. Swaminathan appeals for effective legislations and laws for agro-chemicals with special reference to the sale of spurious chemicals (Jayraj 2007).

3. Support and Sensitization on Biopesticides

A wide range of biopesticides and natural agro-chemicals are available in the Indian market. Encourage the research and extension of natural agrochemicals.

4. Establish Single Independent Nodal Agency

It includes adequate testing laboratories, which will follow the guidelines of USEPA (United States Environment Protection Agency) for technical evaluation, enforcement and licensing of all chemical use in agriculture/public health/allied sectors.

5. Role of Nodal Agencies

Bodies such as IPHA and IAPSM take on the role of consultancy to public and policy advisory to the government on pesticide-related issues. A chapter on pesticides should be formed.

6. Strict Regulations on Pesticides

Banning of Class I (a) agro-chemicals such as arsenic acid, arsenic pentoxide and chromic acid and complete phasing out of pesticides especially I (b) category, which have carcinogenic impacts over human health.

7. Health Monitoring

Health monitoring is very sporadic and almost non-existent in least developed countries. Neither do they have the resource or sometimes the capacity to undertake systematic monitoring of pesticides and even to enforce regulations. Hence, it is recommended that frequent health monitoring of agricultural workers mainly women will be conducted by local primary health centres with the help of local NGOs and medical colleges.

8. Mobile Health Van and Caste-wise Health Survey

Due to poverty and unavailability of transport facilities in remote areas, agricultural workers often neglect to visit health centres. Therefore, mobile health van will be helpful to minimize the existing gap. As well as considering the nature of agricultural workers, there is an urgent need to conduct a massive social survey of pesticide affected Dalit agricultural workers in India.

9. Use of Little Media Channels

As compared to big media channels such as TV and cinema, little media channels such as community radio, local newspapers, magazines, video and traditional folk media channels can be effective to disseminate desired developmental messages and create awareness among the rural masses. These channels are easy, cheap and mobile, and most importantly they use local language and deal with local problems.

10. Ecological Agriculture Movement

This movement looks at agriculture as a holistic system, where other key concerns beside yield increase are considered in making decisions about development. Most emphasis is placed on food sovereignty and security in a framework encompassing production, environment, women's participation and democracy. Such ecological agriculture systems tend to learn from, and build on, traditional farming using local farmers' tools and technology. Today 200,000 farmers in Bangladesh are practicing ecological agriculture within the *Nayakrishi Andolan* (New Agricultural) movement. More than 20,000 farmers in India are practicing low external input agriculture without the use of pesticides; while in one NGO programme in Indonesia, more than 10,000 farmers have reduced pesticide use by 60–80 per cent through community integrated pest management.

Notes

1. See a study that looks into the health effects of acute pesticide among the cotton growers of India by Mancini et al. (2005).
2. The World Trade Agreement of 1994 brought agriculture for the first time in world trade history within its policy framework. The principles and policies of the WTO are based on Ricardo's concept of comparative advantage. The four major elements of the World Trade Agreement in the field of agriculture are: Market access, Domestic support, Export subsidies and Trade-Related Intellectual Property Rights. For India, Trade Liberalization is likely to open opportunities for exports, but poses threat for stiffer competition and greater uncertainties under new world order of price fluctuations. Under WTO, relaxation of quantitative restrictions on non-tariff/phyto/sanitary by importing countries will expose Indian farmers to world market prices. This view feels that the Indian farmer will be jolted out of their 'reverie' under the shadow of the protective cocoon of Government Support (Barua 1999).
3. Food and Agriculture Organization recommends that WHO I.a (extremely hazardous) and I.b (highly hazardous) pesticides should not be used in developing countries. It also suggests that class II (moderately hazardous) pesticides should be avoided. But the practice of spraying these 'powerful' pesticides continues. Preliminary results of environmental sampling tests done in the study area support this statement. Large chemical industries reinforce the myth by adopting aggressive marketing strategies that more

potent pesticides are necessary to prevent crop loss. This scenario has been reported from other countries also.

4. The pesticide residues in food in India, especially vegetables, are the highest in the world. Persistent pesticides such as BHC and DDT remain in the ecosystem for longer periods and contaminate the soil and water. Chemical pesticide residues have often been detected in food grains, vegetables, fruits, oils, cattle feed and fodder in most parts of the country. About 72 per cent of food samples in India have shown the presence of pesticide residue within tolerance levels while in 28 per cent of samples they are above the tolerance level. On a comparative basis, very high level of organic chlorine compounds have been reported in human blood, fat and milk samples in India. As a consequence, India accounts for one-third of all pesticide poisoning cases in the world (Indira Devi 2007).
5. The practice of chewing or smoking while spraying 'to reduce the nauseating feeling' is also hazardous to health. This may also indicate that the farmers were symptomatic enough to self-medicate during a pesticide spraying session. But many are unwilling to follow the necessary precautions attributing to non-availability and high cost of personal protection products, and the prevailing hot and humid weather conditions.
6. *Gutka* (also spelled *gutkha, guttkha* and *guthka*) is a preparation of crushed betel nut, tobacco, catechu, lime and sweet or savoury flavourings. It is manufactured in India and exported to a few other countries. A mild stimulant, it is sold across India in small, individual-sized packets that cost between 1 and 6 rupees per piece. It is consumed much like chewing tobacco, and like tobacco it is considered responsible for oral cancer and other severe negative health effects. In 2008 about 5 million children under 15 are addicted to gutkha. A survey in Uttar Pradesh and Madhya Pradesh yielded precursor of mouth cancers in 16 per cent of the children (http://timesofindia.indiatimes.com/Lucknow/Kidsgetting_addicted_to_tobacco/articleshow/2706674.cms).
7. Country liquor is a distilled alcoholic beverage made from locally available cheap raw material such as sugarcane, rice, palm, coconut and cheap grains, with alcohol content between 25 per cent and 45 per cent. Common varieties of country liquor are *arrack* (from paddy or wheat), *desi sharab* and *tari*. Illicit liquor is mostly produced clandestinely in small production units with raw materials similar to that used for country liquor. With no legal quality control checks on them, alcohol concentration of illicit liquor varies (up to 56%). Adulteration is quite frequent, industrial methylated spirit being a common adulterant, which occasionally causes incidents such as mass poisoning with consumers losing their life or suffering irreversible damage to the eyes. Cheaper than licensed country liquor, illicit liquor is popular among the poorer section of the population. In many parts of India, illicit production of liquor and its marketing is a cottage industry with each village having one or two units operating illegally (Mohan 2001).

8. A recent study has found that women with potential exposure to pesticides at work or at home took longer to get pregnant than women without pesticide connections. The study, conducted by researchers at the University of California, Berkeley, found that women, who worked in agriculture, lived within 200 feet of agriculture fields or used pesticides in their home, took significantly longer to conceive when compared to those who did not. The effect of pesticides on fertility raises considerable concern, especially among women with significant exposure. While a number of studies have been conducted on pesticides and sperm quality, less is known about the possible effects on female fertility (Harley 2008).
9. See Anand Teltumbde, *Impact of Economic Reforms on Dalits in India,* Paper presented at the Seminar on 'Economic Reforms and Dalits in India' by the University of Oxford, Oxford, UK, on 8 November 1996. www.foil.org/inspiration/ambedkar/ecoreforms.html.

References

Arora, P., 2007, 'Pesticide and Human Health', *A Resource for Health Professionals,* 4(1–2), pp. 7–9.

Bag, D., 2000, 'Pesticides and Health Risks', *Economic and Political Weekly,* 6(16), pp. 20–21.

Barua, B., 1999, 'Review of Agricultural Progress: Trends, Development and Outlook for Future', *Journal of Agricultural Finance,* 7(4), pp. 6–9.

Béteille, André, 1972, *Inequality and Social Change*, Oxford University Press, Delhi.

Business Standard, 1999, 'Going off Pesticides', 12 March.

CEPA, 1998, 'Assessment List of Chemicals Known to the State of Cause Cancer or Reproductively Toxic City: The Report 1 of 1998', California.

Chaudhari, P. 1995, *Economic Planning in India*, Oxford University Press, London.

Crime Records, 2007, 'National Crime Records', Serial 10, New Delhi.

CSA, 2007, 'Pesticides, Residues and Regulation: A Case of Vegetables in Hyderabad', Hyderabad, 27 November. Retrieved March 2011, from http://www.Kisanswaraj.in/wp-content/.../pesticides-residues-regulations-csa-pdf

Das, Raju, 1998, The Social and Spatial Character of the Indian State, *Journal of Political Geography*, 17(7): 787–808.

Das, R.J. 2001, Class Capitalism and Agrarian Transition: A Review and Critique of Some Recent Arguments (A Review Article) *Journal of Peasant Studies*, 29:1.

Deshingkar, P., 2010, *Migration, Remote Rural Areas and Chronic Poverty in India.* Working Paper 323, ODI, London.

Devi, Indira, 2007, *Facing Hazards at Work: Agricultural Workers and Pesticide Exposure in Kuttanad, Kerala*, Working Paper, SANDEE.

Devi, P., 2010, 'Pesticides in Agriculture-Boon or A Curse? A Case Study of Kerala', *Economic and Political Weekly*, 26(27), pp. 199–207.

Dreze, J. and A. Sen, 1995, *India: Economic Development and Social Opportunity*, Oxford University Press, London.

EPA-US, 1999, *List of Chemicals Evaluated for Carcinogenic Potential: Office of Pesticide Programme*, EPAUS, California.

FAO, 1990, 'Guidelines for Personal Protection When Working with Pesticides in Tropical Climate', United Nations, FAO, Rome.

Government of India, 2007, Tenth Five-Years Plan, 2002–2007, Planning Commission of India, New Delhi.

Grace, C., Muraleedharan, V., Swaminathan, T. and Ranghhavi, D., 2007, *Use of Pesticides and its Impact on Human Health: A Case of Farmers in South Asia,* Indian Institute of Technology, Madras.

Gupta, P., 2004, 'Pesticide Exposure: Indian Scene', *Journal of Technology,* 198(83), pp. 118–119.

Harley, K., 2008, 'DDT Exposure, Work in Agriculture and Time to Pregnancy Among Farm Workers in California', *Journal of Occupational and Environmental Medicine,* 74(110), pp. 17–21.

Habib, I., 1984, 'Agrarian Relations and Land Reforms', in T. Raychaudhari and I. Habib (eds.), *The Cambridge Economic History of India,* Orient Longman Publications, London.

Human Rights Watch, 2007, 'Hidden Apartheid: Caste Discrimination Against India's 'Untouchables''. Retrieved 12 September 2007, from http://www.hrw.org/reports/2007/india0207/india0207web.pdf

Jeyaratnam, J., 1987, 'Survey of Acute Pesticide Poisoning Among Agricultural Workers in Four Asian Countries', *Bulletin of the World Health Organization,* 65(4), pp. 521–527.

Jayraj, S., 2007, 'Use and Abuse of Chemical Pesticides Need for Safer Pesticide for Sustainable Pest Management', *Journal of Sustainable Agricultural,* 71(101).

Kanekar, A., 1999, 'Pesticides Kill Peasants Instead of Pests', *Journal of TWN Features,* 56(2), pp. 111–125.

Kosambi, D.D., 1965, *The Culture and Civilization of Ancient India: An Historical Outline*, Routledge, London.

Kuruganti, K., 2010, 'Poisoned Pesticides', Info Change News and Features, 16 April. Retrieved February 2011 from http://www.infochangeindia.org.

Mancini, F., Braggen, V., Jiggins, J., Ambatipudi, A.C. and Murphy, H., 2005, 'Acute Pesticide Poisoning Among Female and Male Cotton Growers in India', *International Journal of Occupational Environmental Health*, 11(21), pp. 221–232.

Mohan, D., 2001, 'Alcohol Consumption in India: A Cross Sectional Study', in Demers A., Room R., and Bourgault C. (eds.), *Surveys of Drinking Patterns and Problems in Seven Developing Countries*, Word Health Organization, Geneva.

Patnaik, Utsa, 1990, *Agrarian Relations: The Mode of Production Debate*, Oxford University Press, London.

Pawar, M. and H. Birikar, 2004, *Impact of Indiscriminate Use of Pesticides: Environmental Impact of Agricultural Activities,* Indian Society of Environmental Science and Technology (ISET), Mumbai.

Rangrajan, R., 2001, 'Tasting Toxic', *New Indian Express*, 25 February.

Rengum, S., 2006, *Poverty and Pesticides: Protecting Health and the Environment*, Paper presented at PAN Asia, Hungary.

Sachdeva, S., 2007, 'Pesticides and Their Socio-economic Impact on Agriculture', *Southern Economist,* 41(38), pp. 42–53.

Sabbu, R., 2001, 'Proportion of Agricultural Labour Households on the Rise,' *Economic Times,* 8 September.

Shiva Kumar, S., 2001, 'Proportion of Agricultural Rural Labour Household on the Rise', *Economic Times*, 8 September.

Takagi, K., Kazuhiro, O., Lleji, M., and Masako, A., 1997, 'Use Research and Development of Pesticides in Relationship to Sustainable Agriculture in Japan', *Japan Agricultural Research Quarterly,* 31(2), pp. 13–20.

Tendulkar, S. and Sundaram K., 2000, *Poverty Among Social and Economic Groups in India in the Nineteen Nineties,* Working Paper, 118.

Warriner, D., 1969, *Land Reform in Principle and Practice*, London: Oxford University Press.

WHO, 2004, *The WHO Recommended Classification of Pesticides by Hazard and Guidelines to Classification,*

12

Casteism through the Lens of Discrimination and Distinction

Vishal Jadhav

Have we ever delved into the question as to why do so-called friends/acquaintances seem to share similar identities as ours with respect to community, religion, class, linguistic group and caste? Does this process and outcome seem natural/normal? Do we consciously choose our friends based on these identities and social markers? Does one's last name enable/disable social interaction? Do particular lifestyles such as mannerisms, dressing, food habits, language (dialect), circle of friends and acquaintances predispose an individual as being categorized as belonging to a particular caste? Can skin colour and other physical traits marginalize an individual on the criterion of belonging to a particular caste?

In this chapter, I endeavour to bring out the subtle and invisible ways through which casteism is practiced in India. Sometimes casteism is manifested through overt, deliberate conscious action, but interestingly as I argue, most of the times, it is through unconscious means. By this, I mean when individuals unconsciously practice casteism without knowing that they are actually participating in the process. How is this possible? Bourdieu (1977, 1998) calls this state as *doxa*, meaning a state of naturalized ideas, which one fails to ever question and believes in it. But how do these ideas get reified and naturalized within the individual's cognition? Bourdieu (1990) suggests that the dominant forms of knowledge and ideologies inscribe themselves through the process of socialization within what he calls the 'habitus'.

In this chapter, it is evident by now, I invoke the theorizations and conceptualizations of Bourdieu (1977, 1984, 1998) in order to map the subtle forms of casteism that are practiced in everyday life. Scholars who have researched on caste and casteism have generally focused on the overt, visible forms such as violence, subjugation and hegemony. In this chapter, I wish to elaborate on the ways in which casteism prevails through distinctions. I argue that it is through distinctions that caste discriminations are manifested.

The empirical data employed in this chapter were collected over a period of four years (January 2002 to January 2006) when I was employed as a part-time lecturer in an elite upper-class, educational institution called Fergusson College, located at Pune in India. The universe of study consisted of the students of social sciences and especially those pursuing sociology in the college in these four years. The students were pursuing their three-year integrated graduation course and were in the age groups from 18 to 21 years, though some were older. While teaching sociology, I would involve the students in participatory exercises: one of them was how to understand casteism. I gathered my empirical data through focus groups (FG) that were divided on the basis of caste, class, gender, region (rural/urban), linguistic groups and religion. There were limitations to the FG studies as sustained participation was a key problem. However, it was an interesting exercise as it brought forth the imaginings of the participants regarding caste and was also an eye opening exercise as it demonstrated how casteism can be practiced by an individual even unknowingly. In the four years I was able to conduct several FGs (20 in all) that brought out rich narratives together with a few in-depth interviews (30). Though the universe of my research is rather limited for generalizations to be made conclusively, I contend that this kind of research employing Bourdieu's (1990) theoretical lens provides an in-depth and indispensable tool to understand why casteism still prevails despite the state through the Constitution seeks its eradication.

This chapter is modelled on the research 'Exploration in Caste Stereotypes' carried out by Sinha and Sinha in 1967. In this chapter, these scholars collated caste stereotypes by means of administered questionnaires that were answered by postgraduate students at Bihar University. The questionnaires consisted of positive and negative attributes meant to map caste attributes. Positive aspects were intelligence, bold, brave, discipline and cultured, and the negative aspects were dishonesty, dishonourable, dirty, uncultured, dumb and cowardly among many others. They concluded on the basis of 200 questionnaires that caste stereotypes existed in that positive aspects were attributed to the higher caste and negative to the lower caste. Even though I use this model I differ from their methodology and also in some degree with respect to the queries that they wish to address. I employ an exploratory research design in which I endeavour to examine not only how is casteism understood but also why and through what process and practices does casteism continue – overtly and unconsciously. I stress more on the unconscious and invisible forms of casteism that is manifested through distinctions. Moreover I employ an exploratory research design that stresses on qualitative and interpretative sociological methodology rather than on a quantitative and positivist framework. In my research, which was conducted over a period of four years (January 2002 to January 2006), I was able to interact with approximately 250 students. In all the years, I was able to organize FGs based on caste, class, gender, religion and region. In this chapter, I stress more on the caste/class parameters, though I do extrapolate this vis-à-vis other variables.

Before I begin with the presentation of my research, I wish to briefly introduce Bourdieu's (1977, 1984, 1998) conceptions so that it becomes easier to understand why I employ his theorization to comprehend casteism and discrimination based on caste. Though his theorization is Eurocentric, I contend that it can be employed to examine societal phenomenon outside the spatial perimeter of the global North.

At the core of Bourdieu's work (1998) is his attempt to comprehend how power is reproduced in and through societal relations. How do the privileged manage to maintain their advantage generation after generation? He argues that it is not only the possession of economic capital that matters in the reproduction of power but also the cultural, social and symbolic capital that each individual possesses in different quantities that ensures domination. Bourdieu (1977, 1984, 1998) examines the social construction of objective structures with an emphasis on how people perceive and construct their own social world, but without neglecting how perception and construction is constrained by structures. An important dynamic in this relationship is the ability of individual actors to invent and improvise within the structure of their routines. In this chapter, I am using the Bourdieun perspective to argue how caste can be construed as a form of cultural, social and symbolic capital and how these capitals ensure that casteism survives sometimes knowingly and many a times through a reified, naturalized and unconscious state.

Thus, Bourdieu (1998) proposes a reflexive sociology that examines how symbolic power interfaces with culture, stratification and power. He argues that actors struggle for social recognition and that societal interaction can be examined through the lens of strategies that each individual employs. He argues that each individual is located at various sites within this social universe possessing various kinds of capital – social, economic, cultural and symbolic. He, therefore, argues that it is not economic resources and capital alone that perpetuates power but other forms of capital that necessitate distinctions that operate through cultural and symbolic practices, ranging from mannerisms, cognition, language, artistic tastes, dressing style, eating habits and beliefs among many others. Bourdieu (1998) argues that contestations can actually be examined at these sites of distinctions, and cultural practices that place individuals and groups into locations, sites and hierarchies. He terms these social spaces in and through which individuals compete as 'fields'. Bourdieu (1977) describes the field as a social arena in which actor's manoeuvrer and struggle in pursuit of resources. A field is a network of social relations among the objective positions within it. Each field has certain rules and privileges – certain form is favoured over another. For instance in the field of academics, cultural capital and scholastic capital is preferred over economic capital. Similarly, in the field of politics, social capital may be preferred over cultural capital. Thus, each actor is located differentially in the social space and each of these locations and sites has specific internalized value systems that he terms as 'habitus'. Bourdieu outlines the meaning of habitus as:

> in short, the habitus, the product of history, produces individual and collective practices, and hence history, in accordance with the schemes engendered by history. The system of dispositions – a past which survives in the present and tends to perpetuate itself into the future by making itself present in practices structured according to its principles, an internal law relaying the continuous exercise of the law of external necessities (irreducible to immediate conjunctural constraints) – is the principle of the continuity and regularity which objectivism discerns in the social world without being able to give them a rational basis. (1977: 82)

Thus, by conceptualizing habitus as both a product of history or social structures and also simultaneously ascribing it the function of being the producer of these structures (the 'generative principle' of practice), Bourdieu's (1977, 1984, 1998) theorization allows us to comprehend the moment when structure and agency collapse as a single process. Such an account makes possible a science of the dialectical relations between objective structures (to which the objectivist mode of knowledge gives access) and the structured dispositions within which those structures are actualized and which in their actualization reproduce them, which he terms as the habitus. Similarly Bourdieu (1977) contends that what we understand and believe as natural and normal is because it is a constructed and concealed vision of 'reality'. This naturalized vision of reality Bourdieu terms as *doxa*,

> Every established order tends to produce (to very different degrees and with different means) the naturalization of its own arbitrariness. Of all the mechanisms tending to produce this effect, the most important and the best concealed is undoubtedly the dialectic of the objective chances and the agents' aspirations, out of which arises the sense of limits, commonly called the sense of reality, i.e. the correspondence between the objective classes and the internalized classes, social structures and mental structures, which is the basis of the most ineradicable adherence to established order. (Bourdieu, 1977: 164)

Thus, to sum up the core of Bourdieu's sociological work is a logic of practice that emphasizes the importance of the body and practices within the social world. Bourdieu stressed that mechanisms of social domination and reproduction were primarily focused on bodily know-how and competent practices in the social world. The following social interactions are thus mapped within the framework of Bourdieu's logic of practice.

As mentioned earlier in this chapter, this research was based on the interactions that I had with the students pursuing graduation. There were several advantages that I possessed in the sense of how I was placed and also the fact that I had an opportunity to examine students across a three-year longitudinal period. The first year of graduation is probably a very interesting period to study. This is because the students are adults (as legitimated by the Constitution of India) but more importantly most of these students who enrol for college studies usually do so directly after their high school course. The high school, at least in India as we know, is an intensely circumscribed and regulated space in terms of discipline, uniform, regimentation, schedule, attendance, high levels of surveillance and moral and ethical behaviour. The ambience of college provides a distinctive break from this regimented environment. The students can now dress in any attire they wish and therefore no more uniforms, some can and do work on a part time basis while pursuing this course (which provides them some form of financial independence allowing for greater power of decision making), less surveillance from college authorities and also from parents, as adults they have a legitimate right to take their own decisions regarding future martial choices (and of course experiencing a new sense of and experimenting with sexuality that was regulated in the school environment and especially those students who did not study in co-education environments), in choosing friends and among many other such activities. Moreover, the college campus usually has informal spaces such as the canteens, recreation rooms, spaces for pursuing other curricular activities such as music, sports, drama, art such as social clubs, interaction and interface with civil society groups such as student unions, citizens forums, student and alumni associations, college and industry hiatus among many others. All these spaces then accentuate distinctions rather than uniformities (that previously the high school environment expected) and it is these distinctions that I argue that consciously and unconsciously lead to reproduction of discriminations based on caste, class, religion, linguistic attributes and region.

All these spaces, sites and processes enable students to hone certain skills according to the habitus that they possess. These spaces then become important sociological sites of examining how social interactions operate within them. I began my research by examining some of these sites that propelled me to ask how and why we interact with particular individuals or groups and not others more frequently. I posed this question among the students, and what came out of FG discussions and interviews was really interesting. For instance, one of the exercises given to the FGs was to map out individually the friends circle that one had organized. The outcome of this exercise was really interesting. The friends circle displayed a high correlation on the lines of caste, class, gender, region, religion and linguistic groupings. On further probing this matter with the FGs what emerged was that each of them chooses friends on the basis of 'cultural affinity'. That is to say that a *Brahmin* usually chooses a *Brahmin*, children of professionals choose friends having similar background, it was common to find friends who had similar linguistic backgrounds and rurally moored students preferred friendship with individuals with similar backgrounds. When I employ the term *friendship*, I qualify it to mean those relationships in which individuals spend most of the work and leisure time together and who know each other well for over a period of six months at least. In most cases, however, I found that those students who claimed to be friends carried this bonding over their three-year graduation course.

Though it seems a natural/normal social phenomenon, it is really not so. The habitus of the individual students incline them to choose friends from within particular social locations that conform to their notion of socially and politically correct choices. The habitus as described earlier in the text is really the cognitive framework that is shaped through the process of socialization and that inculcates and inscribes in our bodies certain tastes, dispositions, mannerisms, etc. These value systems are internalized by individuals differentially depending on the location of each actor. Thus, it may seem natural why a child of a doctor would find it easier and convenient to create a bond with the child of a lawyer or an engineer or a civil servant. This is so because each of them shares a specific form of embodied cultural capital that they possess, for example the dressing sense, the language (dialect) of communication, the perceptions regarding the social world around them, the food habits, mannerisms, social networks, lifestyle, and personalities among other such behavioural consistencies.

From the FGs emerged another pertinent set of 'imaginings', that is how differentially located individuals visualized the 'others'. For instance, the *non-Brahmin* students imagined that the *Brahmins* male students exhibited characteristics that were generally effeminate. So were the *Bengali* (male) speaking students. On being asked what constituted this notion of effeminate, the students replied 'they usually prefer sweet food', 'they use soft words in their language', 'they gossip', 'have a very small and restricted circle of confidantes', 'they are cunning', 'intelligent', 'passive' and 'docile'. Similarly from discussions of the FG consisting of *Brahmin* students, what emerged was that the North Indians possessed the following stereotypical traits: brash, unconventional, political, daring, courageous and unreliable among others. The students also imagined the *Maratha* (caste in Maharashtra claiming to have a martial heritage) as head strong, aggressive, political, insensitive, masculine, fool hardy, peasant moorings, brash and uncultured among other traits. The *Marwari* and *Baniya* students (North Indian and communities of traders) were imagined to have the following traits: extremely cunning especially in matters related to finance, efficient, resourceful, politically neutral, unreliable, strict vegetarians, rich, influential, etc. Students who belonged to the Northeast region of India and who in large proportion belonged to the scheduled tribes were deemed to have the following personality stereotypes such as exotic, sportsmen/women, poor communication and scholastic skills, spendthrifts, undisciplined, truthful, Christian, fashionable, dumb, music lovers, having Chinese affinities and therefore were also derogatorily called as *chinkis*, those who enjoy Chinese food (such as noodles, fried rice, etc.) and have lax behaviour patterns among others. Similarly the South Indians (a generic term to describe any individual belonging to the *Dravidian* linguistic zone) are deemed to be intelligent, studious, serious, unfriendly, religious, rice eaters, selfish, meek and shy among other such stereotypical traits.

These imaginings are really stereotypes that have been internalized by students through the process of socialization. For instance, it is at the site of the family that a child learns to recognize the differences about the 'I' and the 'other'. The stories, fables, cinemas, television and other forms of media shape this imaginings and notions about the others such that these become yardstick through which we begin to assess people whom we firstly cognitively categorize as belonging to another social category. We assume that individuals belonging to a particular group share common traits. We generalize these personality traits forgetting that an individual has not only one identity and location but also several at any given moment. Based on these perceptions and cognitive maps, we begin to strategize our social interactions.

These distinctions are then really manifested in the operationalization of actors/agents interaction in the social arenas or fields. In this chapter, I seek to comprehend only one aspect, that is how caste stereotypes are reproduced through these notions of distinctions and how these in the course of time translate into discriminations based on caste sometimes also called *casteism*. It is pertinent to mention here that these distinctions are as argued through the Bourdieu (1990) lens internalized in the habitus such that it becomes doxic in nature. An individual, therefore, assumes that these distinctions are natural and does not question them leading to discrimination.

One of the advantages of examining friendship patterns was that it allowed me to understand why students preferred certain individuals over others. What emerged from the FG discussions was that the correlation between caste and class was very high (80%). This is to say that those students who belonged to the high caste (*savarna*) category usually had friends who either belonged to high castes (and especially from the same caste group or *jati* as the individuals) or high class (irrespective of caste) and vice versa, that is low caste students usually had friends belonging to low caste and class. Additionally, it was noticed that those who belonged to high caste were also economically well off and those belonging to low caste were usually economically depraved.[1] In categorizing high and low caste, I divided the student population on the basis of forward and backward castes as per the provisions of the Constitution of India. The scheduled castes and tribes together with castes that figured in the other backward classes (OBC) list were placed in the category of low caste/class and all others castes such as *Brahmins* (and all their corresponding subcastes or *jatis*), *kshatriyas* (and all their corresponding jatis) and *Vaishyas* (and all subcastes within this broad *varna* category).[2]

Thus, choosing a friend meant that the individual student would look out for persons of similar dispositions or in Bourdieu's terminology, habitus. The habitus is manifested in the way we dress, the food we eat, the mannerisms, preferences, etc. Most of these features are overtly visible. When I enquired with the high caste/class FG regarding how they chose their respective friends the response was rather intriguing. One of the first steps towards entering into a friendship bond is firstly 'sizing up' the other potential candidate. When the students are unfamiliar with each other, they try and find the individual having similar dispositions as his/her own. On enquiring how this process takes place, the FG came up with a set of questions through which they usually 'size up' potential friends – What is the last name of the individual? How has he/she dressed up? Is the dressing formal or informal? Does the individual adorn the latest in fashion or outdated unfashionable clothes? Are the clothes branded? What kind of a wrist watch does the individual possess? Is he/she 'cool' (meaning, is the individual friendly)? Does he/she possess an automobile? Is he/she fluent in English? What is the accent that he/she communicates in English? Does he/she speak a foreign language? How much knowledge does the individual exude while in class? What was the individual's academic record (in the previous high school examination)? Is the individual interested in sports? Which sport? Team games such as cricket, football, volleyball among others or individual sports such as tennis, badminton, chess, billiards, videogames, etc.? What kind of food does the individual consume? Does the individual have any habits such as smoking, drinking and taking drugs among others? Is the individual 'popular' in the class and the college campus? Does the individual already have a large group of friends? How and what are the traits of these friends? What kind of movies/films does the individual prefer to watch? Where does the individual watch these movies – in multiplexes or in ordinary theatre? What is the background of the individual? Where does the individual reside – in city area or in rural area? What do his/her parents do for a living? Are they professionals, industrialists, bureaucrats and state civil servants or agriculturists? How do the teachers treat the individual? How good is the individual's knowledge regarding the restaurants, malls and such other 'interesting' places in the city?

These questions in a way point towards how the individual begins to segregate individuals categories based on stereotypical cultural traits. One then locates a group of potential candidates whom the individual deems to possess the requisite preferred qualities. For instance, how does an individual dress can be really understood as if the individual is wearing expensive, branded clothing then obviously that student belongs to an upper class category. Similarly an individual who regularly adorns only a few sets of clothes which are 'ordinary' implies that the individual is economically not so well located. The food habits one exhibits such as individuals who regularly have their food at expensive restaurants can afford expensive and exotic food (imported chocolates for example), consume particular kind of food (e.g. the *Marwaris* are strict vegetarians) or prefer 'South Indian', 'North Indian', 'Chinese' food, sweet rather than hot and spicy food, etc. imply how the habitus manifests itself as a social and cultural marker – from these traits an individual is generally categorized as belonging to a specific region and caste. For instance, the FG participants claimed it was easy to identify a *Brahmin* from Maharashtra based on the food habits. These individuals would usually eat sweet food, consume a lot of butter and milk products, prefer having their food in specific *Brahmin* food joints and some would follow a religiously sanctioned fasting day (in a week) among others. Similarly, the FGs also came up with how one could identify a student belonging to a particular caste. The last name was usually a highly visible social marker. Also other features such as the accent in which the local language and English is spoken, the way the individual dressed, the food habits, the company that one maintained help in identifying a student belonging to a particular caste.

The kind of sport which they played and showed interest in also showed a high correlation to caste/class. The upper caste/class students were both involved in playing and seeking knowledge of the news in individual sports more often than those students who belonged to the lower caste/class (with the exception of scheduled caste students from the Northeast). Sports such as professional form of swimming, tennis, billiards and golf are rather expensive games in that the equipment, membership of particular clubs and their fees are high. Moreover, these sports were usually played by students who were introduced to it in their early teens. Learning a new sport at the age of 18 and above was uncommon. I discovered a high correlation between these sports and the caste/class background of the student – students who played and patronized these sports belonged to the upper caste/class category. Some individual sports such as body building, boxing, Malkhamb (indigenous form of gymnastics), wrestling and weightlifting among others were popular among the lower caste/class group. One of the reasons for this was that the local municipal corporation has many such sporting complexes all across the city that charge nominal fees for membership. On the other hand, collective or team sports such as volleyball, football, hockey and Kabbadi among others were usually the domain of the low caste/class students.[3]

Another aspect that I examined was how students spend their time while in the campus – what are the activities that they are involved in? Which set of students visit the library often? What kind of reading are they interested in? Which category of students predominates in political activities? Who are involved in social clubs such as film clubs, photography clubs, trekking and adventure clubs and short-term professional courses such as foreign language course, shorthand course and computer courses among others? What emerged from this exercise was that the correlation between high caste/class was extremely strong with activities such as being involved in film clubs, photography, nature walks, trekking and adventure activities and also regarding some professional courses such as learning a foreign language, participating in elocution contests and in conferences and seminars. The lower caste/class students were found to have a large participation in political activities such as affiliation and participation in student political parties and associations. There was also a strong correlation between this group and some specific professional courses such as computer training, shorthand courses, personality development courses, English language learning courses and courses designed to train office supervisors.

What this exercise really brought forth was that these choices which we think are choices are really the differential amounts of embodied cultural capital that each individual and group possesses. For instance, the lower caste/class group prefers to attend rudimentary professional courses which the upper caste/class does not have to attend because these individuals have more than the requisite amount of knowledge regarding the same. Instead they opt for highly specialized courses and social club membership that may provide them with a leverage to enter the market at a higher location than those belonging to the lower caste/class group. For instance, most of the upper caste/class students have a precedence of being educated (in their high school) in English medium and some have studied in elite public and convent schools. They do not need to enrol for English-speaking courses or rudimentary computer courses as usually most of them possess personal computers at home. It is the lower caste/class section that seeks to hone lower level managerial skills in the hope of getting employed in public/private offices. In these patterns, I could also discern how caste/class as a variable constantly featured in the form of friendship, meaning how groups of friends usually belonged to a particular caste/class category and as such displayed proclivities towards following similar kinds of interests.

Perhaps the most visible form of these interactions was manifested in the classroom, canteens and hostels. For instance, what was the pattern in which students occupied spaces within the classroom? I noted and this was corroborated through the FG discussions that the classroom itself as a social space was structured. Students belonging to particular caste/class occupied certain adjoining areas and the remaining space was occupied by the other groups. If one were to understand this seating arrangement through the framework of friends, then it would seem natural. But when we already know that friendship is a function of certain embodied cultural tastes and predispositions called habitus, we may be able to actually discern how caste behaviour occurs unconsciously. Similarly, when we assume the canteen to be a social space, the spatial locations of caste groups becomes self-evident. For instance, one group of friends (caste group) place themselves away from another group on the pretext of the other group being non-vegetarians (though only egg was the non-vegetarian food item sold in the canteen, although students would carry tiffin's/lunch boxes which sometimes had non-vegetarian food in them).

Hostel was a site that really made this phenomenon of caste groupings extremely startling. I argue that when students choose room partner they do so rather unconsciously and this doxic choice is directly related to the habitus of the individuals. From the hostel records, I found out that the students usually chose partners who belonged to similar cultural backgrounds. On being asked why they thought that this occurred they argued that it was because they were most comfortable with such choices. It was easier to accommodate and adjust to students having similar backgrounds than with students having a diverse background. I also enquired with the rector of the hostel (boys) as to why and how this takes place. I was told that the rooms are usually allotted through a random process and sometimes on the basis of first come first serve principle. However, in the course of the year we get complaints from the students as they wish to change room partners. Many times the students change room partners mutually without informing the authorities. What appears from this phenomenon is that because students have to cohabit for a period of three years, they usually choose partners who match their cognition and perception which itself has been shaped by culture through the process of socialization.

To conclude in this chapter, I have argued and demonstrated how distinctions are fundamentally cultural artefacts which have in the process of socialization become embedded in the habitus of the individual. These cognitive frameworks enable us to make choices regarding clothing, food, friends and mannerisms among other such habits. The habitus thus unconsciously dictates the way in which we think, imagine and also interact in a given social space. These distinctions, which are naturalized, then mediate through social agency manifesting in forms of discrimination. The discriminations in most cases are as a result of unconscious actions leading to further reinforcing casteism.

Notes

1. This logic and findings go well with the research findings of Omvedt (1981) and Patil (1979) who are Marxist scholars and who contend that there is a strong correlation between caste and class in India.

2. With the exception of dominant castes such as *Reddy, Kamma, Vokkaliga, Lingayat, Jats, Yadav,* etc. who due to their political and economic resources do not display the same form of marginalization that the scheduled castes and tribes together with other such groups within the OBC category display. Srinivas (1963, 1976) argued that the castes were traditionally linked to the *Jajmani* system, after the term *Jajman*, which means patron. Members of various service castes perform tasks for their patrons, usually members of the land-owning caste of the village. Members of the land-owning castes such as *Kammas and Reddys* of Andhra Pradesh, *Vokkaligas* of Karnataka, *Jats* of North India and Maratha-*Kunbi* of Maharashtra represented the patrons or *jajmans*. Their domination according to him continued in the postcolonial period.
3. Cricket was an exception as this sport is played and consumed with equal fervour by all caste/class of students. It is deemed to be a religion in India with some of the Indian cricket team players being given the status of demigods.

References

Bourdieu, P., 1977, *Outline of a Theory of Practice,* Cambridge University Press.

——, 1984, *Distinction: A Social Critique of the Judgment of Taste*, trans. Richard Nice, Harvard University Press.

——, 1990, *The Logic of Practice*, Polity Press, Cambridge.

——, 1998, *Practical Reason: On the Theory of Action*, Stanford University Press.

Omvedt, G., 1981, 'Capitalist Agriculture and Rural Classes in India', *Economic and Political Weekly*, 16(52), pp. 140–159.

Patil, S., 1979, 'Dialectics of Caste and Class Conflicts', *Economic and Political Weekly*, Annual Number: Class and Caste in India, 14(7/8), pp. 287–296.

Sinha, G.S. and Sinha, R.C., 1967, 'Exploration in Caste Stereotypes', *Social Forces*, 46(1), pp. 42–47.

Srinivas, M.N., 1963, *Caste in Modern India and Other Essays*, Asia Publishing House, Bombay.

Srinivas, M.N., 1976, *The Remembered Village*, Oxford University Press, New Delhi.

Index